The Bumper Vegetarian Cookbook

The Bumper Vegetarian Cookbook

Good Housekeeping

250 tried, trusted, tested recipes ★ delicious results

Compiled by Barbara Dixon

COLLINS & BROWN

First published in the United Kingdom in 2011 by
Collins & Brown
10 Southcombe Street
London
W14 0RA

An imprint of Anova Books Company Ltd

The Good Housekeeping website is
www.allboutyou.com/goodhousekeeping

10 9 8 7 6 5 4 3 2 1

ISBN 978-1-84340-609-9

A catalogue record for this book is available from the British Library.

Repro by Dot Gradations Ltd, UK
Printed and bound by Times Offset, Malaysia

This book can be ordered direct from the publisher at
www.anovabooks.com

Picture Credits:
Neil Barclay (pages 26, 44, 55, 79, 138, 190 and 270); Martin
Brigdale (pages 76, 83, 101, 102, 103, 106, 112, 122, 123, 129,
151, 173 and 212); Nicki Dowey (pages 16, 17, 19, 20, 21, 23,
32, 34, 35, 36, 38, 39, 40, 41, 42, 43, 45, 46, 47, 48, 49, 50,
56, 57, 58, 59, 60, 61, 62, 63, 64, 66, 69, 72, 77, 78, 80, 81,
82, 85, 88, 89, 90, 92, 93, 94, 97, 99, 108, 109, 110, 111, 116,
118, 120, 127, 128, 130, 132, 134, 136, 137, 140, 144, 145,
148, 150, 152, 154, 155, 157, 158, 162, 163, 164, 165, 168,
169, 170, 171, 172, 174, 175, 179, 180, 181, 182, 183, 186,
187, 188, 189, 191, 192, 193, 195, 196, 197, 199, 204, 206,
209, 214, 220, 224, 226, 227, 228, 229, 230, 234, 235, 236,
237, 238, 239, 240, 241, 242, 243, 244, 245, 247, 249, 250,
251, 254, 256, 257, 258, 259, 263, 264, 265, 268, 271, 272
and 273); Will Heap (pages 27, 84, 107, 121, 126, 149, 176 and
194); Craig Robertson (pages 24, 37, 54, 67, 68, 73, 74, 75, 91,
95, 96, 98, 100, 113, 114, 115, 117, 119, 131, 139, 146, 153,
156, 159, 160, 161, 177, 178, 198, 200, 205, 207, 208, 210,
211, 215, 218, 219, 221, 223, 225, 231, 255, 260, 261, 262,
266, 267 and 269); Lucinda Symons (pages 18, 22, 25, 28, 29, 33,
51, 65, 133, 135, 141, 147, 201, 213, 222, 246 and 248)
Home economists: Anna Burges-Lumsden, Joanna Farrow, Emma Jane
Frost, Teresa Goldfinch, Alice Hart, Lucy McKelvie, Kim Morphew,
Katie Rogers, Bridget Sargeson, Sarah Tildesley and Jennifer White.
Stylists: Lucy McKelvie, Wei Tang, Sarah Tildesley, Helen Trent, Fanny
Ward and Mari Mererid Williams

NOTES

Both metric and imperial measures are given for the
recipes. Follow either set of measures, not a mixture of
both, as they are not interchangeable.

All spoon measures are level.
1 tsp = 5ml spoon; 1 tbsp = 15ml spoon.

Ovens and grills must be preheated to the specified
temperature.

Medium eggs should be used except where otherwise
specified.

 Recipes marked with this symbol are suitable
for those on a vegan diet.

DIETARY GUIDELINES

Note that certain recipes contain raw or lightly
cooked eggs. The young, elderly, pregnant women
and anyone with immune-deficiency disease should
avoid these because of the slight risk of salmonella.

Note that some recipes contain alcohol. Check the
ingredients list before serving to children.

Wine: Most wine manufacturing involves animal
by-products. Check the label to ensure the wine is
suitable for vegetarians or vegans.

Honey: Vegans should be aware that some recipes
contain honey; maple or corn syrup can be
substituted.

Contents

Foreword

Gone are the days when vegetarian meant a diet full to the rafters of boiled lentils and mushy tofu. Vegetarian cuisine has become a beacon of creativity and inspiration around the world – with so many ingredients readily available, limitless possibilities of flavour combinations present themselves.

There are as many different types of vegetarian as there are reasons for being one. Vegans are strict vegetarians, not eating any animal products whatsoever (including gelatine and, in some cases, honey). Some vegetarians will eat dairy products such as eggs, cheese and milk. Luckily, this book has something for everyone.

This bumper book is not only written for those who are vegetarian, but for anyone who is after inspiration in the kitchen and wants to follow recipes that are guaranteed to work first time round. It is a comprehensive guide to vegetarian cuisine, with useful ingredients boxes, technique tips and practical advice. It draws inspiration from around the world – from aromatic Indian pulses, to crisp Southeast Asian stir-fries, and Mediterranean sauces to fiery American entries.

When confronted with the task of cooking for a vegetarian, lots of people tend to throw meat-free ingredients into a pan and hope for the best – but this epic book will show that using fewer and more clever ingredients (with good seasoning) gets better results.

So as a meat-eater with a new vegetarian book in my cupboard, I hope you enjoy this all-round title as much as I do.

Meike.

Meike Beck
Cookery Editor

Nutrition

Whether you are already a commited vegetarian, are thinking of giving up meat and fish altogether, or simply fancy having one or two meat-free days a week, you will want to ensure that you and your family are getting a good balanced diet.

A VEGETARIAN DIET

A vegetarian diet is one that excludes meat, poultry and fish. Many vegetarians also avoid other animal products, such as gelatine, animal fats such as lard and suet, and animal rennet in non-vegetarian cheeses. However, the majority of vegetarians do eat dairy produce, including milk, vegetarian cheeses and free-range eggs. Provided a vegetarian diet includes a good range of cereals and grains, pulses, nuts and seeds, fruit and vegetables, dairy and/or soya products, it is unlikely to be lacking nutritionally, but variety is important to ensure a good intake of protein. Vegetable proteins are lacking in one or more of the essential amino acids, but by eating certain foods together, this problem is overcome. For example, you can obtain complete protein by combining cereals with milk or other dairy products; pulses with rice or pasta; pulses or nuts with dairy produce; and nuts with grains. This tends to happen naturally in most vegetarian meals – for example, serving pasta with a cheese sauce, or a lentil or chickpea curry with rice (see Protein, opposite).

A VEGAN DIET

Vegans follow a more restrictive diet, which also excludes all dairy products, eggs, and even foods such as honey, because it is produced by bees. A vegan diet can be deficient in vitamin B12, which is only present in animal and dairy foods. To make up for this, fortified breakfast cereals, yeast extract and/or soya milk should be consumed. Soya products are particularly valuable sources of protein, energy, calcium, minerals, vitamin B12, vitamin D and beneficial omega-3 fatty acids. Vegan recipes in this book are marked with the V symbol.

Many people assume that a vegetarian diet is automatically healthier than a carnivore's. This isn't always the case – there are good and bad vegetarian diets. It is not enough simply to stop eating meat; the nutrients that would normally be obtained from meat must be replaced. It's quite common for vegetarians to rely too heavily on dairy products like cheese and eggs, which can be high in saturated fats and calories. Such a limited diet is not only unhealthy but will also eventually become boring and tedious. As with any diet, variety is important.

It is useful to have a basic understanding of nutrition and the importance of certain foods – even if only to convince meat-eaters that a vegetarian diet is healthy. Here is a brief guide.

PROTEIN

Contrary to popular belief, there are lots of good vegetable sources of protein, such as beans, grains, nuts, soya products and Quorn, as well as eggs,

Balancing a vegetarian or vegan diet

cheese, milk and yogurt. Protein is made up of smaller units called amino acids. They are needed for the manufacture and repair of body cells, so they are very important. The body can manufacture some amino acids itself, but others, known as the 'essential amino acids', must come from food. Animal protein contains almost all of these and is therefore known as 'complete' protein.

With the exception of soya products, vegetable proteins are lacking or low in one or more amino acid. However, by eating certain foods together at the same meal any deficiency is overcome. This isn't as complicated as it sounds and usually happens automatically when menu planning. For example, cereals should be eaten with dairy products, pulses or nuts (for example, muesli with yogurt or milk, chilli beans with rice, nut roast made with breadcrumbs, peanut butter on toast). Pulses and nuts should be eaten with cereals or dairy products (for example, dal with raita, nut burgers with a bap).

VITAMINS

Vitamins are vital for proper body functioning. They can be divided into two categories – fat soluble and water soluble. Fat-soluble vitamins A, D, E and K are found mostly in foods that contain fat. They are stored in the body by the liver. The water-soluble vitamins C and B complex dissolve in water and cannot be stored, so a regular supply is important.

A varied diet should supply all the vitamins our bodies need. Vegetarians and vegans should ensure that their intake of vitamins B12 and D is sufficient, although a deficiency of either is unlikely.

VITAMIN B12

Vitamin B12 is essential for the formation of healthy red blood cells; a deficiency causes a form of anaemia. As it is found only in animal foods (with the exception of uncertain amounts in seaweed and fermented soya products), it is the vitamin most likely to be lacking in a vegan diet. Vegetarians who eat milk, eggs and cheese will get sufficient vitamin B12 from these, but vegans should be careful to include some fortified foods in their diet. Yeast extracts, some brands of breakfast cereals, soya milk and other products marketed for vegans (such as vegetable spreads and pâtés) are all good sources. Get into the habit of reading labels to identify fortified brands.

VITAMIN D

Vitamin D is needed for the growth and formation of healthy teeth and bones. Most of the body's supply comes from the action of sunlight on the skin. Good vegetarian sources of vitamin D are eggs and butter. Some margarines, milk powders and yogurts are fortified – check the labels.

MINERALS

Minerals cannot be manufactured by the body and must be obtained from food. At present, 15 minerals have been identified as being essential to health and others are under investigation. Most people obtain enough minerals provided a good variety of foods is eaten. Iron, calcium and zinc are the three minerals most often discussed in relation to a vegetarian diet.

IRON

Iron is used to make the haemoglobin in red blood cells. Haemoglobin carries oxygen to every cell in the body and a shortage leads to anaemia. Vegetarians are susceptible to anaemia because meat is a rich source of iron, and because the body can absorb iron from meat more efficiently than it can from vegetarian foods. Iron is found in many vegetarian and vegan foods, including leafy green vegetables, cereals, pulses, nuts, eggs and dried fruits (especially apricots). The absorption of iron is greatly increased if vitamin C-rich foods are eaten at the same meal.

Make the most of vitamins

- For maximum vitamin retention, buy fruit and vegetables in peak condition, preferably from a shop with a fast turnover. Eat them as soon as possible. Wilted or old vegetables have a lower vitamin content than fresh.

- Store vegetables in a cool dark place; light is destructive to vitamins, especially the vitamins B and C. Don't leave bottles of milk on the doorstep; Vitamin B2 (riboflavin) is destroyed when exposed to ultra–violet light.

- Steam or boil vegetables until just tender using the minimum amount of water.

- Don't add soda to cooking water. Once the vegetables are cooked and drained, use the water for stocks, gravies and soups.

- Don't prepare vegetables hours in advance and leave them soaking in water. Leave the skins on whenever you can.

- Eat plenty of raw vegetables and fruit.

- Vitamin losses continue after cooking, particularly when warm foods are left waiting around, so eat soon after cooking.

Nutrient	Sourced from

Nutrient   Sourced from

PROTEIN
- Nuts: Hazelnuts, brazils, almonds, cashews, walnuts, pinenuts, macadamias, pecan, peanuts and peanut butter
- Seeds: Sesame, pumpkin, sunflower, linseeds
- Grains/cereals: Wheat (in bread and flour, pasta, etc.), barley, rye, oats, millet, maize (sweetcorn), rice
- Soya products: Tofu, tempeh*, textured vegetable protein, veggie burgers, soya milk (*tempeh is made from soya beans and is a staple protein in Indonesian cooking. It's similar to tofu but has a richer flavour and firmer texture)
- Dairy products: Milk, cheese, yogurt (butter and cream are very poor sources of protein)
- Eggs
- Pulses: Beans, chickpeas and lentils

CARBOHYDRATE
- Fruit
- Milk
- Sugar
- Cereals and grains: Bread, rice, pasta, oats, barley, millet, buckwheat, rye
- Root vegetables: Potatoes, parsnips

VITAMINS
- Vitamin A: Red, orange or yellow vegetables such as carrots, sweet potatoes, peppers and tomatoes; leafy green vegetables such as spinach and watercress; fruits such as apricots, peaches, papayas, orange-fleshed melons
- Vitamin B: Yeasts, whole cereals (especially wheat germ), nuts and seeds, pulses, green vegetables
- Vitamin B12: Eggs, yeast extracts, soya milks, veggie burgers
- Vitamin C: Fruit, salad, vegetables especially leafy green vegetables
- Vitamin E: Vegetable oil, wholegrain cereals, eggs, avocados, nuts
- Vitamin K: Vegetables, cereals

It is decreased by the presence of tannin, which is found in tea, as well as phytates and oxalates in bran.

CALCIUM
Calcium is essential for the growth and development of bones and teeth. Because it is usually associated primarily with milk, eggs, yogurt and cheese, vegans are considered to be at risk of deficiency. However, this is not a problem because calcium is also found in white bread and flour, green vegetables, nuts, sesame seeds, dried fruits, calcium-enriched soya milk and tap water in hard-water areas.

ZINC
Zinc is a trace mineral. Among other things, it is important for the functioning of enzymes and for a healthy immune system. It has been suggested that zinc from plant sources is not readily absorbed by the body. However, there are so many other factors that affect zinc absorption and requirements that it is highly unlikely that vegetarianism would be the cause of a deficiency. As long as a variety of food is included in the diet, a deficiency will be avoided. Good vegetarian sources are sesame seeds, cheese, nuts, pulses and grains.

Breast milk or infant formula contains all the vitamins and minerals a newborn baby needs for the first six months of life. Although breast milk is preferable for a number of reasons, commercial infant formula will provide complete nutrition. Babies should continue to drink breast or formula until they are one year old, but they can have 'doorstep' milk on cereals and in cooked dishes from about six months. For vegan babies, special soya-based formulas are available; ordinary soya milk is nutritionally inadequate.

Weaning should not be introduced until your baby is six months old, but if he or she shows signs of wanting solids earlier than this, speak to your health visitor or midwife. Start with baby rice mixed with breast milk or formula, then try puréed and sieved fruits (such as banana, apple and pear) and vegetables (such as potatoes, carrot and swede). Don't be discouraged if your baby refuses the new food; try again the next day. Introduce one new food at a time and wait three or four days before introducing another new food, in case of an allergic reaction. Avoid wheat-based cereals until baby is six months old because gluten (a constituent of

Vegetarian babies and children

wheat grains) can cause an allergic reaction. Don't give honey until your baby is one year old because of the very small risk of food poisoning. Try to give your child healthy food from the start. Avoid making food very sweet (don't add sugar to breakfast cereals) or very salty (don't add salt to vegetable cooking water). When buying baby foods, look for varieties without added sugar, salt and chemical additives.

From the age of one, your child should be eating (or at least be offered) three small meals a day, along with a mid-morning and a mid-afternoon snack (which could be a glass of milk, some chopped fruit or a piece of cheese). From the age of two, your child can eat much the same as the rest of the family. Avoid nuts unless they are ground into nut butter because there is danger of choking. The Department of Health advises that children should not be given soft-cooked eggs. So make sure that poached eggs are cooked until the yolk is set, and avoid giving children soft scrambled eggs and runny omelettes.

Adolescents need a nutrient-rich diet with lots of calories (girls about 2,100, boys about 2,800 per day). A varied vegetarian diet will easily provide this. Teenage girls should ensure they eat plenty of iron-rich foods. Encourage them to eat vitamin C and iron-rich foods together (see page 11). Vegan adolescents should eat cereals and yeast extracts fortified with vitamin B12 (see page 10).

For some families, a non-meat-eater in their midst can cause problems at meal times. It's important to view this as a positive move for the family as a whole rather than as a problem. There's no doubt that the consumption of too much animal protein is unhealthy, so it's a good idea to use the opportunity to introduce more meat-free meals to all members of the household. Making meals based on rice, potatoes and pasta is a good way to start. It's easy to cook simple nutritious vegetarian meals using these as a base combined with beans, lentils and well-flavoured ingredients such as garlic, tomato, spices, herbs and fresh vegetables. Tasty risottos, pilaffs, vegetable gratins and stuffed baked potatoes are delicious and

Feeding a vegetarian teenager

would usually be made without meat anyway. For particularly steadfast carnivorous members of the family, serve these with grilled meat or fish or sliced cold meat as a last resort until the appeal of vegetarianism sinks in.

Pizzas are surprisingly quick and easy to make and are loved by most teenagers. Piled high with vegetables and served with a large mixed salad, they make a splendid supper. A chunky soup made from a mixture of vegetables and beans or lentils, served with hot garlic bread and followed by yogurt and fruit also makes a healthy meal.

Meat substitutes such as Quorn, and soya products like soya mince are useful additions to the new vegetarian cook's repertoire. Use them to make meat-free versions of traditional family favourites such as shepherd's pie, lasagne, spaghetti bolognese, kebabs and curry.

Start your day

Apricot and Orange Smoothie

400g (14oz) canned apricots in
  natural juice
150g (5oz) apricot yogurt
200–250ml (7–9fl oz) unsweetened
  orange juice

1 Put the apricots, yogurt and orange juice into a blender
or food processor and whiz for 1 minute or until smooth.

2 Chill well, then pour into two glasses and serve.

Serves 2, makes about 450ml (¾ pint)
Preparation Time 5 minutes,
  plus chilling

Nutritional Information (Per Serving)
172 calories, 1g fat (of which trace saturates), 39g carbohydrate, 0.2g salt
Gluten Free · Easy

Taste of the Tropics Smoothie ⓥ

1. Peel and core the pineapple and chop the flesh roughly. Slice the flesh off the central stone of the mango, then peel and chop.

2. Cut two thin slices of kiwi fruit and set aside. Peel the remainder and put into a blender with the pineapple, mango and tropical fruit juice.

3. Blend until smooth and thick, then pour into two glasses. Decorate with the reserved kiwi fruit.

700g (1½lb) pineapple
275g (10oz) mango
1 kiwi fruit
150ml (¼ pint) tropical fruit juice

Cook's Tip
If you prefer a thinner smoothie, add a little water.

Nutritional Information (Per Serving)
262 calories, 1g fat (of which trace saturates), 64g carbohydrate, 0g salt
Gluten Free · Dairy Free · Easy

Serves 2, makes 300ml (½ pint)
Preparation Time 10 minutes

Apple and Almond Yogurt

V

500g (1lb 2oz) natural yogurt or
   soya yogurt
50g (2oz) each flaked almonds
   and sultanas
2 apples

1 Put the yogurt into a bowl and add the almonds and sultanas.

2 Grate the apples, add to the bowl and mix together. Chill in the fridge overnight. Use as a topping for breakfast cereal or serve as a snack.

Try Something Different
Use pears instead of apples.
Replace the sultanas with dried
cranberries.

Serves 4
Preparation Time 5 minutes,
   plus overnight chilling

Nutritional Information (Per Serving)
192 calories, 8g fat (of which 1g saturates), 22g carbohydrate, 0.3g salt
Gluten Free · Easy

Apple Compôte

1 Put the cooking apples into a pan with the lemon juice, caster sugar and 2 tbsp cold water. Cook gently for 5 minutes or until soft. Transfer to a bowl.

2 Sprinkle a little ground cinnamon over the top, cool and chill. It will keep for up to three days.

3 Serve with the raisins, chopped almonds and yogurt.

250g (9oz) cooking apples, peeled and chopped
juice of ½ lemon
1 tbsp golden caster sugar
ground cinnamon

TO SERVE
25g (1oz) raisins
25g (1oz) chopped almonds
1 tbsp natural yogurt or soya yogurt

Cook's Tip
To microwave, put the apples, lemon juice, sugar and water into a microwave-proof bowl, cover loosely with clingfilm and cook on full power in an 850W microwave oven for 4 minutes or until the apples are just soft.

Nutritional Information (Per Serving)
188 calories, 7g fat (of which 1g saturates), 29g carbohydrate, 0g salt
Gluten Free · Easy

Serves 2
Preparation Time 10 minutes, plus chilling
Cooking Time 5 minutes

Porridge with Dried Fruit

200g (7oz) porridge oats
400ml (14fl oz) milk or soya milk,
   plus extra to serve
75g (3oz) mixture of chopped dried
   figs, apricots and raisins

1 Put the oats into a large pan and add the milk and 400ml (14fl oz) water. Stir in the figs, apricots and raisins and heat gently, stirring until the porridge thickens and the oats are cooked.

2 Divide among four bowls and serve with a splash of milk.

Serves 4
Preparation Time 5 minutes
Cooking Time 5 minutes

Nutritional Information (Per Serving)
279 calories, 6g fat (of which 1g saturates), 49g carbohydrate, 0.2g salt
Easy

Toasted Oats with Berries

1 Preheat the grill to medium. Put the hazelnuts into a bowl with the oats. Drizzle with the oil and mix well, then spread out on a baking sheet. Toast the oat mixture for 5–10 minutes until it starts to crisp up. Remove from the heat and set aside to cool.

2 Put the strawberries into a large bowl with the blueberries and yogurt. Stir in the oats and hazelnuts, drizzle with the honey and divide among four dishes. Serve immediately.

25g (1oz) hazelnuts, roughly chopped
125g (4oz) rolled oats
1 tbsp olive oil
125g (4oz) strawberries, sliced
250g (9oz) blueberries
200g (7oz) Greek yogurt or soya yogurt
2 tbsp runny honey

Cook's Tip
Blueberries contain a substance that helps the gut to stay clean and healthy, and, like cranberries, they are rich in antioxidants.

Try Something Different
Use a mixture of raspberries, blackberries, or chopped nectarines or peaches instead of the strawberries and blueberries.

Nutritional Information (Per Serving)
327 calories, 15g fat (of which 3g saturates), 44g carbohydrate, 0.1g salt
Easy

Makes 15 servings
Preparation Time 5 minutes

Granola

300g (11oz) rolled oats
50g (2oz) each chopped Brazil nuts,
  flaked almonds, wheatgerm or rye
  flakes, and sunflower seeds
25g (1oz) sesame seeds
100ml (3½fl oz) sunflower oil
3 tbsp runny honey
100g (3½oz) each raisins and
  dried cranberries

1 Preheat the oven to 140°C (120°C fan oven) mark 1. Put the oats, nuts, wheatgerm or rye flakes, and all the seeds into a bowl. Gently heat the oil and honey in a pan. Pour over the oats and stir to combine. Spread on a shallow baking tray and cook in the oven for 1 hour or until golden, stirring once. Leave to cool.

2 Transfer to a bowl and stir in the dried fruit. Store in an airtight container – the granola will keep for up to a week. Serve with milk or yogurt.

Makes 15 servings
Preparation Time 5 minutes
Cooking Time 1 hour 5 minutes

Nutritional Information (Per Serving)
254 calories, 14g fat (of which 2g saturates), 29g carbohydrate, 0g salt
Dairy Free · Easy

Energy-boosting Muesli

1   Mix the oats with the almonds, seeds and apricots. Store in a sealable container: it will keep for up to one month. Serve with milk or yogurt.

500g (1lb 2oz) porridge oats
100g (3½oz) toasted almonds, chopped
2 tbsp pumpkin seeds
2 tbsp sunflower seeds
100g (3½oz) ready-to-eat dried apricots, chopped
milk or soya milk to serve

Cook's Tip

Oats contain gluten and, strictly speaking, are not suitable for coeliacs. However, because they contain a much smaller amount of gluten than wheat, rye or barley, research shows that most people with coeliac disease can safely eat moderate amounts. The oats must be from a source where there is no risk of contamination from wheat or wheat products during processing or packing. As individual tolerance to gluten varies, if you are a coeliac, seek expert advice before eating oats.

Nutritional Information (Per Serving)
208 calories, 9g fat (of which trace saturates), 28g carbohydrate, 0g salt
Dairy Free • Easy

Makes 15 servings
Preparation Time 5 minutes

Orange Eggy Bread

2 large eggs
150ml (¼ pint) milk
finely grated zest of 1 orange
50g (2oz) butter
8 slices raisin bread, halved
　　diagonally
1 tbsp caster sugar
vanilla ice cream and orange
　　segments to serve (optional)

1 Lightly whisk the eggs, milk and orange zest together in a bowl.

2 Heat the butter in a large frying pan over a medium heat. Dip the slices of raisin bread into the egg mixture, then fry on both sides until golden.

3 Sprinkle the bread with the sugar and serve immediately with ice cream and orange slices, if you like.

Serves 4
Preparation Time 10 minutes
Cooking Time 15 minutes

Nutritional Information (Per Serving)
358 calories, 13g fat (of which 7g saturates), 54g carbohydrate, 1.2g salt
Easy

Breakfast Bruschetta

1 Put the banana into a bowl with the blueberries. Spoon in the quark cheese and mix well.

2 Toast the slices of bread on both sides, then spread with the blueberry mixture. Drizzle with the honey and serve immediately.

1 ripe banana, peeled and sliced
250g (9oz) blueberries
200g (7oz) quark cheese (see Cook's Tip, page 35)
4 slices pumpernickel or wheat-free wholegrain bread
1 tbsp runny honey

Nutritional Information (Per Serving)
145 calories, 1g fat (of which 0g saturates), 30g carbohydrate, 0.4g salt
Easy

Serves 4
Preparation Time 5 minutes
Cooking Time 5 minutes

French Toast

2 medium eggs
150ml (¼ pint) semi-skimmed milk
a generous pinch of freshly grated
    nutmeg or ground cinnamon
4 slices white bread, or fruit bread,
    crusts removed and each slice cut
    into four fingers
50g (2oz) butter
vegetable oil for frying
1 tbsp golden caster sugar

1 Put the eggs, milk and nutmeg or cinnamon into a shallow dish and beat together.

2 Dip the pieces of bread into the mixture, coating them well.

3 Heat half the butter with 1 tbsp oil in a heavy-based frying pan. When the butter is foaming, fry the egg-coated bread pieces in batches, until golden on both sides, adding more butter and oil as needed. Sprinkle with sugar to serve.

Cook's Tips

Use leftover bread for this tasty breakfast or brunch dish.

For a savoury version, use white bread and omit the spice and sugar; serve with tomato ketchup, or with bacon and maple syrup.

Serves 4
Preparation Time 5 minutes
Cooking Time 10 minutes

Nutritional Information (Per Finger)
259 calories, 20g fat (of which 9g saturates), 15g carbohydrate, 0.7g salt
Easy

Lemon and Blueberry Pancakes

1 Sift the flour, baking powder and bicarbonate of soda into a bowl, tipping in the contents left in the sieve. Add the sugar and lemon zest. Pour in the yogurt and milk. Break the eggs into the mixture and whisk together.

2 Melt 25g (1oz) butter in a pan, add to the bowl with the blueberries and stir everything together.

3 Heat a dot of butter with the oil in a frying pan over a medium heat until hot. Add four large spoonfuls of the mixture to the pan to make four pancakes. After about 2 minutes, flip them over and cook for 1–2 minutes. Repeat with the remaining mixture, adding a dot more butter each time.

4 Serve with natural yogurt and some fruit compote.

125g (4oz) wholemeal plain flour
1 tsp baking powder
¼ tsp bicarbonate of soda
2 tbsp golden caster sugar
finely grated zest of 1 lemon
125g (4oz) natural yogurt
2 tbsp milk
2 medium eggs
40g (1½oz) butter
100g (3½oz) blueberries
1 tsp sunflower oil
natural yogurt and fruit compote
   to serve

Try Something Different
Instead of blueberries and lemon, use 100g (3½oz) chopped ready-to-eat dried apricots and 2 tsp grated fresh root ginger.

Nutritional Information (Per Serving)
290 calories, 13g fat (of which 6g saturates), 39g carbohydrate, 0.6g salt
Easy

Serves 4
Preparation Time 15 minutes
Cooking Time 10–15 minutes

Blueberry Muffins

250g (9oz) wheat-free flour
2 tsp wheat-free baking powder
1 tsp bicarbonate of soda
125g (4oz) golden caster sugar
75g (3oz) ground almonds
finely grated zest of 1 lemon
125g (4oz) dried blueberries
1 medium egg
1 tsp vanilla extract
250ml (9fl oz) skimmed milk
50g (2oz) unsalted butter, melted

1 Preheat the oven to 200°C (180°C fan oven) mark 6. Line a muffin tin with 12 paper muffin cases.

2 Put the flour, baking powder and bicarbonate of soda into a bowl, then stir in the caster sugar, ground almonds, lemon zest and dried blueberries.

3 Put the egg, vanilla extract, milk and butter into a jug and mix together with a fork. Pour this liquid into the dry ingredients and lightly fold together.

4 Spoon the mixture into the muffin cases to three-quarters fill them and bake in the oven for 15 minutes or until the muffins are risen, pale golden and just firm.

5 Transfer the muffins to a wire rack and leave to cool slightly before serving.

Try Something Different
Use chopped dried apricots, dried sour cherries or dried cranberries instead of the blueberries.

START YOUR DAY

Makes 12
Preparation Time 15 minutes
Cooking Time 15 minutes

Nutritional Information (Per Muffin)
228 calories, 8g fat (of which 3g saturates), 36g carbohydrate, 0.1g salt
Easy

Breakfast Cupcakes

1. Preheat the oven to 190°C (170°C fan oven), mark 5. Line a 12-hole muffin tin with paper muffin cases.

2. Using a hand-held electric whisk, whisk the butter and caster sugar in a bowl, or beat with a wooden spoon, until pale and creamy. Gradually whisk in the eggs until just combined. Using a metal spoon, fold in the apricot jam, flour, oatbran and baking powder until combined. Divide the mixture equally between the paper cases.

3. Bake for 20 minutes or until golden and risen. Leave to cool in the tin for 5 minutes, then transfer to a wire rack to cool completely.

4. For the icing, sift the icing sugar into a bowl, then add enough orange juice to achieve a smooth, thick icing. Spoon a little on top of each cake, then sprinkle with the granola. Stand the cakes upright on the wire rack and leave for about 1 hour to set.

175g (6oz) unsalted butter, softened
100g (3½oz) caster sugar
3 medium eggs
75g (3oz) apricot jam
150g (5oz) self-raising flour, sifted
75g (3oz) oatbran
½ tsp baking powder

FOR THE ICING AND DECORATION
225g (8oz) icing sugar
1–2 tbsp orange juice
75g (3oz) mixed berry granola

To Store
Store in an airtight container. They will keep for 3–5 days.

Freezing Tip
To freeze Complete the recipe to the end of step 3. Open-freeze, then wrap and freeze.

To use Thaw for about 1 hour, then complete the recipe.

Nutritional Information (Per Cupcake)
327 calories, 14g fat (of which 8g saturates), 48g carbohydrate, 0.3g salt
Easy

Makes 12
Preparation Time 30 minutes
Cooking Time 20 minutes, plus cooling and setting

Soups and starters

Beetroot Soup

Bloody Mary Soup with Bruschetta

Broad Bean, Pea and Mint Soup

Courgette and Leek Soup

Curried Parsnip Soup

Sweet Potato Soup

Pasta and Chickpea Soup with Pesto

Green Lentil and Coconut Soup

Spicy Bean and Courgette Soup

Pumpkin and Butternut Squash Soup

Spring Vegetable Broth

Red Onions with Rosemary Dressing

Chilli Onions with Goat's Cheese

Asparagus and Quail Egg Salad

Beef Tomatoes with Bulgur

Red Pepper Pesto Croûtes

Goat's Cheese Parcels

Mushroom Baskets

Cheese and Egg Tartlets

Mini Poppadoms

Beetroot Soup

1 tbsp olive oil

1 onion, finely chopped

750g (1lb 11oz) raw beetroot, peeled and cut into 1cm (½in) cubes

275g (10oz) potatoes, roughly chopped

2 litres (3½ pints) hot vegetable stock

juice of 1 lemon

8 tbsp soured cream

50g (2oz) mixed root vegetable crisps

salt and ground black pepper

2 tbsp chopped chives to garnish

1 Heat the oil in a large pan, add the onion and cook for 5 minutes. Add the beetroot and potatoes and cook for a further 5 minutes.

2 Add the hot stock and lemon juice, then bring to the boil. Season with salt and pepper, reduce the heat and simmer, half-covered, for 25 minutes. Cool slightly, then purée in a blender until smooth.

3 Pour the soup into a clean pan and reheat gently. Divide the soup among eight warmed bowls. Add 1 tbsp soured cream to each bowl, sprinkle with black pepper, top with a few vegetable crisps and sprinkle the chopped chives on top to serve.

Freezing Tip

To freeze Complete the recipe to the end of step 2, then freeze the soup in a sealed container. It will keep for up to three months.

To use Thaw in the fridge overnight. Reheat gently and simmer over a low heat for 5 minutes.

Serves 8
Preparation Time 15 minutes
Cooking Time 40–45 minutes

Nutritional Information (Per Serving)
216 calories, 9g fat (of which 3g saturates), 31g carbohydrate, 1.5g salt
Gluten Free • Easy

Bloody Mary Soup
with Bruschetta

V

1 Put the tomatoes into a large shallow dish and scatter with the spring onions, lemon zest and basil.

2 Blend together the oil, vinegar, 1 crushed garlic clove, the sugar, vodka, Worcestershire sauce and Tabasco. Season to taste with salt and pepper and pour over the tomatoes. Cover and leave to marinate for 2 hours at room temperature.

3 Put the tomato salad and tomato juice into a blender and whiz until very smooth. Transfer to a bowl and leave to chill in the fridge for 1 hour.

4 Just before serving, preheat the grill. Put the bread on the grill rack and toast lightly on both sides. Rub each one with the remaining crushed garlic, drizzle with oil and garnish with fresh basil leaves. Spoon the soup into bowls, drizzle with oil, sprinkle with black pepper and serve at once with the bruschetta.

700g (1½lb) ripe plum tomatoes, thinly sliced
6 spring onions, trimmed and finely chopped
grated zest of ½ lemon
2 tbsp freshly chopped basil, plus fresh basil leaves to garnish
125ml (4fl oz) extra virgin olive oil, plus extra to drizzle
2 tbsp balsamic vinegar
2–3 garlic cloves, crushed
a pinch of sugar
50ml (2fl oz) chilled vodka
1 tbsp vegetarian Worcestershire sauce
a few drops of Tabasco
150ml (¼ pint) tomato juice
8 thin slices bruschetta
salt and ground black pepper

Cook's Tip
This recipe is not suitable for children because it contains alcohol.

SOUPS AND STARTERS

Nutritional Information (Per Serving)
468 calories, 23g fat (of which 4g saturates), 52g carbohydrate, 1.5g salt
Dairy Free • Easy

Serves 4
Preparation Time 15 minutes, plus marinating and chilling
Cooking Time 5 minutes

33

Broad Bean, Pea and
Mint Soup

1 tbsp olive oil

1 medium onion, finely chopped

1.1kg (2½lb) fresh broad beans
    (pre-podded weight), podded

700g (1½lb) fresh peas (pre-podded
    weight), podded

1.1 litres (2 pints) hot vegetable stock

2 tbsp freshly chopped mint, plus
    extra sprigs to garnish

3 tbsp crème fraîche, plus extra
    to garnish (optional)

salt and ground black pepper

1 Heat the oil in a large pan and fry the onion gently for 15 minutes until softened.

2 Meanwhile, blanch the broad beans by cooking them for 2–3 minutes in a large pan of boiling water. Drain and refresh under cold water. Slip the beans out of their skins.

3 Put the beans and peas into the pan with the onion and stir for 1 minute. Add the hot stock and bring to the boil. Simmer for 5–8 minutes until the vegetables are tender, then cool for a few minutes. Stir in the mint, then whiz in batches in a blender or food processor until smooth. Alternatively, use a stick blender.

4 Return the soup to the rinsed-out pan, stir in the crème fraîche and check the seasoning. Reheat gently, then ladle into warmed bowls and garnish with a little crème fraîche, if you like, and a sprig of mint.

Serves 4
Preparation Time 20 minutes
Cooking Time 30 minutes

Nutritional Information (Per Serving)
176 calories, 4g fat (of which 1g saturates), 22g carbohydrate, 0.1g salt
Easy

Courgette and Leek Soup

1 Heat the oil in a large pan. Add the onion and leeks and cook for 5–10 minutes. Add the courgettes and cook, stirring, for a further 5 minutes.

2 Add the hot stock and 3 rosemary sprigs, then bring to the boil. Season with salt and pepper, reduce the heat and simmer for 20 minutes.

3 Preheat the grill to medium-high. Slice the bread diagonally into eight and grill for 1–2 minutes on one side until golden. Turn the bread over, sprinkle with the cheese and season. Grill for a further 1–2 minutes. Keep the croûtes warm.

4 Leave the soup to cool a little. Remove the rosemary stalks and whiz the soup in batches in a blender or food processor until smooth. Pour into a clean pan and reheat gently.

5 Ladle into warmed bowls, garnish with the croûtes and sprinkle with the remaining rosemary leaves.

1 tbsp olive oil
1 onion, finely chopped
2 leeks, trimmed and sliced
900g (2lb) courgettes, grated
1.3 litres (2¾ pints) hot
    vegetable stock
4 short rosemary sprigs
1 small baguette
125g (4oz) grated Gruyère cheese
    (see Cook's Tip)
salt and ground black pepper

Cook's Tip
Vegetarian cheeses: some vegetarians prefer to avoid cheeses that have been produced by the traditional method, because this uses animal-derived rennet. Most supermarkets and cheese shops now stock an excellent range of vegetarian cheeses, produced using vegetarian rennet, which comes from plants, such as thistle and mallow, that contain enzymes capable of curdling milk.

Nutritional Information (Per Serving)
246 calories, 9g fat (of which 3g saturates), 32g carbohydrate, 1g salt
Easy

Serves 8
Preparation Time 15 minutes
Cooking Time 35–40 minutes

Curried Parsnip Soup

40g (1½ oz) butter
1 onion, sliced
700g (1½lb) parsnips, peeled, cored and finely diced
1 tsp curry powder (see Cook's Tip)
½ tsp ground cumin
1.2 litres (2 pints) vegetable stock
150ml (¼ pint) single cream
salt and ground black pepper
paprika to sprinkle

1 Melt the butter in a large pan, add the onion and fry gently for 5–7 minutes. Add the parsnips and fry gently for about 3 minutes.

2 Stir in the curry powder and cumin and cook for a further 2 minutes.

3 Add the stock, season to taste with salt and pepper and bring to the boil. Reduce the heat, cover the pan and simmer for 35 minutes or until the vegetables are tender.

4 Leave the soup to cool a little, then whiz in batches in a blender or food processor until smooth. Return the soup to the pan and adjust the seasoning. Add the cream and reheat but do not boil.

5 Ladle the soup into warmed bowls, sprinkle each with a little paprika and serve.

Cook's Tip
Curry Powder
Bought curry powders are readily available, but for optimum flavour make your own.

To make your own curry powder: Put 1 tbsp each cumin and fenugreek seeds, ½ tsp mustard seeds, 1½ tsp each poppy seeds, black peppercorns and ground ginger, 4 tbsp coriander seeds, ½ tsp hot chilli powder and 2 tbsp ground turmeric into an electric blender or grinder. Grind to a fine powder. Store in an airtight container and use within one month.

Serves 6
Preparation Time 20 minutes
Cooking Time 50 minutes

Nutritional Information (Per Serving)
184 calories, 12g fat (of which 7g saturates), 17g carbohydrate, 0.2g salt
Easy

Sweet Potato Soup

1 Heat the oil in a large pan over a gentle heat and fry the onion for about 10 minutes until soft. Add the coriander seeds and chillies to the pan and cook for 1–2 minutes.

2 Add the squash, sweet potatoes and tomatoes and cook for 5 minutes. Add the hot stock, cover and bring to the boil. Simmer gently for 15 minutes or until the vegetables are soft. Using a blender, purée the soup in batches until smooth. Season with salt and pepper. Reheat gently, then divide among eight warmed bowls. Sprinkle with black pepper.

1 tbsp olive oil
1 large onion, finely chopped
2 tsp coriander seeds, crushed
2 fresh red chillies, seeded and chopped (see Cook's Tips)
1 butternut squash, about 750g (1lb 11oz), peeled and roughly chopped
2 sweet potatoes, roughly chopped
2 tomatoes, peeled and diced
1.7 litres (3 pints) hot vegetable stock
salt and ground black pepper

Cook's Tips

Chillies vary enormously in strength, from quite mild to blisteringly hot, depending on the type of chilli and its ripeness. Taste a small piece first to check it's not too hot for you.

Be extremely careful when handling chillies not to touch or rub your eyes with your fingers, as they will sting. Wash knives immediately after handling chillies. As a precaution, use rubber gloves when preparing them if you like.

SOUPS AND STARTERS

Nutritional Information (Per Serving)
78 calories, 2g fat (of which trace saturates), 14g carbohydrate, 0.8g salt
Gluten Free · Dairy Free · Easy

Serves 8
Preparation Time 20 minutes
Cooking Time 35 minutes

Pasta and Chickpea Soup
with Pesto

3 tbsp olive oil
1 onion, chopped
2 garlic cloves, finely chopped
1 small leek, trimmed and sliced
1 tsp freshly chopped rosemary
400g can chickpeas
1.2 litres (2 pints) vegetable stock
4 ripe tomatoes, skinned and chopped
1 courgette, diced
125g (4oz) shelled peas
125g (4oz) French beans, halved
125g (4oz) shelled broad beans
50g (2oz) dried pastina (small
   soup pasta)
2 tbsp freshly chopped parsley
salt and ground black pepper
pesto (see Cook's Tip) and freshly
   grated pecorino or Parmesan (see
   Cook's Tip, page 35) to serve

1 Heat the oil in a large saucepan, add the onion, garlic, leek and rosemary and fry gently for 5–6 minutes until softened but not coloured. Add the chickpeas with their liquid, the stock and tomatoes. Bring to the boil, then reduce the heat, cover the pan and simmer for 40 minutes.

2 Add the courgette, peas, French beans and broad beans. Return to the boil, then reduce the heat and simmer for 10 minutes. Add the pasta and parsley and simmer for 6–8 minutes until al dente. Season to taste with salt and pepper.

3 Ladle into warmed bowls and serve topped with a spoonful of pesto and a sprinkling of cheese.

Cook's Tip
Pesto
Roughly chop 75g (3oz) basil, 50g (2oz) Parmesan, 25g (1oz) pinenuts and ½ crushed garlic clove and put into a food processor. With the motor running, add 50–75ml (2–3fl oz) extra virgin olive oil to make a paste. Season well with salt and pepper.

Serves 6
Preparation Time 25 minutes
Cooking Time about 1 hour

Nutritional Information (Per Serving)
211 calories, 8g fat (of which 1g saturates), 26g carbohydrate, 0.3g salt
Easy

Green Lentil and Coconut Soup ⓥ

1 Put the lentils into a sieve and wash thoroughly under cold running water. Drain well.

2 Heat the oil in a large saucepan. Add the potatoes and fry gently for 5 minutes until beginning to colour. Remove with a slotted spoon and drain on kitchen paper.

3 Add the onion to the pan and fry gently for 10 minutes until soft. Add the garlic, turmeric and cumin and fry for 2–3 minutes. Add the coconut, stock, coconut milk and lentils and bring to the boil, then reduce the heat, cover the pan and simmer gently for 20 minutes or until the lentils are just tender.

4 Add the potatoes and lemon zest and season to taste with salt and pepper. Cook gently for a further 5 minutes or until the potatoes are tender. Ladle into warmed bowls, garnish with toasted coconut and the coriander sprigs, if you like, and serve hot.

225g (8oz) whole green lentils
4 tbsp sunflower oil
350g (12oz) floury potatoes, peeled and diced
1 large onion, chopped
2 garlic cloves, crushed
¼ tsp ground turmeric
2 tsp ground cumin
50g (2oz) creamed coconut
750ml (1¼ pints) vegetable stock
300ml (½ pint) coconut milk
finely grated zest of 1 lemon
salt and ground black pepper
toasted fresh coconut and coriander sprigs (optional) to garnish

Nutritional Information (Per Serving)
442 calories, 22g fat (of which 10g saturates), 48g carbohydrate, 0.3g salt
Dairy Free • Easy

Serves 4
Preparation Time 20 minutes
Cooking Time 40 minutes

Spicy Bean and Courgette
Soup

2 tbsp olive oil
175g (6oz) onions, finely chopped
2 garlic cloves, crushed
2 tsp ground coriander
1 tbsp paprika
1 tsp mild curry powder
450g (1lb) courgettes, trimmed,
   halved and sliced
225g (8oz) potatoes, peeled
   and diced
400g can red kidney beans, drained
   and rinsed
425g can flageolet beans, drained
   and rinsed
1.5 litres (2½ pints) vegetable stock
salt and ground black pepper
crusty bread to serve

1 Heat the oil in a pan. Add the onions and garlic and sauté for 2 minutes. Add the spices and cook, stirring, for 1 minute. Mix in the courgettes and potatoes and cook for 1–2 minutes.

2 Add the remaining ingredients and bring to the boil, then reduce the heat, cover the pan and simmer for 25 minutes, stirring occasionally, or until the potatoes are tender. Adjust the seasoning if necessary.

3 Ladle into warmed bowls and serve with crusty bread.

Cook's Tip
Courgettes are baby marrows. Look for small, firm vegetables. They lose their flavour as they grow larger.

Serves 4
Preparation Time 10 minutes
Cooking Time 30 minutes

Nutritional Information (Per Serving)
289 calories, 8g fat (of which 1g saturates), 43g carbohydrate, 1.5g salt
Dairy Free · Easy

Pumpkin and Butternut
Squash Soup

1 Preheat the oven to 220°C (200°C fan oven) mark 7. Put the pumpkin, squash, shallots, garlic and coriander seeds into a large roasting tin and toss with the melted butter. Season the vegetables well with salt and pepper and bake for about 30 minutes until golden and just cooked through.

2 Meanwhile, in separate pans, heat the stock and milk.

3 Transfer the vegetables to a large pan, then pour the hot stock into the roasting tin and stir to loosen the remaining bits in the tin. Add this to the vegetables in the pan, then stir in the milk.

4 Put three-quarters of the soup into a blender or food processor and whiz until smooth. Mash the remaining soup mixture, then stir the two together and reheat gently. Ladle into warmed bowls, garnish with basil and swirls of soured cream, then serve with crusty bread or small Yorkshire puddings.

900g (2lb) pumpkin, peeled and
  roughly diced
750g (1lb 10oz) butternut squash,
  peeled and roughly diced
125g (4oz) shallots, roughly chopped
1 fat garlic clove, chopped
1 tsp coriander seeds, crushed
125g (4oz) butter, melted
600ml (1 pint) vegetable stock
600ml (1 pint) full-fat milk
salt and ground black pepper
basil sprigs and soured cream
  to garnish
crusty bread or small Yorkshire
  puddings to serve

Nutritional Information (Per Serving)
398 calories, 32.5g fat (of which 21g saturates), 19g carbohydrate, 0.8g salt
Easy

Serves 4
Preparation Time 20 minutes
Cooking Time 40 minutes

Spring Vegetable Broth

1 tbsp olive oil

4 shallots, chopped

1 fennel bulb, chopped

1 leek, trimmed and chopped

5 small carrots, chopped

1.1 litres (2 pints) hot vegetable stock

2 courgettes, chopped

1 bunch of asparagus, chopped

2 × 400g cans cannellini beans, drained and rinsed

50g (2oz) Gruyère or Parmesan cheese shavings (see Cook's Tip, page 35) to serve

1 Heat the oil in a large pan. Add the shallots, fennel, leek and carrots and fry for 5 minutes or until they start to soften.

2 Add the hot stock, cover and bring to the boil. Add the courgettes, asparagus and beans, then reduce the heat and simmer for 5–6 minutes until the vegetables are tender.

3 Ladle into warmed bowls, sprinkle with a little cheese and serve.

Try Something Different

This broth is also good with a tablespoon of pesto (see Cook's Tip, page 38) added to each bowl, and served with chunks of crusty bread.

Serves 4
Preparation Time 20 minutes
Cooking Time 20 minutes

Nutritional Information (Per Serving)
264 calories, 6g fat (of which 3g saturates), 35g carbohydrate, 2.4g salt
Easy

Red Onions
with Rosemary Dressing

1 Preheat the barbecue. Soak eight wooden skewers in water for 20 minutes. Thread the onion wedges on to the skewers. Brush with about 3 tbsp oil, then season well with salt and pepper.

2 Barbecue the onion kebabs for 30–35 minutes, turning from time to time and brushing with oil when necessary, until tender and lightly charred.

3 To make the dressing, mix the vinegar with the remaining oil and the rosemary. Drizzle the rosemary dressing over the cooked onions and serve.

3 large red onions, root intact,
   each cut into eight wedges
6 tbsp olive oil
4 tbsp balsamic vinegar
2 tsp freshly chopped rosemary
salt and ground black pepper

Nutritional Information (Per Serving)
91 calories, 6g fat (of which trace saturates), 9g carbohydrate, trace salt
Gluten Free · Dairy Free · Easy

Serves 8
Preparation Time 20 minutes
Cooking Time 30–35 minutes

Chilli Onions with Goat's Cheese

75g (3oz) unsalted butter, softened
2 medium red chillies, seeded and
    finely chopped (see Cook's Tips,
    page 37)
1 tsp crushed dried chillies
6 small red onions
3 × 100g (3½oz) goat's cheese logs,
    with rind (see Cook's Tip, page 35)
salt and ground black pepper
balsamic vinegar to serve

1 Preheat the oven to 200°C (180°C fan oven) mark 6. Put the butter into a small bowl, beat in the fresh and dried chillies and season well with salt and pepper.

2 Cut off the root from one of the onions, sit it on its base, then make several deep cuts in the top to create a star shape, slicing about two-thirds of the way down the onion. Do the same with the other five onions, then divide the chilli butter equally among them, pushing it down into the cuts.

3 Put the onions into a small roasting tin, cover with foil and bake for 40–45 minutes until soft.

4 About 5 minutes before the onions are ready, slice each goat's cheese in two, leaving the rind intact, then put on a baking sheet and bake for 2–3 minutes.

5 To serve, put each onion on top of a piece of goat's cheese and drizzle with balsamic vinegar.

Serves 6
Preparation Time 15 minutes
Cooking Time 45 minutes

Nutritional Information (Per Serving)
276 calories, 23g fat (of which 16g saturates), 5g carbohydrate, 0.9g salt
Gluten Free · Easy

Asparagus and Quail Egg Salad

1. Add the quail's eggs to a pan of boiling water and cook for 2 minutes, then drain and plunge into cold water. Cook the asparagus in lightly salted boiling water for 2 minutes or until just tender. Drain, plunge into cold water and leave to cool.

2. Whisk together the lemon juice, oil and seasoning. Stir in the spring onions and put to one side.

3. Peel the quail's eggs and cut in half. Put into a large bowl with the asparagus, watercress, dill and tarragon. Pour the dressing over and lightly toss all the ingredients together. Adjust the seasoning and serve.

24 quail's eggs
24 asparagus spears, trimmed
juice of ½ lemon
5 tbsp olive oil
4 large spring onions, finely sliced
100g (3½oz) watercress, roughly chopped
a few fresh dill and tarragon sprigs
salt and ground black pepper

Nutritional Information (Per Serving)
127 calories, 11g fat (of which 2g saturates), 1g carbohydrate, 0.1g salt
Gluten Free · Dairy Free · Easy

Serves 8
Preparation Time 30 minutes
Cooking Time 2 minutes

Beef Tomatoes with Bulgur

125g (4oz) bulgur wheat
20g (¾oz) flat-leafed parsley,
    finely chopped
75g (3oz) feta cheese, chopped (see
    Cook's Tip, page 35)
1 courgette, chopped
50g (2oz) flaked almonds, toasted
4 large beef tomatoes
1 tbsp olive oil

1 Preheat the oven to 180°C (160°C fan oven) mark 4. Cook the bulgur according to the pack instructions. Chop the parsley, feta and courgette and stir into the bulgur with the almonds.

2 Chop the top off each tomato and scoop out the seeds. Put on to a baking sheet and spoon in the bulgur mixture. Drizzle with the oil and cook in the oven for 15–20 minutes until the cheese is starting to soften. Serve.

Try Something Different

Try quinoa instead of the bulgur wheat. Put the quinoa in a bowl of cold water and mix well, then soak for 2 minutes. Drain. Put into a pan with twice its volume of water and bring to the boil. Simmer for 20 minutes. Remove from the heat, cover and leave to stand for 10 minutes.

Serves 4
Preparation Time 10 minutes
Cooking Time 30–35 minutes

Nutritional Information (Per Serving)
245 calories, 14g fat of which 4g saturates), 21g carbohydrate, 0.7g salt
Easy

Red Pepper Pesto Croûtes

1 Preheat the oven to 200°C (180°C fan oven) mark 6. Brush both sides of the bread with oil and put on a baking sheet. Cook in the oven for 15–20 minutes.

2 Spread 1 tsp pesto on each croûte, top with a pepper strip and pinenuts and serve.

1 thin French stick, sliced into
    24 rounds
olive oil to brush
fresh pesto (see Cook's Tip, page 38)
4 pepper pieces (from a jar of
    marinated peppers), each sliced
    into 6 strips
pinenuts to garnish

Nutritional Information (Per Croûte)
90 calories, 5g fat (of which 1g saturates), 10g carbohydrate, 0.3g salt
Easy

Serves 24
Preparation Time 20 minutes
Cooking Time 15–20 minutes

Goat's Cheese Parcels

125g (4oz) fresh spinach leaves
2 tbsp sunflower oil
1 onion, finely chopped
1 large garlic clove, chopped
250g (9oz) soft goat's cheese (see
  Cook's Tip, page 35)
275g (10oz) filo pastry, thawed
  if frozen
50g (2oz) butter, melted
sesame seeds to sprinkle
salt and ground black pepper

1 Plunge the spinach into a pan of boiling water, bring back to the boil for 1 minute, then drain and refresh under very cold water. Squeeze out all the excess liquid and chop finely.

2 Heat the oil in a pan, add the onion and garlic and cook until translucent, then allow to cool. Combine the spinach, onion mixture and goat's cheese in a bowl and season generously.

3 Cut the pastry into twenty-four 12.5cm (5in) squares. Brush one square with melted butter, cover with a second square and brush with more butter. Put to one side and cover with a damp teatowel. Repeat with the remaining squares, to make twelve sets.

4 Put a dessertspoonful of the filling on each square and join up the corners to form a parcel. Brush with a little more butter, sprinkle with sesame seeds and chill for 20 minutes. Meanwhile, preheat the oven to 220°C (200°C fan oven) mark 7. Bake for about 5 minutes or until the pastry is crisp and browned.

Serves 6
Preparation Time 45 minutes,
  plus cooling
Cooking Time 10 minutes

Nutritional Information (2 parcels per serving)
345 calories, 22g fat (of which 12g saturates), 26g carbohydrate, 0.8g salt
Easy

Mushroom Baskets

1. Whiz the flour and butter in a food processor until the mixture resembles fine breadcrumbs. Add the egg and pulse until the mixture comes together. Knead lightly on a floured surface and shape into six balls. Wrap and chill for 30 minutes. Roll out the pastry on a lightly floured surface and line six loose-based tart tins, 9cm (3½in) across the base. Prick the bases and chill for 20 minutes. Meanwhile, preheat the oven to 200°C (180°C fan oven) mark 6. Line the pastry case with greaseproof paper, fill with baking beans and bake blind for 15–20 minutes. Remove the paper and beans, prick the pastry base all over with a fork and cook for a further 5–10 minutes until golden. Reduce the oven temperature to 180°C (160°C fan oven) mark 4.

2. To make the filling, heat the butter in a pan, add the onion and cook for 10 minutes. Add the sliced mushrooms and garlic and cook for 5 minutes, then remove and set aside. Put the dried mushrooms and their liquid into the pan with the sherry. Bring to the boil and bubble for 10 minutes, then add the cream and cook for 5 minutes or until syrupy.

3. To serve, warm the pastry in the oven for 5 minutes. Add the reserved mushrooms to the sauce, season and heat through. Pour into the cases, garnish with thyme and serve with salad.

Freezing Tip

To freeze Complete the recipe to the end of step 1, then cool, wrap and freeze the baskets.

To use Thaw, then complete the recipe.

250g (9oz) plain flour, plus extra
   to dust
150g (5oz) chilled butter, cubed
1 large egg
fresh thyme sprigs to garnish
green salad to serve

FOR THE FILLING
50g (2oz) butter
225g (8oz) onion, finely chopped
450g (1lb) mixed mushrooms, sliced
1 garlic clove, crushed
15g (½oz) dried mushrooms, soaked
   in 300ml (½ pint) boiling water for
   10 minutes
300ml (½ pint) medium-dry sherry
300ml (½ pint) double cream
salt and ground black pepper

SOUPS AND STARTERS

Nutritional Information (Per Serving)
659 calories, 48g fat (of which 29g saturates), 37g carbohydrate, 0.5g salt
Easy

Serves 6
Preparation Time 40 minutes,
   plus chilling
Cooking Time 50 minutes

Cheese and Egg Tartlets

12 thin slices white bread
25g (1oz) butter, melted
2 hard-boiled eggs, finely chopped
50g (2oz) Cheddar, grated (see
    Cook's Tip, page 35)
2–3 tbsp mayonnaise
mustard and cress
salt and ground black pepper

1 Preheat the oven to 180°C (160°C fan oven) mark 4. Flatten the bread slightly with a rolling pin and cut out rounds with a 7.5cm (3in) fluted cutter. Brush with melted butter and press into the holes of a bun tin. Sit another bun tin on top to keep the bread pressed down and bake for 15–20 minutes until golden brown and crisp. Cool on a wire rack.

2 Mix the hard-boiled eggs with the cheese and mayonnaise. Season with salt and pepper. Divide between the tartlet cases and sprinkle with the mustard and cress.

Get Ahead

To prepare ahead Complete the recipe to the end of step 1, cool, then store the tartlet cases in airtight containers for up to two weeks.

To use Complete the recipe.

Serves 12
Preparation Time 15 minutes
Cooking Time 15–20 minutes

Nutritional Information (Per Serving)
134 calories, 7g fat (of which 3g saturates), 13g carbohydrate, 0.5g salt
Easy

Mini Poppadoms

1. Preheat the oven to 200°C (180°C fan oven) mark 6. Pierce the aubergines several times with a sharp knife, put on a baking sheet and cook in the oven for about 1 hour or until very soft. Leave to cool.

2. Peel the aubergines. Wrap the flesh in a clean cloth and squeeze to remove any excess juice. Add the garlic, tahini and lemon juice and mash well with a fork or blend in a food processor. Stir in the chopped coriander and enough water to give a dipping consistency. Season with salt and pepper.

3. Put a little purée on each of the poppadoms and garnish with paprika and coriander sprigs. Serve with Spicy Red Pepper Dip.

2 large aubergines
1–2 garlic cloves, crushed
1 tbsp tahini (see Cook's Tips)
juice of ½ lemon
3 tbsp freshly chopped coriander, plus extra sprigs to garnish
1 pack mini poppadoms (40 in pack)
salt and ground black pepper
paprika to garnish
Spicy Red Pepper Dip to serve (see Cook's Tips)

Cook's Tips

Tahini is a thick, creamy paste that is made from ground sesame seeds. You can buy it in supermarkets and health food shops (see page 283).

Spicy Red Pepper Dip

Preheat the grill. Chargrill 3 large halved red peppers (about 450g/1lb) total weight as above, then peel and seed. Put the flesh into a food processor or blender with 200g tub reduced-fat soft cheese and ½ tsp hot pepper sauce and whiz until smooth. Cover and leave to chill for at least 2 hours to let the flavours develop. Taste and adjust the seasoning if necessary. Serves 8.

Nutritional Information (Per Serving)
128 calories, 6g fat (of which 1g saturates), 16g carbohydrate, 0.4g salt
Gluten Free · Dairy Free · Easy

Serves 8
Preparation Time 5 minutes, plus cooling
Cooking Time about 1 hour

Salads

Tomato, Mozzarella and Red Pesto Salad

Japanese Noodle Salad

Thai Noodle Salad

Sprouted Bean and Mango Salad

Chicory, Stilton and Walnut Salad

Panzanella

Grilled Ciabatta and Mozzarella Salad

Halloumi and Avocado Salad

Feta, Peach and Watercress Salad

Roasted Root Vegetable Salad

Spinach and Carrot Salad

Winter Leaf Salad

Winter Coleslaw

Warm Tofu, Fennel and Bean Salad

Warm Salad with Quorn and Berries

Warm Pear and Walnut Caesar Salad

Tomato, Mozzarella
and Red Pesto Salad

225g (8oz) baby plum tomatoes,
  halved
225g (8oz) baby mozzarella, drained
  (see Cook's Tip below and
  page 35)
100g jar red pepper pesto
175g (6oz) pitted black olives,
  drained
100g (3½oz) mixed salad leaves
salt and ground black pepper

1 Put the tomatoes, mozzarella, pesto and olives into a large bowl and toss together. Season with pepper. Check the seasoning before adding any salt, though, as the olives are already salty. Cover the bowl and put to one side.

2 Just before serving, toss the salad leaves with the tomato and mozzarella mixture.

Cook's Tip
If you can't find baby mozzarella, buy larger buffalo mozzarella instead – available from most major supermarkets – and cut it into large cubes.

Serves 4
Preparation Time 10 minutes

Nutritional Information (Per Serving)
400 calories, 36g fat (of which 12g saturates), 3g carbohydrate, 2.9g salt
Gluten Free · Easy

Japanese Noodle Salad

1 Dry-fry the sesame seeds in a frying pan until golden.
Set aside.

2 Cook the noodles in a pan of lightly salted boiling water for
5 minutes or until tender but firm. Drain and cool under cold
running water. Drain again and put into a bowl.

3 Add the toasted sesame seeds, tamari, sesame oil and vinegar
and toss to coat the noodles. Chill until needed or for up to
24 hours. To serve, top with spring onions.

2 tbsp sesame seeds
200g (7oz) Japanese 100% wheat-
    free soba noodles
2–3 tbsp tamari (wheat-free Japanese
    soy sauce)
1 tbsp sesame oil
1 tbsp rice vinegar
salt
1 small bunch of spring onions, finely
    sliced, to serve

Try Something Different
Thinly sliced mushrooms, diced
red pepper, cubes of tofu (not
silken) or cooked broccoli or
asparagus spears can all be
added. Add to the salad just
before serving, and mix well.

SALADS

Nutritional Information (Per Serving)
268 calories, 10g fat (of which 1g saturates), 39g carbohydrate, 2g salt
Gluten Free · Dairy Free · Easy

Serves 4
Preparation Time 2 minutes,
    plus chilling
Cooking Time 7 minutes

Thai Noodle Salad

200g (7oz) sugarsnap peas, trimmed

250g pack Thai stir-fry rice noodles

100g (3½oz) cashew nuts

300g (11oz) carrots, peeled and cut into batons

10 spring onions, sliced diagonally

300g (11oz) bean sprouts

20g (¾oz) fresh coriander, roughly chopped, plus coriander sprigs to garnish

1 red bird's-eye chilli, seeded and finely chopped (see Cook's Tip below and page 37)

2 tsp sweet chilli sauce

4 tbsp sesame oil

6 tbsp soy sauce

juice of 2 limes

salt and ground black pepper

1 Bring a pan of lightly salted water to the boil and blanch the sugarsnap peas for 2–3 minutes until just tender to the bite. Drain and refresh under cold water.

2 Put the noodles into a bowl, cover with boiling water and leave to soak for 4 minutes. Rinse under cold water and drain very well.

3 Toast the cashews in a dry frying pan until golden – about 5 minutes.

4 Put the sugarsnaps in a large glass serving bowl. Add the carrots, spring onions, bean sprouts, chopped coriander, chopped chilli, cashews and noodles. Mix together the chilli sauce, sesame oil, soy sauce and lime juice and season well with salt and pepper. Pour over the salad and toss together, then garnish with coriander sprigs and serve.

Cook's Tip

Red bird's-eye chillies are always very hot. The smaller they are, the hotter they are.

Serves 4
Preparation Time 20 minutes, plus soaking
Cooking Time 7–8 minutes

Nutritional Information (Per Serving)
568 calories, 29g fat (of which 4g saturates), 65g carbohydrate, 2.9g salt
Dairy Free · Easy

Sprouted Bean and
Mango Salad

1 To make the dressing, put the mango chutney into a small bowl and add the lime zest and juice. Whisk in the oil and season with salt and pepper.

2 Quarter the tomatoes, discard the seeds and then dice. Put into a large bowl with the onion, peppers, mango, coriander and sprouted beans. Pour in the dressing and mix well. Serve immediately.

3 tbsp mango chutney
grated zest and juice of 1 lime
2 tbsp olive oil
4 plum tomatoes
1 small red onion, finely chopped
1 red pepper, seeded and finely diced
1 yellow pepper, seeded and finely diced
1 mango, finely diced
4 tbsp freshly chopped coriander
150g (5oz) sprouted beans
salt and ground black pepper

Try Something Different
Use papaya instead of mango.

Ginger and Chilli Dressing
Mix together 2 tsp grated fresh root ginger, 1 tbsp sweet chilli sauce, 2 tsp white wine vinegar and 2 tbsp walnut oil. Season with salt.

Peanut Dressing
Mix together 1 tbsp peanut butter, ¼ of a whole dried chilli, crushed, 4 tsp white wine vinegar, 3 tbsp walnut oil, 1 tsp sesame oil and a dash of soy sauce.

SALADS

Nutritional Information (Per Serving)
103 calories, 4g fat (of which 1g saturates), 15g carbohydrate, 0.1g salt
Dairy Free · Easy

Serves 6
Preparation Time 15 minutes

Chicory, Stilton and
Walnut Salad

200g (7oz) Stilton, crumbled (see
   Cook's Tip, page 35)
75ml (3fl oz) double cream
nutmeg to grate
a little milk
2 Cox's Orange Pippin apples, cored
   and sliced
juice of ½ lemon
1 head each green and red chicory
3 handfuls of watercress
50g (2oz) walnuts, toasted
salt and ground black pepper

1 Put 125g (4oz) Stilton into a pan with the cream and a grating of nutmeg. Stir over a gentle heat until bubbling. Thin with a little milk if too thick.

2 Toss the apples in the lemon juice in a bowl. Cut the chicory into bite-size pieces and add to the bowl with the watercress. Season with salt and pepper and toss. Divide among six plates along with the toasted walnuts and remaining Stilton. Drizzle the dressing over the salad and serve at once.

Get Ahead

To prepare ahead Complete the recipe to the end of step 1 up to one day in advance and keep chilled.

To use Reheat the Stilton sauce gently just before serving. Complete the recipe.

SALADS

Serves 6
Preparation Time 15 minutes
Cooking Time 5 minutes

Nutritional Information (Per Serving)
270 calories, 24g fat (of which 12g saturates), 5g carbohydrate, 0.8g salt
Gluten Free · Easy

Panzanella

1 Put the bread into a large bowl with the tomatoes, capers, thyme, onion, garlic, chillies, oil, olives and sun-dried tomatoes. Season well with salt and pepper, then toss together and leave in a cool place for at least 30 minutes.

2 Toss the salad thoroughly again. Tear the basil into pieces and scatter over the salad with the Parmesan shavings. Garnish with thyme sprigs and then serve.

2–3 thick slices from a day-old country loaf, about 100g (3½oz), torn or cut into cubes
450g (1lb) ripe tomatoes, roughly chopped
2 tbsp capers
1 tsp freshly chopped thyme
1 small red onion, thinly sliced
2 garlic cloves, finely chopped
2 small red chillies, seeded and finely chopped (see Cook's Tips, page 37)
4 tbsp extra virgin olive oil
125g (4oz) pitted black olives
50g (2oz) sun-dried tomatoes, roughly chopped
8 fresh basil leaves
25g (1oz) Parmesan, pared into shavings with a vegetable peeler (see Cook's Tip, page 35)
salt and ground black pepper
fresh thyme sprigs to garnish

Cook's Tip
Panzanella is a Tuscan salad, which uses stale bread.

Get Ahead
This salad is best made 2–3 hours ahead to let the flavours mingle.

SALADS

Nutritional Information (Per Serving)
228 calories, 14g fat (of which 3g saturates), 21g carbohydrate, 0.6g salt
Easy

Serves 4
Preparation Time 20 minutes, plus chilling

59

Grilled Ciabatta and
Mozzarella Salad

8 thick slices Italian bread, such
    as ciabatta
2 tsp olive paste or sun-dried
    tomato paste
2 × 150g packs mozzarella cheese,
    drained and sliced (see Cook's Tip,
    page 35)
4 tbsp olive oil, plus extra to drizzle
2 tbsp balsamic vinegar
280g jar marinated artichoke hearts
    in oil, drained and sliced (see
    Cook's Tip)
100g (3½oz) rocket salad
50g (2oz) sun-dried tomato halves
salt and ground black pepper

1 Preheat the grill. Toast the bread slices on one side. Spread the untoasted side with olive or sun-dried tomato paste, then top with mozzarella slices and drizzle lightly with oil.

2 Mix the vinegar, salt and pepper in a bowl and whisk in the 4 tbsp oil. Add the artichoke hearts.

3 Place the bread slices under the grill for 2–3 minutes until the mozzarella browns lightly.

4 Toss the rocket salad with the artichoke mixture and divide among four plates. Top with two slices of grilled bread and the sun-dried tomatoes and serve.

Cook's Tip
Find marinated artichokes in supermarkets; alternatively, buy canned artichoke hearts, drain, slice and cover in olive oil. They will keep in the refrigerator for up to one week.

Serves 4
Preparation Time 10 minutes
Cooking Time 5 minutes

Nutritional Information (Per Serving)
613 calories, 33g fat (of which 13g saturates), 56g carbohydrate, 2.4g salt
Easy

Halloumi and Avocado Salad

1 To make the dressing, whisk the lemon juice with the oil and mint, then season with salt and pepper.

2 Coat the halloumi with the flour. Heat the oil in a large frying pan and fry the cheese for 1 minute on each side or until it forms a golden crust.

3 Meanwhile, in a large bowl, add half the dressing to the salad leaves and avocado and toss together. Arrange the hot cheese on top and drizzle the remaining dressing over it. Garnish with rocket leaves and serve with lemon halves to squeeze over the salad.

250g (9oz) halloumi cheese, sliced into eight (see Cook's Tip below and page 35)
1 tbsp flour, seasoned
2 tbsp olive oil
200g (7oz) mixed leaf salad
2 ripe avocados, halved, stoned, peeled and sliced
fresh rocket leaves to garnish
lemon halves to serve

FOR THE MINT DRESSING
3 tbsp lemon juice
8 tbsp olive oil
3 tbsp freshly chopped mint
salt and ground black pepper

Cook's Tip
Halloumi is a firm cheese made from ewe's milk. It is best used sliced and cooked.

Nutritional Information (Per Serving)
397 calories, 34g fat (of which 13g saturates), 11g carbohydrate, 2.3g salt
Easy

Serves 4
Preparation Time 10 minutes
Cooking Time 2 minutes

Feta, Peach and
Watercress Salad

3 slices walnut bread, cubed
1 tbsp olive oil
4 peaches, halved, stoned
    and cut into wedges
50g bag watercress
50g bag rocket
200g (7oz) feta cheese, roughly
    broken up (see Cook's Tip,
    page 35)
25g (1oz) each walnuts and mixed
    seeds (such as linseeds, pinenuts
    and sesame seeds)
1 tbsp toasted sesame oil
3 tbsp extra virgin olive oil
2 tbsp red wine vinegar
a few mint leaves, chopped
salt and ground black pepper
1 lemon, cut into six wedges, to serve

1 Preheat the oven to 200°C (180°C fan oven) mark 6. Put the cubed bread on a baking tray, drizzle with the olive oil and bake for 10 minutes until golden. Put the peaches into a large bowl with the watercress, rocket, feta and nuts and seeds.

2 Mix together the sesame and extra virgin olive oils and the vinegar, add the mint leaves and season with salt and pepper. Add half the dressing to the bowl and toss.

3 Divide the salad among six plates, then drizzle with the remaining dressing. Serve each with a lemon wedge to squeeze over.

Serves 6
Preparation Time 15 minutes
Cooking Time 10 minutes

Nutritional Information (Per Serving)
271 calories, 22g fat (of which 7g saturates), 10g carbohydrate, 1.4g salt
Easy

Roasted Root Vegetable Salad v

1 Preheat the oven to 190°C (170°C fan oven) mark 5. Put the squash and carrots into a large deep roasting tin. Scatter the thyme sprigs over them, drizzle with 1 tbsp oil and season with salt and pepper. Roast for 20 minutes.

2 Take the tin out of the oven, give it a good shake to make sure the vegetables aren't sticking, then add the onions. Drizzle the remaining oil over and toss to coat. Roast for a further 20 minutes or until all the vegetables are tender.

3 Remove the roasted vegetables from the oven and discard any twiggy sprigs of thyme. Drizzle the vinegar over, stir in and leave to cool.

4 To serve, put the chickpeas into a large serving bowl. Add the cooled vegetables, the pinenuts and rocket (reserving a few leaves to garnish). Toss everything together and garnish with the reserved rocket leaves.

1 butternut squash, halved, seeded and cubed
1½ large carrots, cut into chunks
3 fresh thyme sprigs
1½ tbsp olive oil
2 red onions, cut into wedges
1 tbsp balsamic vinegar
400g can chickpeas, drained and rinsed
25g (1oz) pinenuts, toasted
100g (3½oz) wild rocket
salt and ground black pepper

Get Ahead

To prepare ahead Complete the recipe to the end of step 3, then cool, cover and chill for up to two days.

To use Complete the recipe.

Nutritional Information (Per Serving)
290 calories, 14g fat (of which 2g saturates), 33g carbohydrate, 0.7g salt
Gluten Free · Dairy Free · Easy

Serves 4
Preparation Time 20 minutes, plus cooling
Cooking Time 40 minutes

Spinach and Carrot Salad

350g (12oz) carrots, sliced
225g (8oz) green beans, trimmed
350g (12oz) baby leaf spinach
1 garlic clove, crushed
2 tsp each soy sauce and honey
1 tbsp cider vinegar
4 tbsp olive oil
ground black pepper

1 Cook the carrots in lightly salted boiling water for 3–4 minutes, adding the beans for the last minute. Drain and rinse in cold water. Drain well, then put both in a bowl with the spinach.

2 Put the garlic into a small bowl. Add the soy sauce, honey, vinegar and oil. Season with pepper and whisk together thoroughly. Pour some of the dressing over the carrot, bean and spinach mixture and toss together well. Serve the remaining dressing separately.

Try Something Different
Add a handful of sultanas
or raisins, or lightly toasted
sesame seeds.

Serves 4
Preparation Time 5 minutes
Cooking Time 4 minutes

Nutritional Information (Per Serving)
173 calories, 12g fat (of which 2g saturates), 12g carbohydrate, 0.8g salt
Gluten Free · Dairy Free · Easy

Winter Leaf Salad

1 Put the dressing ingredients into a jar with a lid. Season with salt and pepper and shake well to mix.

2 Tear all the salad leaves into bite-size pieces and put into a large bowl. Add the walnuts and toss to mix.

3 To serve, shake the dressing again, then pour it over the salad and toss well.

75g (3oz) lamb's lettuce
1 small head radicchio
2 small red chicory
75g (3oz) walnuts, toasted
 and roughly chopped

FOR THE DRESSING
2 tbsp white wine vinegar
2 tbsp walnut oil
4 tbsp olive oil
salt and ground black pepper

Try Something Different
Add orange segments for a really refreshing salad.

SALADS

Nutritional Information (Per Serving)
196 calories, 20g fat (of which 2g saturates), 2g carbohydrate, 0.6g salt
Gluten Free · Dairy Free · Easy

Serves 6
Preparation Time 10 minutes

Winter Coleslaw

4 oranges
400g can chickpeas, drained
   and rinsed
450g (1lb) carrots, coarsely grated
½ red cabbage, about 550g (1¼lb),
   finely shredded
75g (3oz) sultanas
6 tbsp freshly chopped coriander
4 tbsp extra virgin olive oil
3 tbsp red wine vinegar
salt and ground black pepper

1 Using a sharp knife, cut a thin slice of peel and pith from each end of the oranges. Put the oranges, cut side down, on a board and cut off the peel and pith. Remove any remaining pith. Cut out each segment, leaving the membrane behind. Squeeze the juice from the membrane into a bowl.

2 Put the orange segments and juice into a serving bowl with the chickpeas, carrots, cabbage, sultanas and coriander. Add the oil and vinegar and season well with salt and pepper.

3 Toss everything together to coat thoroughly.

Get Ahead

To prepare ahead Complete the recipe. Store the coleslaw in a sealable container in the refrigerator for up to two days.

Serves 6
Preparation Time 15 minutes

Nutritional Information (Per Serving)
265 calories, 10g fat (of which 1g saturates), 38g carbohydrate, 0.4g salt
Gluten Free · Dairy Free · Easy

Warm Tofu, Fennel
and Bean Salad

1 Heat 1 tbsp oil in a large frying pan. Add the onion and fennel and cook over a medium heat for 5–10 minutes until soft.

2 Add the vinegar and heat through for 2 minutes. Stir in the butter beans and parsley, season with salt and pepper, then tip into a bowl.

3 Slice the smoked tofu horizontally into four and then into eight triangles. Add to the pan with the remaining 1 tsp oil. Cook for 2 minutes on each side or until golden.

4 Divide the bean mixture among four plates, then add two slices of tofu to each plate.

1 tbsp olive oil, plus 1 tsp
1 red onion, finely sliced
1 fennel bulb, finely sliced
1 tbsp cider vinegar
400g can butter beans, drained
    and rinsed
2 tbsp freshly chopped flat-leafed
    parsley
200g (7oz) smoked tofu
salt and ground black pepper

SALADS

Nutritional Information (Per Serving)
150 calories, 6g fat (of which 1g saturates), 15g carbohydrate, 0.8g salt
Gluten Free · Dairy Free · Easy

Serves 4
Preparation Time 10 minutes
Cooking Time 15 minutes

Warm Salad with Quorn
and Berries

2 tbsp olive oil
1 onion, sliced
175g pack Quorn pieces
2 tbsp raspberry vinegar
150g (5oz) blueberries
225g (8oz) mixed salad leaves
salt and ground black pepper

1 Heat the oil in a frying pan, add the onion and cook for 5 minutes or until soft and golden. Increase the heat and add the Quorn pieces. Cook, stirring, for 5 minutes or until golden brown. Season with salt and pepper, put into a large bowl and put to one side.

2 Add the vinegar, 75ml (2½fl oz) water and the blueberries to the frying pan. Bring to the boil and bubble for 1–2 minutes until it reaches a syrupy consistency.

3 Gently toss together the Quorn mixture, blueberry mixture and salad leaves. Serve immediately.

Serves 4
Preparation Time 5 minutes
Cooking Time 12 minutes

Nutritional Information (Per Serving)
152 calories, 7g fat (of which 1g saturates), 8g carbohydrate, 0.3g salt
Gluten Free • Dairy Free • Easy

Warm Pear and Walnut
Caesar Salad

1 Put the walnuts into a non-stick frying pan and dry-fry over a medium heat for about 1 minute until lightly toasted. Set aside.

2 Heat the oil and butter in the frying pan, then add the pears. Fry for 2 minutes on each side or until golden. Remove with a slotted spoon.

3 To serve, put the salad leaves into a large bowl. Add the walnuts, pears, croûtons, Parmesan and blue cheese. Add the salad dressing and toss lightly, or serve the dressing separately in a small bowl. Serve immediately, garnished with chives.

50g (2oz) walnut pieces
1 tbsp walnut or mild olive oil
a small knob of butter
3 firm rosy pears, quartered, cored and thickly sliced
1 bag Caesar salad with croûtons, dressing and Parmesan (see Cook's Tip, page 35)
100g (3½oz) blue cheese, such as Roquefort, Stilton or Danish blue, crumbled (see as above)
1 bunch of chives, roughly chopped

Get Ahead

To prepare ahead Complete the recipe to the end of step 2, then leave the pears in the frying pan and set aside for up to 4 hours.

To use Warm the pears in the pan for 1 minute, then complete the recipe.

SALADS

Nutritional Information (Per Serving)
397 calories, 31g fat (of which 8g fat saturates), 19g carbohydrate, 1.3g salt
Easy

Serves 6
Preparation Time 10 minutes
Cooking Time 5 minutes

Light bites and snacks

Beans on Toast

Tomato Crostini with Feta and Basil

Roast Mushrooms with Pesto

Mozzarella Mushrooms

Mushrooms with Cashew Nuts

Rösti Potatoes with Fried Eggs

Glamorgan Sausages

Falafel, Rocket and Soured Cream Wraps

Spicy Bean and Tomato Fajitas

Veggie Pitta

Chickpea Patties

Vegetable Tempura

Lemon Hummus with Black Olives

Cheese Scone Twists

Beans on Toast

1 tbsp olive oil
2 garlic cloves, finely sliced
400g can borlotti or cannellini beans,
   drained and rinsed
400g can chickpeas, drained
   and rinsed
400g can chopped tomatoes
leaves from 2 fresh rosemary sprigs,
   finely chopped
4 thick slices Granary bread
25g (1oz) Parmesan (see Cook's Tip,
   page 35)
chopped fresh chives to serve
   (optional)

1 Heat the oil in a pan over a low heat, add the garlic and cook for 1 minute, stirring gently.

2 Add the beans and chickpeas to the pan with the tomatoes and bring to the boil. Add the rosemary, then reduce the heat and simmer for 8–10 minutes until thickened.

3 Meanwhile, toast the bread and put on to plates. Grate the Parmesan into the bean mixture, stir once, then spoon over the bread. Serve immediately, scattered with chives, if you like.

Try Something Different
This will be just as good with toasted soda bread or seeded bread, mixed beans instead of borlotti or cannellini, and grated Gruyère cheese or Cheddar instead of Parmesan.

LIGHT BITES AND SNACKS

Serves 4
Preparation Time 5 minutes
Cooking Time 10 minutes

Nutritional Information (Per Serving)
364 calories, 9g fat (of which 2g saturates), 55g carbohydrate, 2.1g salt
Easy

Tomato Crostini with Feta
and Basil

1 Put the garlic, chopped basil, pinenuts, oil, lime zest and juice into a food processor and whiz to a smooth paste. Add the feta cheese and whiz until smooth. Thin with 1 tbsp water if necessary. Season with salt and pepper.

2 Put the tomatoes, salsa and olives into a bowl and gently toss together.

3 Toast the bread. Divide the tomato mixture among the slices of toast and spoon the basil and feta mixture on top. Garnish with basil leaves and serve.

1 small garlic clove, crushed
3 tbsp freshly chopped basil, plus extra basil leaves to garnish
25g (1oz) pinenuts
2 tbsp extra virgin olive oil
grated zest and juice of 1 lime
50g (2oz) feta cheese (see Cook's Tip, page 35)
4 large tomatoes, preferably vine-ripened, thickly sliced
150g tub fresh tomato salsa
50g (2oz) pitted black olives, roughly chopped
4 thick slices country-style bread
salt and ground black pepper

Nutritional Information (Per Serving)
242 calories, 17g fat (of which 3g saturates), 18g carbohydrate, 1.5g salt
Easy

Serves 4
Preparation Time 20 minutes
Cooking Time 3 minutes

Roast Mushrooms with Pesto

8 portabella mushrooms
8 tbsp fresh Pesto (see Cook's Tip,
    page 38)
toasted ciabatta, salad and basil
    leaves to serve

1 Preheat the oven to 200°C (180°C fan oven) mark 6. Put the mushrooms into an ovenproof dish, then spoon 1 tbsp fresh pesto on top of each one.

2 Pour 150ml (¼ pint) boiling water into the dish, then cook for 15 minutes or until the mushrooms are soft and the topping is hot. Serve with toasted ciabatta and salad, and scatter a few small basil leaves over the mushrooms.

Serves 4
Preparation Time 5 minutes
Cooking Time 15 minutes

Nutritional Information (Per Serving)
258 calories, 23g fat (of which 6g saturates), 1g carbohydrate, 0.5g salt
Easy

Mozzarella Mushrooms

1 Preheat the oven to 200°C (180°C fan oven) mark 6. Lay the mushrooms side by side in a roasting tin and season with salt and pepper. Top each mushroom with a slice of red pepper and a basil leaf. Lay a slice of mozzarella on top of each mushroom and season again. Roast in the oven for 15–20 minutes until the mushrooms are tender and the cheese has melted.

2 Meanwhile, toast the muffin halves until golden. Put a mozzarella mushroom on top of each muffin half. Serve immediately with a green salad.

8 large portabella mushrooms
8 slices marinated red pepper
8 fresh basil leaves
150g (5oz) mozzarella cheese, cut into eight slices (see Cook's Tip, page 35)
4 English muffins, halved
salt and ground black pepper
green salad to serve

Nutritional Information (Per Serving)
137 calories, 9g fat (of which 5g saturates), 5g carbohydrate, 0.4g salt
Easy

Serves 4
Preparation Time 2–3 minutes
Cooking Time 15–20 minutes

Mushrooms with Cashew Nuts

1 tbsp vegetable oil
25g (1oz) unsalted cashew nuts
225g (8oz) brown-cap
   mushrooms, sliced
1 tbsp lemon juice
4 tbsp freshly chopped coriander,
   plus fresh sprigs to garnish
1 tbsp single cream or soya
   cream (optional)
salt and ground black pepper

1 Heat the oil in a wok or large frying pan. Add the cashew nuts and cook over a high heat for 2–3 minutes until golden. Add the mushrooms and cook for a further 2–3 minutes until tender, stirring frequently.

2 Stir in the lemon juice and coriander and season to taste with salt and pepper. Heat until bubbling. Remove the pan from the heat and stir in the cream, if using. Adjust the seasoning, if necessary, and serve immediately, garnished with coriander sprigs.

Try Something Different
Chinese Garlic Mushrooms
Replace the nuts with 2 crushed garlic cloves and stir-fry for only 20 seconds before adding the mushrooms. Replace the lemon juice with rice wine or dry sherry.

Serves 4
Preparation Time 5 minutes
Cooking Time 5–8 minutes

Nutritional Information (Per Serving)
75 calories, 6g fat (of which 1g saturates), 2g carbohydrate, 0.1g salt
Gluten Free • Easy

Rösti Potatoes with Fried Eggs

1 Put the potatoes into a pan of cold water. Cover, bring to the boil and parboil for 5–8 minutes. Drain and leave to cool for 15 minutes.

2 Preheat the oven to 150°C (130°C fan oven) mark 2. Put a baking tray inside to warm. Peel the potatoes and coarsely grate them lengthways into long strands. Divide into eight portions and shape into mounds.

3 Melt half the butter in a large non-stick frying pan. When it is beginning to brown, add four of the potato mounds, spacing them well apart, and flatten them a little. Fry slowly for 6–7 minutes until golden brown, then turn them and brown the other side for 6–7 minutes. Transfer to a warmed baking tray and keep warm in the oven while you fry the rest.

4 Just before serving, carefully break the eggs into the hot pan and fry for about 2 minutes until the white is set and the yolk is still soft. Season with salt and pepper and serve at once, with the rösti. Garnish with sprigs of parsley.

900g (2lb) red potatoes, scrubbed
   and left whole
40g (1½oz) butter
4 large eggs
salt and ground black pepper
sprigs of flat-leafed parsley to garnish

Nutritional Information (Per Serving)
324 calories, 16g fat (of which 7g saturates), 36g carbohydrate, 0.4g salt
Gluten Free · Easy

Serves 4
Preparation Time 20 minutes,
   plus cooling
Cooking Time 20–25 minutes

Glamorgan Sausages

150g (5oz) Caerphilly cheese, grated
  (see Cook's Tip, page 35)
200g (7oz) fresh white breadcrumbs
3 spring onions, finely chopped
1 tbsp freshly chopped flat-leafed
  parsley
leaves from 4 thyme sprigs
3 large eggs, 1 separated
vegetable oil for frying
salt and ground black pepper
green salad and chutney to serve

1 Preheat the oven to 140°C (120°C fan oven) mark 1. Mix the cheese with 150g (5oz) breadcrumbs, the spring onions and herbs in a large bowl. Season well.

2 Add the 2 whole eggs plus the extra yolk and mix well to combine. Cover and chill for 5 minutes.

3 Lightly beat the egg white in a shallow bowl. Tip the rest of the breadcrumbs on to a large plate.

4 Take 2 tbsp of the cheese mixture and shape into a small sausage, about 4cm (1½in) long. Roll first in the egg white, then in the breadcrumbs to coat. Repeat to make 12 sausages in total.

5 Heat 2 tsp oil in a large heavy-based pan until hot and fry the sausages in two batches for 6–8 minutes, turning until golden all over. Keep them warm in the oven while cooking the rest. Serve with salad and chutney.

Serves 4
Preparation Time 25 minutes
Cooking Time 15 minutes

Nutritional Information (Per Serving)
403 calories, 20g fat (of which 9g saturates), 39g carbohydrate, 1.7g salt
Easy

Falafel, Rocket and
Soured Cream Wraps

1 Lay the tortillas on a board and spread each one with a little soured cream.

2 Divide the rocket among the wraps and sprinkle with coriander, celery and falafel.

3 Roll up as tightly as you can, then wrap each roll in clingfilm and chill for up to 3 hours or until ready to use. To serve, unwrap and cut each roll into quarters.

6 large flour tortillas
200g (7oz) soured cream
100g (3½oz) wild rocket
a small handful of fresh
    coriander, chopped
1 celery stick, finely chopped
180g pack ready-made falafel,
    roughly chopped or crumbled

Nutritional Information (Per Serving)
270 calories, 9g fat (of which 4g saturates), 42g carbohydrate, 0.5g salt
Easy

Serves 6
Preparation Time 5 minutes,
    plus chilling

Spicy Bean and Tomato
Fajitas

1 Heat the oil in a large pan, add the onion and cook gently for 5 minutes. Add the garlic and spices and cook for a further 2 minutes.

2 Add the tomato purée and cook for 1 minute, then add the tomatoes, beans and hot stock. Season well with salt and pepper and bring to the boil, then reduce the heat and simmer for 15 minutes, stirring occasionally.

3 Halve, stone and peel the avocados, then chop. Put the avocado into a bowl, add the lime juice and chopped coriander and mash. Season to taste.

4 Warm the tortillas: either wrap them in foil and heat in the oven at 180°C (160°C fan oven) mark 4 for 10 minutes, or put on to a plate and microwave on full power for 45 seconds (based on a 900W oven).

5 Spoon some beans down the centre of each tortilla. Fold up the bottom to keep the filling inside, then wrap the sides in so they overlap. Spoon on the avocado and soured cream. Sprinkle with chilli powder and coriander sprigs and serve with lime wedges.

2 tbsp sunflower oil
1 onion, sliced
2 garlic cloves, crushed
½ tsp hot chilli powder, plus extra
    to garnish
1 tsp each ground coriander and
    ground cumin
1 tbsp tomato purée
400g can chopped tomatoes
200g can red kidney beans, drained
    and rinsed
400g can borlotti beans, drained
    and rinsed
400g can flageolet beans, drained
    and rinsed
150ml (¼ pint) hot vegetable stock
2 ripe avocados
juice of ½ lime
1 tbsp freshly chopped coriander,
    plus sprigs to garnish
6 ready-made flour tortillas
150ml (¼ pint) soured cream
salt and ground black pepper
lime wedges to serve

Serves 6
Preparation Time 15 minutes
Cooking Time 25 minutes

Nutritional Information (Per Serving)
512 calories, 20g fat (of which 6g saturates), 71g carbohydrate, 1.5g salt
Easy

Veggie Pitta

V

1 Split the pitta bread and spread with the hummus.

2 Fill the pitta with the cashew nuts, mushrooms, cucumber and a generous helping of fresh watercress or salad leaves. Serve with extra hummus, if you like, and season with pepper.

1 wholemeal pitta bread
1 tbsp hummus (to make your own, see page 84), plus extra to serve
15g (½oz) unsalted cashew nuts
2 closed-cup mushrooms, finely sliced
¼ cucumber, chopped
fresh watercress or mixed salad leaves
ground black pepper

Try Something Different
Add a diced ripe avocado. It is rich in omega fats and good for your skin.

Nutritional Information (Per Serving)
322 calories, 11g fat (of which 2g saturates), 47g carbohydrate, 1.2g salt
Easy

Serves 1
Preparation Time 8 minutes

Chickpea Patties

2 x 400g cans chickpeas, drained
    and rinsed
4 garlic cloves, crushed
1 tsp ground cumin
1 small red onion, chopped
20g pack fresh coriander
2 tbsp plain flour, plus extra to dust
olive oil for frying
mixed salad and lemon wedges
    to serve

1 Pat the chickpeas dry with kitchen paper, then put them into a food processor with the garlic, cumin, onion and coriander. Whiz until smooth, then stir in the flour.

2 With floured hands, shape the chickpea mixture into 12 small, round patties and chill in the fridge for 20 minutes.

3 Heat a little oil in a non-stick frying pan over a medium heat and fry the patties in batches for about 2 minutes on each side or until heated through and golden. Serve warm with mixed salad and lemon wedges.

Freezing Tip
To freeze Make the patties, then cool, put in a freezerproof container and freeze. They will keep for up to one month.

To use Thaw overnight at a cool room temperature, then reheat in the oven at 180°C (160°C fan oven) mark 4 for 20 minutes.

Serves 4
Preparation Time 20 minutes,
    plus chilling
Cooking Time about 15 minutes

Nutritional Information (Per Serving)
344 calories, 17g fat (of which 2g saturates), 37g carbohydrate, 1g salt
Dairy Free · Easy

Vegetable Tempura

1. Sift 125g (4oz) flour, the cornflour and arrowroot into a large bowl with a pinch each of salt and pepper. Gradually whisk in 300ml (½ pint) ice-cold water to form a thin batter. Cover and chill.

2. To make the dipping sauce, put the ginger, sherry and soy sauce into a heatproof bowl and pour in 200ml (7fl oz) boiling water. Stir well to mix, then put to one side.

3. Put the vegetables into a large bowl and sprinkle with 2 tbsp flour. Toss well to coat. Heat the oil in a wok or deep-fryer to 170°C (test by frying a small cube of bread: it should brown in 40 seconds).

4. Dip a handful of the vegetables in the batter, then remove with a slotted spoon, taking up a lot of the batter with the vegetables. Add to the hot oil and deep-fry for 3–5 minutes until crisp and golden. Remove with a slotted spoon and drain on kitchen paper; keep them hot while you cook the remaining batches. Serve immediately, garnished with coriander sprigs and accompanied by the dipping sauce.

125g (4oz) plain flour, plus 2 tbsp extra to sprinkle
2 tbsp cornflour
2 tbsp arrowroot
125g (4oz) cauliflower, cut into small florets
2 large carrots, cut into matchsticks
16 button mushrooms
2 courgettes, sliced
2 red peppers, seeded and sliced
vegetable oil for deep-frying
salt and ground black pepper
fresh coriander sprigs to garnish

FOR THE DIPPING SAUCE
25g (1oz) piece fresh root ginger, peeled and grated
4 tbsp dry sherry
3 tbsp soy sauce

LIGHT BITES AND SNACKS

Nutritional Information (Per Serving)
450 calories, 21g fat (of which 3g saturates), 55g carbohydrate, 2.1g salt
Dairy Free · A Little Effort

Serves 4
Preparation Time 20 minutes
Cooking Time 15 minutes

Lemon Hummus
with Black Olives

2 × 400g cans chickpeas, drained
    and rinsed
1 garlic clove (use fresh garlic when
    possible, see Cook's Tip), crushed
zest and juice of 1 lemon
4 tbsp olive oil
25g (1oz) pitted black olives,
    roughly chopped
1 tsp paprika, plus a little extra
    to sprinkle (optional)
sticks of raw vegetables and
    breadsticks to serve

1 Put the chickpeas and garlic into a food processor, add the lemon zest and juice and whiz to combine. With the motor running, drizzle in the oil to make a thick paste. If the hummus is too thick, add 1–2 tbsp cold water and whiz again.

2 Spoon into a bowl and stir in the olives and paprika. Sprinkle with a little extra paprika, if you like, and serve with raw vegetables and breadsticks for dipping.

Cook's Tip
Raw garlic is renowned for its curative and protective powers, which include lowering blood pressure and cholesterol levels.

Fresh garlic has juicy mild cloves and is available from May and throughout the summer. It is the classic form of garlic to use for making (for example) pesto, salsa verde, garlic mayonnaise and chilled soups.

Serves 4
Preparation Time 15 minutes

Nutritional Information (Per Serving)
284 calories, 16g fat (of which 2g saturates), 25g carbohydrate, 1.2g salt
Gluten Free · Dairy Free · Easy

Cheese Scone Twists

1 Preheat the oven to 220°C (200°C fan oven) mark 7. Lightly grease two (or three) baking sheets. Sift the flour, baking powder and a pinch of salt together into a bowl, then rub in the butter. Add half the cheese and stir in enough milk to make a soft, but not sticky, dough. Knead briefly to bring together.

2 Roll out on a floured worksurface to a thickness of 1cm (½in). Cut out rounds with a 7.5cm (3in) cutter and remove the centres using a 4cm (1½in) cutter.

3 Lightly knead the trimmings, including the 4cm (1½in) rounds, and roll out again. Cut out more scone rings until all the dough is used.

4 Twist each ring to form a figure of eight and space well apart on the baking trays. Brush with milk and sprinkle with the remaining cheese. Bake for about 12 minutes until well risen and golden brown. Leave to cool on a wire rack.

75g (3oz) butter, plus extra to grease
450g (1lb) self-raising flour, plus extra to dust
2 tsp baking powder
125g (4oz) mature Cheddar, finely grated (see Cook's Tip, page 35)
about 300ml (½ pint) milk, plus extra to glaze
salt

Try Something Different
Add a pinch of cayenne pepper to the flour in step 1 and sprinkle with 25g (1oz) Parmesan in step 4.

LIGHT BITES AND SNACKS

Nutritional Information (Per Serving)
193 calories, 8g fat (of which 5g saturates), 26g carbohydrate, 0.6g salt
Easy

Makes 14
Preparation Time 15 minutes
Cooking Time 12 minutes

Vegetable mains

Grilled Vegetables with Walnut Sauce

Grilled Mediterranean Vegetables

Spicy Roasted Roots

Roasted Ratatouille

Pumpkin with Chickpeas

Leek and Broccoli Bake

Spring Vegetable Stew

Tomato and Butterbean Stew

Mushroom and Bean Hotpot

Aubergine and Lentil Curry

Mauritian Vegetable Curry

Thai Vegetable Curry

Chilli Vegetable and Coconut Stir-fry

Aubergines in a Hot Sweet and Sour Sauce

Bean Sprouts with Peppers and Chillies

Summer Vegetable Stir-fry

Grilled Vegetables
with Walnut Sauce

2 large carrots, peeled
1 fennel bulb
225g (8oz) sweet potatoes
225g (8oz) Jerusalem
    artichokes, scrubbed
225g (8oz) thick asparagus spears
8 baby leeks
4–6 tbsp olive oil
salt and ground black pepper

FOR THE WALNUT SAUCE
50g (2oz) day-old bread,
    crusts removed
75g (3oz) walnuts, toasted
2 garlic cloves, chopped
1 tbsp red wine vinegar
2 tbsp chopped parsley
90ml (3fl oz) olive oil
50ml (2fl oz) walnut oil

1 First make the walnut sauce. Crumble the bread into a bowl, add 2 tbsp water, then squeeze dry. Put the bread into a food processor with the toasted walnuts, garlic, vinegar and parsley and whiz until fairly smooth. Add the olive and walnut oils and whiz briefly to form a thick sauce. Season with salt and pepper and transfer to a serving dish.

2 Preheat the grill to medium-high. Prepare the vegetables. Cut the carrots into 5mm (¼in) slices; thinly slice the fennel lengthways; peel and thinly slice the sweet potatoes; thinly slice the Jerusalem artichokes. Trim the asparagus and leeks, but leave whole.

3 Baste the vegetables with the oil and grill in batches, turning once, for 2–6 minutes on each side until charred and tender (see Cook's Tip); keep warm in a low oven while grilling the rest.

4 Transfer all the grilled vegetables to a warmed serving plate and season with a little salt and pepper. Serve accompanied by the walnut sauce.

Cook's Tip
The root vegetables take longest to cook through, while the asparagus and leeks only need a short time under the grill.

Serves 4
Preparation Time 25 minutes
Cooking Time 15–20 minutes

Nutritional Information (Per Serving)
598 calories, 48g fat (of which 6g saturates), 35g carbohydrate, 0.3g salt
Dairy Free · Easy

Grilled Mediterranean
Vegetables

1 Blanch the garlic cloves in boiling water for 5 minutes. Drain.

2 Put all the vegetables and the garlic into a shallow glass dish, pour the oil over them and season with salt and pepper. Cover and chill for up to 6 hours.

3 Preheat the barbecue, griddle or grill. Lay the vegetables in a single layer on the grill rack (you may need to do two batches) and cook for about 10 minutes, turning once or twice, until they are slightly charred. Serve hot or cold.

6 garlic cloves, peeled and left whole
2 red peppers, seeded and cut into thick strips
4 courgettes, quartered lengthways and cut into sticks
2 aubergines, cut into sticks the same size as the courgettes
2 small red onions, cut into wedges
100ml (3½fl oz) olive oil
salt and ground black pepper

VEGETABLE MAINS

Nutritional Information (Per Serving)
234 calories, 18g fat (of which 3g saturates), 16g carbohydrate, trace salt
Gluten Free · Dairy Free · Easy

Serves 4
Preparation Time 10 minutes, plus chilling
Cooking Time 20 minutes

Spicy Roasted Roots

3 carrots, sliced lengthways
3 parsnips, sliced lengthways
3 tbsp olive oil
1 butternut squash, chopped
2 red onions, cut into wedges
2 leeks, sliced
3 garlic cloves, roughly chopped
2 tbsp mild curry paste
salt and ground black pepper

1 Preheat the oven to 200°C (180°C fan oven) mark 6. Put the carrots and parsnips into a large roasting tin, drizzle with 1 tbsp oil and cook for 40 minutes.

2 Add the butternut squash, onions, leeks and garlic to the roasting tin. Season with salt and pepper, then drizzle with the remaining 2 tbsp oil.

3 Roast for 45 minutes until the vegetables are tender and golden. Stir in the curry paste and return to the oven for a further 10 minutes. Serve immediately.

Freezing Tip

To freeze Complete the recipe, then cool, wrap and freeze for up to one month.

To use Thaw overnight at room temperature, then reheat at 200°C (180°C fan oven) mark 6 for 20 minutes in an ovenproof dish with 200ml (7fl oz) hot stock.

VEGETABLE MAINS

Serves 8
Preparation Time 25 minutes
Cooking Time about 1½ hours

Nutritional Information (Per Serving)
134 calories, 8g fat (of which 1g saturates), 14g carbohydrate, 0.1g salt
Gluten Free • Dairy Free • Easy

Roasted Ratatouille

1. Preheat the oven to 240°C (220°C fan oven) mark 9. Put the peppers, aubergine, onions, garlic, oil and fennel seeds into a roasting tin. Season with sea salt flakes and pepper and toss together.

2. Transfer to the oven and cook for 30 minutes (tossing frequently during cooking) or until the vegetables are charred and beginning to soften.

3. Stir the passata through the vegetables and put the roasting tin back in the oven for 50–60 minutes, stirring occasionally. Garnish with the thyme sprigs and serve.

400g (14oz) red peppers, seeded and roughly chopped
700g (1½lb) aubergines, stalk removed, cut into chunks
450g (1lb) onions, peeled and cut into wedges
4 or 5 garlic cloves, unpeeled and left whole
150ml (¼ pint) olive oil
1 tsp fennel seeds
200ml (7fl oz) passata
sea salt and ground black pepper
a few fresh thyme sprigs to garnish

Try Something Different
Replace half the aubergines with 400g (14oz) courgettes; use a mix of green and red peppers; garnish with fresh basil instead of thyme.

VEGETABLE MAINS

Pumpkin with Chickpeas

900g (2lb) pumpkin or squash,
    such as butternut, crown prince
    or kabocha (see Cook's Tip),
    peeled, seeded and chopped
    into roughly 2cm (¾in) cubes
1 garlic clove, crushed
2 tbsp olive oil
2 × 400g cans chickpeas, drained
½ red onion, thinly sliced
1 large bunch of coriander,
    roughly chopped
salt and ground black pepper
steamed spinach to serve

FOR THE TAHINI SAUCE
1 large garlic clove, crushed
3 tbsp tahini paste
juice of 1 lemon

1 Preheat the oven to 220°C (200°C fan oven) mark 7. Toss the pumpkin or squash in the garlic and oil and season. Put into a roasting tin and roast for 25 minutes or until soft.

2 Meanwhile, put the chickpeas into a pan with 150ml (¼ pint) water over a medium heat, to warm through.

3 To make the tahini sauce, put the garlic into a bowl, add a pinch of salt, then whisk in the tahini paste. Add the lemon juice and 4–5 tbsp cold water – enough to make a consistency somewhere between single and double cream – and season.

4 Drain the chickpeas, put into a large bowl, then add the pumpkin, onion and coriander. Pour the tahini sauce over them and toss carefully. Adjust the seasoning and serve while warm, with spinach.

Cook's Tip
Kabocha is a Japanese variety of winter squash and has a dull-coloured deep green skin with whitish stripes. Its flesh is an intense yellow-orange colour.

Serves 6
Preparation Time 15 minutes
Cooking Time 25–30 minutes

Nutritional Information (Per Serving)
228 calories, 12g fat (of which 2g saturates),22g carbohydrate, 0.6g salt
Gluten Free · Dairy Free · Easy

Leek and Broccoli Bake

1 Preheat the oven to 200°C (180°C fan oven) mark 6. Heat the oil in a large flameproof dish, add the onion, aubergine and leeks and cook for 10–12 minutes until golden and softened.

2 Add the broccoli, mushrooms, cherry tomatoes, half the rosemary and 300ml (½ pint) boiling water. Season with salt and pepper. Stir well, then cover and cook in the oven for 30 minutes.

3 Meanwhile, put the Parmesan into a bowl. Add the remaining rosemary and season with pepper. When the vegetables are cooked, remove the lid and sprinkle the Parmesan mixture on top. Cook, uncovered, in the oven for a further 5–10 minutes until the topping is golden.

2 tbsp olive oil
1 large red onion, cut into wedges
1 aubergine, chopped
2 leeks, trimmed and cut into chunks
1 broccoli head, cut into florets and stalks chopped
3 large flat mushrooms, chopped
2 × 400g cans cherry tomatoes
3 rosemary sprigs, chopped
50g (2oz) Parmesan, freshly grated (see Cook's Tip, page 35)
salt and ground black pepper

Try Something Different
Use sliced courgettes instead of aubergine.

VEGETABLE MAINS

Nutritional Information (Per Serving)
245 calories, 13g fat (of which 4g saturates), 18g carbohydrate, 0.4g salt
Gluten Free · Easy

Serves 4
Preparation Time 20 minutes
Cooking Time 45–55 minutes

Spring Vegetable Stew

225g (8oz) new potatoes, scrubbed
75g (3oz) unsalted butter
4 shallots, blanched in boiling water,
    drained, peeled and thinly sliced
1 garlic clove, crushed
2 tsp freshly chopped thyme
1 tsp grated lime zest
6 baby leeks, trimmed and sliced
    into 5cm (2in) lengths
125g (4oz) baby carrots, scrubbed
125g (4oz) podded peas
125g (4oz) podded broad beans
300ml (½ pint) vegetable stock
1 Little Gem lettuce, shredded
4 tbsp freshly chopped herbs, such as
    chervil, chives, mint and parsley
salt and ground black pepper

1 Put the potatoes into a pan of lightly salted water. Bring to the boil, cover and par-boil for 5 minutes. Drain and refresh under cold water.

2 Meanwhile, melt half the butter in a large sauté pan, add the shallots, garlic, thyme and lime zest and fry gently for 5 minutes or until softened and lightly golden. Add the leeks and carrots and sauté for a further 5 minutes. Stir in the potatoes, peas and broad beans, then pour in the stock and bring to the boil. Reduce the heat, cover the pan and simmer gently for 10 minutes. Remove the lid and cook, uncovered, for a further 5–8 minutes until all the vegetables are tender.

3 Add the shredded lettuce to the stew with the chopped herbs and remaining butter. Heat through until the butter is melted. Check the seasoning and serve at once.

Serves 4
Preparation Time 20 minutes
Cooking Time 30–35 minutes

Nutritional Information (Per Serving)
270 calories, 17g fat (of which 10g saturates), 23g carbohydrate, 0.6g salt
Gluten Free • Dairy Free • Easy

Tomato and Butterbean Stew

1. Preheat the oven to 180°C (160°C fan oven) mark 4. Heat the oil in a flameproof casserole over a medium heat. Add the onion and garlic and cook for 10 minutes until golden and soft. Add the leeks and cook, covered, for 5 minutes.

2. Add the tomatoes, beans and hot stock and season well with salt and pepper. Bring to the boil, then cover and cook in the oven for 35–40 minutes until the sauce has thickened. Remove from the oven, stir in the vinegar and spoon into warmed bowls.

2 tbsp olive oil
1 onion, finely sliced
2 garlic cloves, finely chopped
2 large leeks, sliced
2 × 400g cans cherry tomatoes
2 × 400g cans butter beans, drained and rinsed
150ml (¼ pint) hot vegetable stock
1–2 tbsp balsamic vinegar
salt and ground black pepper

VEGETABLE MAINS

Nutritional Information (Per Serving)
286 calories, 8g fat (of which 1g saturates), 41g carbohydrate, 1.8g salt
Dairy Free · Easy

Serves 4
Preparation Time 10 minutes
Cooking Time 50–55 minutes

95

Mushroom and Bean Hotpot

3 tbsp olive oil
700g (1½lb) chestnut mushrooms,
    roughly chopped
1 large onion, finely chopped
2 tbsp plain flour
2 tbsp mild curry paste (see
    Cook's Tip)
150ml (¼ pint) dry white wine
400g can chopped tomatoes
2 tbsp sun-dried tomato paste
2 × 400g cans mixed beans,
    drained and rinsed
3 tbsp mango chutney
3 tbsp roughly chopped fresh
    coriander and mint

1 Heat the oil in a large pan over a low heat, then fry the mushrooms and onion until the onion is soft and dark golden. Stir in the flour and curry paste and cook for 1–2 minutes.

2 Add the wine, tomatoes, sun-dried tomato paste and beans and bring to the boil, then reduce the heat and simmer gently for 30 minutes or until most of the liquid has reduced. Stir in the chutney and herbs before serving.

Cook's Tip
Check the ingredients in the curry paste: some brands may not be suitable for vegetarians.

Serves 6
Preparation Time 15 minutes
Cooking Time 30 minutes

Nutritional Information (Per Serving)
280 calories, 10g fat (of which 1g saturates), 34g carbohydrate, 1.3g salt
Dairy Free · Easy

Thai Vegetable Curry

V

1 Put the curry paste into a large pan, add the ginger and cashew nuts and stir-fry over a medium heat for 2–3 minutes.

2 Add the coconut milk, cover and bring to the boil. Stir the carrots into the pan, then reduce the heat and simmer for 5 minutes. Add the broccoli florets and simmer for a further 5 minutes or until tender.

3 Stir the coriander and lime zest into the pan with the spinach. Squeeze the lime juice over and serve with basmati rice.

2–3 tbsp red Thai curry paste (see Cook's Tip)
2.5cm (1in) piece fresh root ginger, peeled and finely chopped
50g (2oz) cashew nuts
400ml can coconut milk
3 carrots, cut into thin batons
1 broccoli head, cut into florets
20g (¾ oz) fresh coriander, roughly chopped
zest and juice of 1 lime
2 large handfuls of spinach leaves
basmati rice to serve

Try Something Different

Replace carrots and/or broccoli with alternative vegetables – try baby sweetcorn, sugarsnap peas or mangetouts and simmer for only 5 minutes until tender.

Cook's Tip

Check the ingredients in the Thai curry paste: some contain shrimp and are therefore not suitable for vegetarians.

Chilli Vegetable
and Coconut Stir-fry

2 tbsp sesame oil

2 green chillies, seeded and finely chopped (see Cook's Tips, page 37)

2.5cm (1in) piece fresh root ginger, peeled and finely grated

2 garlic cloves, crushed

1 tbsp Thai green curry paste (see Cook's Tip, page 99)

125g (4oz) carrots, cut into fine matchsticks

125g (4oz) baby sweetcorn, halved

125g (4oz) mangetouts, halved on the diagonal

2 large red peppers, seeded and finely sliced

2 small pak choi, quartered

4 spring onions, finely chopped

300ml (½ pint) coconut milk

2 tbsp peanut satay sauce

2 tbsp light soy sauce

1 tsp soft brown sugar

4 tbsp freshly chopped coriander, plus extra sprigs to garnish

ground black pepper

roasted peanuts to garnish

rice or noodles to serve

1 Heat the oil in a wok or large non-stick frying pan over a medium heat, add the chillies, ginger and garlic and stir-fry for 1 minute. Add the curry paste and fry for a further 30 seconds.

2 Add the carrots, sweetcorn, mangetouts and red peppers. Stir-fry over a high heat for 3–4 minutes, then add the pak choi and spring onions. Cook, stirring, for a further 1–2 minutes.

3 Pour in the coconut milk, satay sauce, soy sauce and sugar and season with pepper. Bring to the boil and cook for 1–2 minutes, then add the chopped coriander. Garnish with the peanuts and coriander sprigs and serve with rice or noodles.

Serves 4
Preparation Time 25 minutes
Cooking Time about 10 minutes

Nutritional Information (Per Serving)
200 calories, 11g fat (of which 2g saturates), 21g carbohydrate, 1.4g salt
Dairy Free · Easy

Aubergines in a Hot
Sweet and Sour Sauce

1 Heat the oil in a wok or large frying pan, add the onions, ginger and chopped chillies and stir-fry for about 4 minutes or until softened. Add the cumin and coriander seeds, cloves and cinnamon and cook for 2–3 minutes.

2 Add 300ml (½ pint) water to the pan, then stir in the paprika, lime juice, sugar, salt and aubergines. Bring to the boil, then cover the pan, reduce the heat and simmer for about 20 minutes or until the aubergines are tender.

3 Uncover the pan and bring the sauce back to the boil. Bubble for 3–4 minutes until the liquid is thick enough to coat the aubergine pieces. Garnish with whole red chillies, if you like, and serve with rice.

3 tbsp vegetable oil
200g (7oz) onions, thinly sliced
2.5cm (1in) piece fresh root ginger, peeled and finely chopped
2 red chillies, finely chopped (see Cook's Tips, page 37), plus extra whole red chillies to garnish (optional)
1½ tsp cumin seeds
1½ tsp coriander seeds
3 cloves
5cm (2in) cinnamon stick
1 tbsp paprika
juice of 2 limes
3–4 tbsp dark muscovado sugar
1–2 tsp salt
450g (1lb) aubergines, cut into 2.5cm (1in) pieces
rice to serve

Try Something Different
Braised Aubergines
Omit the cumin, coriander, cloves, cinnamon and paprika. Add the aubergines to the onion mixture at the end of step 1 and stir-fry for 1–2 minutes. Add 1 tbsp sugar, 1 tsp salt, 3–4 tbsp yellow bean sauce and the water; complete the recipe.

VEGETABLE MAINS

Nutritional Information (Per Serving)
136 calories, 7g fat (of which 1g saturates), 17g carbohydrate, 2.5g salt
Gluten Free · Dairy Free · Easy

Serves 4
Preparation Time 10 minutes
Cooking Time 35 minutes

101

Bean Sprouts with Peppers and Chillies

3 tbsp vegetable oil
2 garlic cloves, chopped
2.5cm (1in) piece fresh root ginger,
    peeled and chopped
6 spring onions, cut into 2.5cm
    (1in) pieces
1 red pepper, seeded and thinly sliced
1 yellow pepper, seeded and
    thinly sliced
2 green chillies, seeded and finely
    chopped (see Cook's Tips,
    page 37)
350g (12oz) bean sprouts
1 tbsp dark soy sauce
1 tbsp sugar
1 tbsp malt vinegar
a few drops of sesame oil (optional)
boiled rice with 2 tbsp freshly
    chopped coriander stirred through
    to serve

1 Heat the oil in a wok or large frying pan. Add the garlic, ginger, spring onions, peppers, chillies and bean sprouts and stir-fry over a medium heat for 3 minutes.

2 Add the soy sauce, sugar and vinegar and fry, stirring, for a further minute.

3 Sprinkle with a few drops of sesame oil, if you like, then serve immediately with coriander rice.

Summer Vegetable Stir-fry

1. Blanch the carrots in lightly salted boiling water for 2 minutes, then drain and pat dry.

2. Toast the sesame seeds in a hot dry wok or large frying pan over a medium heat, stirring until they turn golden. Tip on to a plate.

3. Return the wok or frying pan to the heat, add the sunflower oil and heat until it is smoking. Add the garlic to the oil and stir-fry for 20 seconds. Add the carrots, courgettes, yellow pepper and asparagus and stir-fry over a high heat for 1 minute.

4. Add the tomatoes and season to taste with salt and pepper. Stir-fry for 3–4 minutes until the vegetables are just tender. Add the vinegar and sesame oil, toss well and sprinkle with the toasted sesame seeds. Serve immediately.

125g (4oz) baby carrots, scrubbed and trimmed
1 tbsp sesame seeds
2 tbsp sunflower oil
2 garlic cloves, roughly chopped
125g (4oz) baby courgettes, halved lengthways
1 large yellow pepper, seeded and cut into thick strips
125g (4oz) thin asparagus spears, trimmed
125g (4oz) cherry tomatoes, halved
2 tbsp balsamic or sherry vinegar
1 tsp sesame oil
salt and ground black pepper

Try Something Different

Vary the vegetables, but always blanch the harder ones first. For a winter vegetable stir-fry, use cauliflower and broccoli florets, carrot sticks, 2–3 sliced spring onions and a little chopped fresh root ginger.

VEGETABLE MAINS

15 minutes
3 minutes

Side dishes

Asparagus and Mangetouts with Lemon Sauce
Baked Tomatoes and Fennel
Baked Potatoes with Mustard Seeds
Braised Chicory in White Wine
Braised Red Cabbage
Charred Courgettes
Courgettes with Sesame Seeds
Roasted Butternut Squash
Roasted Root Vegetables
Roasted Mediterranean Vegetables
Roasted Rosemary Potatoes
Sage-roasted Parsnips, Apples and Prunes
Lemon and Orange Carrots
Sweet Roasted Fennel
Spinach with Tomatoes
Green Beans and Flaked Almonds
Stir-fried Beans with Cherry Tomatoes
Stir-fried Green Vegetables

Asparagus and Mangetouts
with Lemon Sauce

225g (8oz) asparagus spears, trimmed and cut diagonally into three pieces
1 tbsp sesame seeds
1 tbsp vegetable oil
1 tsp sesame oil
225g (8oz) mangetouts
1 garlic clove, crushed
2 tbsp dry sherry
1 tbsp caster sugar
2 tsp light soy sauce
grated zest and juice of 1 lemon
1 tsp cornflour
salt
strips of lemon zest to garnish

1 Cook the asparagus in a pan of lightly salted boiling water for about 5 minutes until just tender. Drain well.

2 Meanwhile, toast the sesame seeds in a hot wok or large frying pan until golden. Tip on to a plate.

3 Return the wok or frying pan to the heat and add the vegetable and sesame oils. Add the mangetouts, garlic and asparagus and stir-fry for 2 minutes.

4 Put the sherry, sugar, soy sauce, lemon zest and juice, cornflour and 5 tbsp water into a bowl and mix well.

5 Pour the mixture into the pan and cook, stirring, until the sauce thickens and coats the vegetables. Sprinkle with the toasted sesame seeds, garnish with lemon zest and serve immediately.

Serves 4
Preparation Time 5–10 minutes
Cooking Time 10 minutes

Nutritional Information (Per Serving)
114 calories, 6g fat (of which 1g saturates), 10g carbohydrate, trace salt
Dairy Free • Easy

Baked Tomatoes and Fennel Ⓥ

1 Preheat the oven to 200°C (180°C fan oven) mark 6. Put the fennel into a roasting tin and pour the white wine over it. Snip the thyme sprigs over the fennel, drizzle with the oil and roast for 45 minutes.

2 Halve the tomatoes, add to the roasting tin and continue to roast for 30 minutes or until tender, basting with the juices halfway through.

900g (2lb) fennel, trimmed and
  cut into quarters
75ml (2½fl oz) white wine
5 thyme sprigs
75ml (2½fl oz) olive oil
900g (2lb) ripe beef or plum tomatoes

Cook's Tip
This is an ideal accompaniment to a vegetarian frittata.

Nutritional Information (Per Serving)
127 calories, 9g fat (of which 1g saturates), 7g carbohydrate, 0.1g salt
Gluten Free · Dairy Free · Easy

Serves 6
Preparation Time 10 minutes
Cooking Time 1¼ hours

Baked Potatoes
with Mustard Seeds

6 baking potatoes, about 1.4kg (3lb), scrubbed
2 tbsp sunflower oil
1 tbsp coarse sea salt
4–5 large garlic cloves, unpeeled
50g (2oz) butter
6 tbsp crème fraîche
2 tbsp mustard seeds, toasted and lightly crushed
salt and ground black pepper
fresh oregano sprigs to garnish

1 Preheat the oven to 200°C (180°C fan oven) mark 6. Prick the potato skins all over with a fork, rub with oil and sprinkle with salt. Cook in the oven for 1 hour. Twenty minutes before the end of the cooking time, put the garlic cloves in a small roasting tin and cook for 20 minutes.

2 Squeeze the potatoes gently to check they are well cooked, then remove the potatoes and garlic from the oven and leave to cool slightly. When cool enough to handle, slice the tops off the potatoes and scoop the flesh into a warm bowl. Squeeze the garlic out of its skin and add it to the potato flesh with the butter, crème fraîche and mustard seeds. Season to taste with salt and pepper, then mash well. Return the potato mixture to the hollowed skins.

3 Put the filled potatoes on a baking sheet and return to the oven for 15 minutes or until golden brown. Garnish with oregano sprigs and serve hot.

Freezing Tip
To freeze Complete the recipe to the end of step 2, then cool, wrap and freeze for up to one month.

To use Thaw overnight at cool room temperature. Cook at 200°C (180°C fan oven) mark 6 for 20–25 minutes or until piping hot to the centre.

Serves 6
Preparation Time 15–20 minutes
Cooking Time 1¼ hours

Nutritional Information (Per Serving)
315 calories, 17g fat (of which 9g saturates), 38g carbohydrate, 1g salt
Gluten Free • Easy

Braised Chicory in White Wine

1 Preheat the oven to 190°C (170°C fan oven) mark 5. Grease a 1.7 litre (3 pint) ovenproof dish with 15g (½oz) butter and lay the chicory in the dish.

2 Season to taste, add the wine and dot the remaining butter over the top. Cover with foil and cook in the oven for 1 hour or until soft. Scatter with chives to serve.

50g (2oz) butter, softened
6 heads of chicory, trimmed
100ml (3½fl oz) white wine
salt and ground black pepper
snipped chives to serve

Nutritional Information (Per Serving)
80 calories, 7g fat (of which 5g saturates), 3g carbohydrate, 0.1g salt
Gluten Free · Easy

Serves 6
Preparation Time 5 minutes
Cooking Time about 1 hour

Braised Red Cabbage

V

1 tbsp olive oil
1 red onion, halved and sliced
2 garlic cloves, crushed
1 large red cabbage, about 1kg
    (2¼lb), shredded
2 tbsp light muscovado sugar
2 tbsp red wine vinegar
8 juniper berries
¼ tsp ground allspice
300ml (½ pint) vegetable stock
2 pears, cored and sliced
salt and ground black pepper
fresh thyme sprigs to garnish

1 Heat the oil in a large pan, add the onion and fry for 5 minutes. Add the remaining ingredients, except the pears, and season with salt and pepper. Bring to the boil, then reduce the heat, cover and simmer for 30 minutes.

2 Add the pears and cook for a further 15 minutes or until nearly all the liquid has evaporated and the cabbage is tender. Serve hot, garnished with thyme.

Get Ahead

To prepare ahead Red cabbage improves if made a day ahead. Complete the recipe to the end of step 1, cover and chill.

To use Reheat the cabbage gently, add the pears and complete the recipe.

Serves 6
Preparation Time 15 minutes
Cooking Time about 50 minutes

Nutritional Information (Per Serving)
63 calories, 1g fat (of which 0g saturates), 12g carbohydrate, 0.9g salt
Gluten Free · Dairy Free · Easy

Charred Courgettes

1. Preheat the barbecue or griddle. Score a criss-cross pattern on the fleshy side of the courgettes. Brush lightly with oil and sprinkle with sea salt.

2. Cook the courgettes on the barbecue or griddle for 10 minutes or until just tender, turning occasionally.

4 courgettes, halved lengthways
olive oil to brush
coarse sea salt to sprinkle

Try Something Different
Mix the olive oil with a good pinch of dried chilli flakes and a small handful of chopped fresh rosemary leaves.

Use a mixture of yellow and green courgettes if you like.

SIDE DISHES

Nutritional Information (Per Serving)
36 calories, 2g fat (of which trace saturates), 2g carbohydrate, 0g salt
Gluten Free · Dairy Free · Easy

Serves 4
Preparation Time 5 minutes
Cooking Time 10 minutes

Courgettes with
Sesame Seeds

2 tbsp sesame seeds
2 tbsp vegetable oil
4 garlic cloves, crushed
900g (2lb) courgettes, thinly sliced
1 spring onion, thickly sliced
½ tsp salt
1 tbsp sesame oil
ground black pepper
banana leaves to serve (optional, see Cook's Tip)

1 Toast the sesame seeds in a hot wok or large frying pan until golden. Tip on to a plate.

2 Heat the vegetable oil in the wok or frying pan. Add the garlic and fry for 2 minutes.

3 Add the courgettes and stir-fry for 7–8 minutes. Stir in the spring onion, salt and sesame oil and season to taste with pepper. Cook for a further 1 minute, then add the toasted sesame seeds. Stir once and serve hot or cold on a bed of banana leaves, if you like.

Cook's Tip
Banana leaves are sometimes used instead of plates in Southeast Asia; they make an unusual presentation and are available from some Asian food shops.

SIDE DISHES

Serves 6
Preparation Time 5 minutes
Cooking Time 12 minutes

Nutritional Information (Per Serving)
107 calories, 9g fat (of which 1g saturates), 3g carbohydrate, 0.4g salt
Gluten Free · Dairy Free · Easy

Roasted Butternut Squash

1. Preheat the oven to 220°C (200°C fan oven) mark 7. Cut the squash in half lengthways and scoop out the seeds. Cut in half again, then put into a roasting tin. Drizzle with the oil, season with salt and pepper and roast for 40 minutes.

2. Meanwhile, put the butter into a bowl with the thyme and chilli. Mix together well. Add a little to each slice of cooked butternut squash and serve.

2 butternut squash
2 tbsp olive oil
25g (1oz) butter
2 tbsp freshly chopped thyme leaves
1 red chilli, seeded and finely chopped (see Cook's Tips, page 37)
salt and ground black pepper

Try Something Different
Use crushed garlic instead of chilli.

Nutritional Information (Per Serving)
165 calories, 12g fat (of which 5g saturates), 11g carbohydrate, 0.1g salt
Gluten Free · Easy

Serves 4
Preparation Time 15 minutes
Cooking Time 40 minutes

Roasted Root Vegetables

1 large potato, cut into large chunks
1 large sweet potato, cut into
    large chunks
3 carrots, cut into large chunks
4 small parsnips, halved
1 small swede, cut into large chunks
3 tbsp olive oil
2 fresh rosemary and 2 fresh
    thyme sprigs
salt and ground black pepper

1 Preheat the oven to 200°C (180°C fan oven) mark 6. Put all the vegetables into a large roasting tin. Add the oil.

2 Use scissors to snip the herbs over the vegetables, then season with salt and pepper and toss everything together. Roast for 1 hour or until tender.

Try Something Different
Use other combinations of vegetables: try celeriac instead of parsnips, fennel instead of swede, peeled shallots instead of carrots.

Serves 4
Preparation Time 15 minutes
Cooking Time 1 hour

Nutritional Information (Per Serving)
251 calories, 10g fat (of which 1g saturates), 39g carbohydrate, 0.2g salt
Gluten Free • Dairy Free • Easy

Roasted Mediterranean
Vegetables

1. Preheat the oven to 220°C (200°C fan oven) mark 7. Put the tomatoes into a large roasting tin with the onions, peppers, courgettes and garlic. Drizzle with the oil and sprinkle with thyme, sea salt flakes and black pepper.

2. Roast, turning occasionally, for 35–40 minutes until tender.

4 plum tomatoes, halved
2 onions, quartered
4 red peppers, seeded and
    cut into strips
2 courgettes, cut into thick slices
4 garlic cloves, unpeeled
6 tbsp olive oil
1 tbsp freshly chopped thyme leaves
sea salt flakes and ground
    black pepper

Cook's Tips
To make a nutritionally complete meal, sprinkle with toasted sesame seeds and serve with hummus (see page 84).

Use oregano instead of thyme.

SIDE DISHES

Nutritional Information (Per Serving)
252 calories, 18g fat (of which 3g saturates), 19g carbohydrate, 0.4g salt
Gluten Free · Dairy Free · Easy

Serves 4
Preparation Time 10 minutes
Cooking Time 35–40 minutes

115

Roasted Rosemary Potatoes

750g (1lb 11oz) new potatoes
3 tbsp olive oil
8 rosemary stalks, each about 18cm
   (7in) long
salt and ground black pepper

1 Preheat the barbecue or grill. Cook the potatoes, unpeeled, in lightly salted boiling water for 10 minutes or until nearly tender. Drain, cool a little, then toss in the oil. Season well. Strip most of the leaves from the rosemary stalks, leaving a few at the tip; set the stripped leaves to one side.

2 Thread the potatoes on to the rosemary stalks, place on the barbecue or grill and scatter with the leaves. Cook for 10–15 minutes, turning from time to time, until tender and lightly charred.

Cook's Tip

Skewering the potatoes helps them to cook more quickly and makes them easier to handle on a barbecue. Using rosemary stalks adds a wonderful flavour.

SIDE DISHES

Serves 8
Preparation Time 10 minutes
Cooking Time 20–25 minutes

Nutritional Information (Per Serving)
102 calories, 4g fat (of which 1g saturates), 15g carbohydrate, trace salt
Gluten Free • Dairy Free • Easy

Sage-roasted Parsnips,
Apples and Prunes

1 Heat 3–4 tbsp oil in a large flameproof roasting tin, add the parsnips in batches and fry over a medium heat until a rich golden brown all over. Remove from the tin and set aside. Add 3–4 tbsp oil to the same tin. Fry the apples until golden brown. Remove from the tin and set aside.

2 Preheat the oven to 200°C (180°C fan oven) mark 6. Put the parsnips back into the tin, season with salt and pepper and roast for 15 minutes.

3 Add the apples and continue roasting for 10 minutes. Put the prunes in the tin and roast for a further 5 minutes. At the end of this time, test the apples: if they're still firm, roast everything for a further 5–10 minutes until the apples are soft and fluffy.

4 Put the tin on the hob over a very low heat. Add the butter and sage, drizzle with honey, if you like, and spoon into a hot serving dish.

6–8 tbsp olive oil
1.8kg (4lb) parsnips, peeled, quartered and cored
6 apples, peeled, cored and quartered
16 ready-to-eat prunes
50g (2oz) butter
1–2 tbsp freshly chopped sage leaves
1–2 tbsp clear honey (optional)
salt and ground black pepper

Get Ahead
To prepare ahead Fry the parsnips and apples, then cool, cover and chill for up to one day.

To use Complete the recipe.

SIDE DISHES

Nutritional Information (Per Serving)
313 calories, 16g fat (of which 5g saturates), 40g carbohydrate, 0.2g salt
Gluten Free • Easy

Serves 8
Preparation Time 20 minutes
Cooking Time 45–55 minutes

Lemon and Orange Carrots

900g (2lb) carrots, cut into
    long batons
150ml (¼ pint) orange juice
juice of 2 lemons
150ml (¼ pint) dry white wine
50g (2oz) butter
3 tbsp light muscovado sugar
4 tbsp freshly chopped coriander
    to garnish

1 Put the carrots, orange and lemon juices, wine, butter and sugar into a pan. Cover and bring to the boil.

2 Remove the lid and cook until almost all the liquid has evaporated, about 10 minutes. Serve sprinkled with the coriander.

Freezing Tip

To freeze Cook the carrots for only 5 minutes, then cool and freeze with the remaining liquid.

To use Thaw for 5 hours, then reheat in a pan for 5–6 minutes, or cook on full power in a 900W microwave for 7–8 minutes.

Serves 8
Preparation Time 10 minutes
Cooking Time 10–15 minutes

Nutritional Information (Per Serving)
127 calories, 6g fat (of which 3g saturates), 17g carbohydrate, 0.2g salt
Gluten Free · Easy

Sweet Roasted Fennel

1 Preheat the oven to 200°C (180°C fan oven) mark 6. Trim and quarter the fennel and put into a large roasting tin.

2 Drizzle the fennel with the oil and melted butter and squeeze the lemon juice over. Add the lemon halves to the roasting tin. Sprinkle with sugar and season generously with salt and pepper. Add the thyme and cover with a damp piece of non-stick baking parchment.

3 Roast for 30 minutes, then remove the baking parchment and cook for a further 20–30 minutes until lightly charred and tender.

700g (1½lb) fennel (about 3 bulbs)
3 tbsp olive oil
50g (2oz) butter, melted
1 lemon, halved
1 tsp caster sugar
2 large thyme sprigs
salt and ground black pepper

Nutritional Information (Per Serving)
192 calories, 19g fat (of which 8g saturates), 4g carbohydrate, 0.2g salt
Gluten Free • Easy

Serves 4
Preparation Time 10 minutes
Cooking Time about 1 hour

Spinach with Tomatoes

50g (2oz) butter
2 garlic cloves, crushed
450g (1lb) baby plum tomatoes,
    halved
250g (9oz) baby spinach leaves
a large pinch of freshly grated nutmeg
salt and ground black pepper

1 Heat half the butter in a pan, add the garlic and cook until just soft. Add the tomatoes and cook for 4–5 minutes until just beginning to soften.

2 Put the spinach and a little water into a clean pan, cover and cook for 2–3 minutes until just wilted. Drain well, chop roughly and stir into the tomatoes.

3 Add the remaining butter and heat through gently. Season well with salt and pepper, stir in the nutmeg and serve.

Serves 6
Preparation Time 10 minutes
Cooking Time 15 minutes

Nutritional Information (Per Serving)
85 calories, 7g fat (of which 5g saturates), 3g carbohydrate, 0.3g salt
Gluten Free · Easy

Green Beans and
Flaked Almonds

1 Bring a large pan of water to the boil. Add the green beans and cook for 4–5 minutes. Drain.

2 Meanwhile, heat the oil in a large frying pan. Add the almonds and cook for 1–2 minutes until golden. Turn off the heat, add the drained beans to the frying pan and toss. Squeeze over a little lemon juice just before serving.

200g (7oz) green beans
1 tsp olive oil
25g (1oz) flaked almonds
½ lemon

Try Something Different

Use basil-infused oil and increase the amount of oil to 2 tbsp.

Use pinenuts instead of almonds, drizzle with balsamic vinegar and scatter with basil leaves to serve.

SIDE DISHES

Nutritional Information (Per Serving)
57 calories, 5g fat (of which trace saturates), 2g carbohydrate, 0g salt
Gluten Free · Dairy Free · Easy

Serves 4
Preparation Time 5 minutes
Cooking Time 5–7 minutes

Stir-fried Beans with
Cherry Tomatoes

350g (12oz) green beans, trimmed
2 tsp olive oil
1 large garlic clove, crushed
150g (5oz) cherry or baby plum
    tomatoes, halved
2 tbsp freshly chopped flat-leafed
    parsley
salt and ground black pepper

1 Cook the beans in lightly salted boiling water for 4–5 minutes, then drain well.

2 Heat the oil in a wok or large frying pan over a high heat. Stir-fry the beans with the garlic and tomatoes for 2–3 minutes until the beans are tender and the tomatoes are just beginning to soften without losing their shape. Season well with salt and pepper, stir in the parsley and serve.

Serves 6
Preparation Time 10 minutes
Cooking Time about 8 minutes

Nutritional Information (Per Serving)
30 calories, 2g fat (of which trace saturates), 3g carbohydrate, 0g salt
Gluten Free · Dairy Free · Easy

Stir-fried Green Vegetables

1 Heat the oil in a wok or large frying pan, add the courgettes and stir-fry for 1–2 minutes.

2 Add the mangetouts and cook for 1 minute. Add the butter and peas and cook for 1 minute. Season to taste with salt and pepper and serve immediately.

2 tbsp vegetable oil
225g (8oz) courgettes, thinly sliced
175g (6oz) mangetouts
25g (1oz) butter
175g (6oz) frozen peas, thawed
salt and ground black pepper

Try Something Different
Try other vegetables, such as thinly sliced leeks, spring onions or pak choi.

Nutritional Information (Per Serving)
100 calories, 8g fat (of which 3g saturates), 5g carbohydrate, 0.1g salt
Gluten Free · Easy

Serves 6
Preparation Time 5 minutes
Cooking Time 3–4 minutes

Egg and cheese dishes

Baked Eggs

2 tbsp olive oil
125g (4oz) mushrooms, chopped
225g (8oz) fresh spinach
2 medium eggs
2 tbsp single cream
salt and ground black pepper

1 Preheat the oven to 200°C (180°C fan oven) mark 6. Heat the oil in a large frying pan, add the mushrooms and stir-fry for 30 seconds. Add the spinach and stir-fry until wilted. Season to taste, then divide the mixture between two shallow ovenproof dishes.

2 Carefully break an egg into the centre of each dish, then spoon 1 tbsp single cream over it.

3 Cook in the oven for about 12 minutes or until just set – the eggs will continue to cook a little once they're out of the oven. Grind a little more pepper over the top, if you like, and serve.

126

Serves 2
Preparation Time 10 minutes
Cooking Time 15 minutes

Nutritional Information (Per Serving)
238 calories, 21g fat (of which 5g saturates), 2g carbohydrate, 0.6g salt
Gluten Free · Easy

Poached Eggs with Mushrooms

1. Preheat the oven to 200°C (180°C fan oven) mark 6. Arrange the mushrooms in a single layer in a small roasting tin and dot with the butter. Roast for 15 minutes or until golden brown and soft.

2. Meanwhile, bring a wide shallow pan of water to the boil. When the mushrooms are half-cooked and the water is bubbling furiously, break the eggs into the pan, spaced well apart, then take the pan off the heat. The eggs will take about 6 minutes to cook.

3. When the mushrooms are tender, put them on a warmed plate, cover and return to the turned-off oven to keep warm.

4. Put the roasting tin over a medium heat on the hob and add the spinach. Cook, stirring, for about 30 seconds or until the spinach has just started to wilt.

5. The eggs should be set by now, so divide the mushrooms among four warmed plates and top with a little spinach, a poached egg and a teaspoonful of pesto.

Try Something Different

For a more substantial meal, serve on 100% rye bread or German pumpernickel.

8 medium-sized flat or
  portabella mushrooms
40g (1½oz) butter
8 medium eggs
225g (8oz) baby spinach leaves
4 tsp fresh pesto (see Cook's Tip,
  page 38)

EGG AND CHEESE DISHES

Nutritional Information (Per Serving)
276 calories, 23g fat (of which 9g saturates), 1g carbohydrate, 0.7g salt
Gluten Free · Easy

Serves 4
Preparation Time 15 minutes
Cooking Time 20 minutes

Piperade

2 tbsp olive oil
1 medium onion, finely chopped
1 garlic clove, finely chopped
1 red pepper, seeded and chopped
375g (13oz) tomatoes, peeled, seeded
   and chopped
a pinch of cayenne pepper
8 large eggs
salt and ground black pepper
freshly chopped flat-leafed parsley
   to garnish
fresh bread to serve (optional)

1 Heat the oil in a heavy-based frying pan. Add the onion and garlic and cook gently for 5 minutes. Add the red pepper and cook for 10 minutes or until softened.

2 Add the tomatoes, increase the heat and cook until they are reduced to a thick pulp. Season well with cayenne pepper, salt and pepper.

3 Lightly whisk the eggs and add to the frying pan. Using a wooden spoon, stir gently until they've just begun to set but are still creamy. Garnish with parsley and serve with bread, if you like.

Serves 4
Preparation Time 20 minutes
Cooking Time 20 minutes

Nutritional Information (Per Serving)
232 calories, 17g fat (of which 4g saturates), 7g carbohydrate, 0.4g salt
Gluten Free · Dairy Free · Easy

Egg Fu Yung

1 Heat the oil in a wok or large frying pan, add the spring onions, mushrooms, bamboo shoots, green pepper and peas and stir-fry for 2–3 minutes.

2 Season the eggs with salt and chilli powder. Pour the eggs into the pan and continue to cook, stirring, until the egg mixture is set.

3 Sprinkle with the soy sauce and stir well. Serve immediately, garnished with spring onion curls.

3 tbsp groundnut or vegetable oil
8 spring onions, finely sliced, plus extra spring onion curls to garnish (see Cook's Tip)
125g (4oz) shiitake or oyster mushrooms, sliced
125g (4oz) canned bamboo shoots, drained and chopped
½ green pepper, seeded and finely chopped
125g (4oz) frozen peas, thawed
6 medium eggs, beaten
2 good pinches of chilli powder
1 tbsp light soy sauce
a pinch of salt

Cook's Tip

To make spring onion curls, trim spring onions into 7.5cm (3in) lengths, shred finely, then place in a bowl of water with ice cubes for 30 minutes.

EGG AND CHEESE DISHES

Nutritional Information (Per Serving)
232 calories, 18g fat (of which 4g saturates), 6g carbohydrate, 0.9g salt
Dairy Free · Easy

Serves 4
Preparation Time 10 minutes
Cooking Time about 5 minutes

Classic French Omelette

2–3 medium eggs
1 tbsp milk or water
25g (1oz) unsalted butter
salt and ground black pepper
sliced or grilled tomatoes and freshly
    chopped flat-leafed parsley to serve

1 Whisk the eggs in a bowl, just enough to break them down – over-beating spoils the texture of the omelette. Season with salt and pepper and add the milk or water.

2 Heat the butter in an 18cm (7in) omelette pan or non-stick frying pan until it is foaming, but not brown. Add the eggs and stir gently with a fork or wooden spatula, drawing the mixture from the sides to the centre as it sets and letting the liquid egg in the centre run to the sides. When set, stop stirring and cook for 30 seconds or until the omelette is golden brown underneath and still creamy on top: don't overcook. If you are making a filled omelette (see Try Something Different), add the filling at this point.

3 Tilt the pan away from you slightly and use a palette knife to fold over one-third of the omelette to the centre, then fold over the opposite third. Slide the omelette out on to a warmed plate, letting it flip over so that the folded sides are underneath. Serve immediately, with tomatoes sprinkled with parsley.

Try Something Different
Blend 25g (1oz) mild goat's cheese (see Cook's Tip, page 35) with 1 tbsp crème fraîche; put in the centre of the omelette before folding.

Serves 1
Preparation Time 5 minutes
Cooking Time 5 minutes

Nutritional Information (Per Serving)
449 calories, 40g fat (of which 19g saturates), 1g carbohydrate, 1g salt
Gluten Free • Dairy Free • Easy

Mushroom Soufflé Omelette

1. Heat a non-stick frying pan for 30 seconds. Add the mushrooms and cook, stirring, for 3 minutes to brown slightly, then stir in the crème fraîche and turn off the heat.

2. Lightly beat the egg yolks in a bowl, add 2 tbsp cold water and season with salt and pepper.

3. In a separate clean, grease-free bowl, whisk the egg whites until stiff but not dry, then gently fold into the egg yolks. Do not over-mix. Heat an 18cm (7in) non-stick frying pan over a medium heat. Add the butter, then the egg mixture, tilting the pan to cover the bottom. Cook for 3 minutes or until the underside is golden brown.

4. Meanwhile, preheat the grill. Gently reheat the mushrooms and add the chives. Put the omelette under the grill for 1 minute or until the surface is just firm and puffy. Tip the mushroom mixture on top. Run a spatula around and underneath the omelette to loosen it, then carefully fold it and turn out on to a warmed plate. Serve immediately.

50g (2oz) small chestnut mushrooms, sliced
3 tbsp crème fraîche
2 medium eggs, separated
15g (½oz) butter
5 fresh chives, roughly chopped
salt and ground black pepper

Nutritional Information (Per Serving)
440 calories, 42g fat (of which 23g saturates), 2g carbohydrate, 0.6g salt
Gluten Free · Easy

Serves 1
Preparation Time 5 minutes
Cooking Time 7–10 minutes

Sweet Potato and
Goat's Cheese Tortilla

2 large sweet potatoes, peeled
   and thinly sliced
3 tbsp olive oil
3 peppers (mixed red and yellow),
   seeded and roughly chopped
1 fennel bulb, thinly sliced
3 garlic cloves, crushed
1 small onion, thinly sliced
3 medium eggs
284ml carton single cream
125g (4oz) each fresh soft goat's
   cheese and Taleggio cheese,
   chopped (see Cook's Tip,
   page 35)
75g (3oz) young spinach leaves,
   watercress leaves or fresh basil
salt and ground black pepper

1 Preheat the oven to 220°C (200°C fan oven) mark 7. Put the potatoes into a large roasting tin, season with salt and pepper and drizzle with half the oil. Toss well. Put the peppers, fennel, garlic and onion into a second tin. Season, drizzle with the remaining oil and toss well. Put both tins into the oven and roast for 30–35 minutes until the vegetables are tender.

2 Whisk together the eggs, cream and cheese and season with plenty of coarsely ground black pepper.

3 Line the base and sides of a 20.5cm (8in) round, 7.5cm (3in) deep cake tin with non-stick baking parchment.

4 Reduce the oven temperature to 170°C (150°C fan oven) mark 3. Layer the roasted vegetables in the tin with the spinach, watercress or basil, adding a little egg mix as you go. Pour in any remaining egg mix and cook the tortilla in the centre of the oven for about 1 hour 15 minutes or until the egg is set and the top golden. Serve warm or cold.

Get Ahead

To prepare ahead Complete the recipe up to 24 hours in advance. Cool in the tin, cover and keep chilled.

To use To serve hot, turn out the tortilla, slice and lay it flat on a lightly greased baking sheet. Cover with foil and reheat in a hot oven for 10–15 minutes.

Serves 8
Preparation Time 15 minutes
Cooking Time 1 hour 50 minutes

Nutritional Information (Per Serving)
316 calories, 22g fat (of which 11g saturates), 20g carbohydrate, 0.7g salt
Easy

Courgette and
Parmesan Frittata

1 Melt 25g (1oz) butter in an 18cm (7in) non-stick frying pan and cook the onion for about 10 minutes or until softened. Add the courgettes and fry gently for 5 minutes or until they begin to soften.

2 Beat the eggs in a bowl and season with salt and pepper.

3 Add the remaining butter to the pan and heat, then pour in the eggs. Cook for 2–3 minutes until golden underneath and cooked around the edges. Meanwhile, preheat the grill to medium.

4 Sprinkle the grated cheese over the frittata and grill for 1–2 minutes until just set. Scatter with Parmesan shavings, cut the frittata into quarters and serve with a green salad.

40g (1½oz) butter
1 small onion, finely chopped
225g (8oz) courgettes, finely sliced
6 medium eggs, beaten
25g (1oz) Parmesan, freshly grated, plus shavings to garnish (see Cook's Tip, page 35)
salt and ground black pepper
green salad to serve

Try Something Different
Cherry Tomato and Rocket Frittata
Replace the courgettes with 175g (6oz) ripe cherry tomatoes, frying them for 1 minute only, until they begin to soften. Immediately after pouring in the eggs, scatter 25g (1oz) rocket leaves over the surface. Continue cooking as in step 3.

Nutritional Information (Per Serving)
229 calories, 19g fat (of which 9g saturates), 2g carbohydrate, 0.6g salt
Gluten Free · Easy

Serves 4
Preparation Time 10 minutes
Cooking Time 15–20 minutes

Mixed Mushroom Frittata

1 tbsp olive oil
300g (11oz) mixed mushrooms, sliced
2 tbsp freshly chopped thyme
zest and juice of ½ lemon
50g (2oz) watercress, chopped
6 medium eggs, beaten
salt and ground black pepper
stoneground wholegrain bread
    (optional) and a crisp green salad
    to serve

1 Heat the oil in a large deep frying pan over a medium heat. Add the mushrooms and thyme and stir-fry for 4–5 minutes until starting to soften and brown. Stir in the lemon zest and juice, then bubble for 1 minute. Reduce the heat.

2 Preheat the grill. Add the watercress to the beaten eggs, season with salt and pepper and pour into the pan. Cook on the hob for 7–8 minutes until the sides and base are firm but the centre is still a little soft.

3 Transfer to the grill and cook for 4–5 minutes until just set. Cut into wedges and serve with chunks of bread, if you like, and a salad.

Serves 4
Preparation Time 15 minutes
Cooking Time 15–20 minutes

Nutritional Information (Per Serving)
148 calories, 12g fat (of which 3g saturates), 0g carbohydrate, 0.3g salt
Dairy Free · Gluten Free

Spinach and Goat's
Cheese Frittata

1 Preheat the grill to high. Blanch the leeks in a pan of lightly salted boiling water for 2 minutes. Add the spring onions and spinach just before the end of the cooking time. Drain, rinse in cold water and dry on kitchen paper.

2 Whisk together the eggs, milk and nutmeg. Season with salt and pepper. Stir the goat's cheese into the egg mixture with the leeks, spinach and spring onions.

3 Heat the oil in a non-stick frying pan. Pour in the frittata mixture and fry gently for 4–5 minutes, then finish under the hot grill for 4–5 minutes until the top is golden and just firm. Serve with mixed salad.

200g (7oz) baby leeks, trimmed
 and chopped
4 spring onions, chopped
125g (4oz) baby leaf spinach
6 large eggs
4 tbsp milk
freshly grated nutmeg
125g (4oz) soft goat's cheese,
 chopped (see Cook's Tip, page 35)
1 tbsp olive oil
salt and ground black pepper
mixed salad leaves to serve

Try Something Different
Use a different cheese, such as Stilton (see Cook's Tip, page 35).

Nutritional Information (Per Serving)
281 calories, 21g fat (of which 9g saturates), 3g carbohydrate, 0.9g salt
Gluten Free • Easy

Serves 4
Preparation Time 10 minutes
Cooking Time 12 minutes

Twice-baked Soufflés

1 Preheat the oven to 180°C (160°C fan oven) mark 4. Grease eight 150ml (¼ pint) ramekins and baseline with greaseproof paper. Dust with the almonds.

2 Cook the cauliflower in lightly salted boiling water until tender. Drain, plunge into iced water and drain again. Blend with the milk until smooth. Melt the butter in a pan, add the flour and mix to a smooth paste. Stir in the cauliflower purée and bring to the boil. Cool a little. Beat in the cheeses and egg yolks and season. Whisk the whites to a soft peak and fold in. Spoon the mixture into the ramekins, put into a roasting tin and fill halfway up the sides with hot water. Cook for 20–25 minutes until firm to the touch. Remove from the tin and cool completely. Run a knife around the edge of the soufflés and turn out on to a baking sheet.

3 Preheat the oven to 200°C (180°C fan oven) mark 6. Bring the cream to the boil in a wide pan. Bubble until reduced by one-third. Add the mustard and season. Spoon a little cream over the soufflés and bake for 15–20 minutes until golden. Serve with dressed rocket leaves and cherry tomatoes.

50g (2oz) butter, plus extra to grease
25g (1oz) ground almonds,
   lightly toasted
250g (9oz) cauliflower florets
150ml (¼ pint) milk
40g (1½oz) plain flour
75g (3oz) Cheddar cheese, finely
   grated (see Cook's Tip, page 35)
75g (3oz) Emmenthal cheese,
   finely grated (see as above)
3 large eggs, separated
300ml (½ pint) double cream
1 tbsp grainy mustard
salt and ground black pepper
rocket leaves and cherry tomatoes
   drizzled with olive oil and balsamic
   vinegar to serve

Freezing tip

To freeze Prepare the recipe to the first baking, turn out on to a baking sheet and cool, then wrap separately, label and freeze for up to one month.

To use Complete the recipe. Cook the soufflés from frozen at 200°C (180°C fan oven) mark 6 for 25–30 minutes until golden.

EGG AND CHEESE DISHES

Serves 8
Preparation Time 20 minutes,
   plus cooling
Cooking Time 1¼ hours

Nutritional Information (Per Serving)
377 calories, 34g fat (of which 20g saturates), 7g carbohydrate, 0.6g salt
A Little Effort

Grilled Sweet Potatoes
with Feta and Olives

1 Preheat the barbecue or griddle. Peel the sweet potato and cut lengthways into eight wedges. Put them into a pan of boiling water and bring back to the boil, then simmer for 3 minutes. Drain and refresh in cold water. Drain, dry well on kitchen paper, then brush lightly with oil. Season with salt and pepper, then barbecue or grill for 10–15 minutes until well browned and cooked through.

2 Meanwhile, mash the cheese, herbs, olives, garlic and 4 tbsp oil together. Serve the sweet potato with the feta cheese mixture, garnished with flat-leafed parsley.

1 large sweet potato, weighing about 500g (1lb 2oz)
4 tbsp olive oil, plus extra to brush
200g (7oz) feta cheese (see Cook's Tip, page 35)
2 tsp dried Herbes de Provence
50g (2oz) pitted black olives, chopped
1 garlic clove, crushed
salt and ground black pepper
flat-leafed parsley sprigs to garnish

Cook's Tip
Herbes de Provence, an aromatic dried mixture made up of rosemary, thyme, basil, bay and savory, is a wonderful complement to barbecued or grilled food.

EGG AND CHEESE DISHES

Nutritional Information (Per Serving)
324 calories, 23g fat (of which 9g saturates), 21g carbohydrate, 2.5g salt
Gluten Free • Easy

Serves 4
Preparation Time 15 minutes
Cooking Time 15–20 minutes

Cheese and Vegetable Bake

250g (9oz) macaroni
1 cauliflower, cut into florets
2 leeks, trimmed and finely chopped
100g (3½oz) frozen peas
25g (1oz) wholemeal breadcrumbs
crusty bread to serve

FOR THE CHEESE SAUCE

15g (½oz) butter
15g (½oz) plain flour
200ml (7fl oz) skimmed milk
75g (3oz) Parmesan, grated (see
    Cook's Tip, page 35)
2 tsp Dijon mustard
salt and ground black pepper

1 Cook the macaroni in a large pan of boiling water for 6 minutes, adding the cauliflower and leeks for the last 4 minutes and the peas for the last 2 minutes.

2 Meanwhile, make the cheese sauce. Melt the butter in a pan and add the flour. Cook for 1–2 minutes, then take off the heat and gradually stir in the milk. Bring to the boil slowly, stirring until the sauce thickens. Stir in 50g (2oz) Parmesan and the mustard. Season with salt and pepper.

3 Preheat the grill to medium. Drain the pasta and vegetables and put back into the pan. Add the cheese sauce and mix well. Spoon into a large shallow 2 litre (3½ pint) ovenproof dish and scatter the remaining Parmesan and the breadcrumbs over the top. Grill for 5 minutes or until golden and crisp. Serve hot with bread.

Cook's Tip
Microwave Cheese Sauce
Put the butter, flour and milk into a large microwave-proof bowl and whisk together. Cook in a 900W microwave oven on full power for 4 minutes, whisking every minute, until the sauce has thickened. Stir in the cheese until it melts. Stir in the mustard and season to taste.

Serves 4
Preparation Time 15 minutes
Cooking Time 15 minutes

Nutritional Information (Per Serving)
471 calories, 13g fat (of which 7g saturates), 67g carbohydrate, 0.8g salt
Easy

Cheese Fondue Tarts

1 Preheat the oven to 220°C (200°C fan oven) mark 7 and grease a 12-cup bun tin or muffin pan. On a lightly floured surface, roll out the pastry to 3mm (⅛in) thick. Cut out twelve 10cm (4in) rounds and put into the tin. Prick the bases and chill for 10 minutes. Line with greaseproof paper and fill with baking beans. Bake for 15–20 minutes, then remove the paper and beans and bake for 5 minutes or until golden.

2 Meanwhile, put the cheese, garlic, cream, lemon juice and paprika into a pan, heat and stir to make a smooth sauce. Mix the cornflour with the vodka, add to the pan and cook for 1–2 minutes. Stir in the dill.

3 Spoon the mixture into the pastry cases, scatter with dill and serve warm.

butter to grease
flour to dust
425g pack puff pastry, thawed if frozen
200g (7oz) each Jarlsberg and Gouda cheese, grated (see Cook's Tip, page 35)
1 garlic clove, crushed
150ml (¼ pint) single cream
juice of 1 small lemon
½ tsp paprika
2 tsp cornflour
50ml (2fl oz) vodka
2 tbsp freshly chopped dill, plus extra to garnish

Nutritional Information (Per Serving) (2 tarts per serving)
337 calories, 22g fat (of which 3g saturates), 28g carbohydrate, 0.6g salt
Easy

Serves 6
Preparation Time 20 minutes, plus chilling
Cooking Time 25 minutes

Mediterranean Kebabs

1 large courgette, cut into chunks
1 red pepper, seeded and cut
    into chunks
12 cherry tomatoes
125g (4oz) halloumi cheese, cubed
    (see Cook's Tip, page 35)
100g (3½oz) natural yogurt
1 tsp ground cumin
2 tbsp olive oil
squeeze of lemon
1 lemon, cut into eight wedges
couscous tossed with freshly chopped
    flat-leafed parsley to serve

1 Preheat the barbecue or grill. Soak eight wooden skewers in water for 20 minutes. Put the courgette into a large bowl with the red pepper, cherry tomatoes and halloumi cheese. Add the yogurt, cumin, oil and a squeeze of lemon and mix.

2 Push a lemon wedge on to each skewer, then divide the vegetables and cheese among the skewers. Grill the kebabs, turning regularly, for 8–10 minutes until the vegetables are tender and the halloumi is nicely charred. Serve with couscous.

Serves 4
Preparation Time 15 minutes
Cooking Time 8–10 minutes

Nutritional Information (Per Serving)
164 calories, 13g fat (of which 5g saturates), 7g carbohydrate, 1.1g salt
Gluten Free · Easy

Roasted Stuffed Peppers

1 Preheat the oven to 180°C (160°C fan oven) mark 4. Use a little of the butter to grease a shallow ovenproof dish and put the peppers in it side by side, ready to be filled.

2 Heat the remaining butter and 1 tbsp oil in a pan. Add the mushrooms and fry until they're golden and there's no excess liquid left in the pan. Stir in the chives, then spoon the mixture into the pepper halves.

3 Crumble the feta over the mushrooms. Mix the breadcrumbs and Parmesan in a bowl, then sprinkle over the peppers.

4 Season with salt and pepper and drizzle with the remaining oil. Roast in the oven for 45 minutes or until golden and tender. Serve warm.

40g (1½oz) butter
4 Romano peppers, halved, with stalks on and seeded
3 tbsp olive oil
350g (12oz) chestnut mushrooms, roughly chopped
4 tbsp finely chopped fresh chives
100g (3½oz) feta cheese (see Cook's Tip, page 35)
50g (2oz) fresh white breadcrumbs
25g (1oz) freshly grated Parmesan (see as above)
salt and ground black pepper

Get ahead

To prepare ahead Complete the recipe to the end of step 4, up to one day ahead. Cover and chill.

To use Reheat under the grill for 5 minutes.

Nutritional Information (Per Serving)
189 calories, 14g fat (of which 6g saturates), 11g carbohydrate, 0.9g salt
Easy

Serves 8
Preparation Time 20 minutes
Cooking Time 45 minutes

Pulses

Lentils with Red Pepper

Lentil Casserole

Lentil Chilli

Warm Lentil and Egg Salad

Spicy Vegetable Kebabs

Smoked Sesame Tofu

Curried Tofu Burgers

Sweet Chilli Tofu Stir-fry

Tofu Laksa Curry

Chickpea and Butternut Pot

Spiced Chickpeas with Sweet Potatoes

Chickpeas with Spinach

Moroccan Chickpea Stew

Chickpea Curry

Chickpea and Chilli Stir-fry

Black-eye Bean Chilli

Chilli Bean Cake

Spiced Bean and Vegetable Stew

Mixed Beans with Lemon Vinaigrette

Cannellini Bean and Sunblush Tomato Salad

Simple Bean Salad

Split Pea Roti

Lentils with Red Pepper

1 tbsp olive oil
1 very small onion, finely chopped
1 celery stick, diced
1 carrot, diced
2 bay leaves, torn
150g (5oz) Puy lentils
600ml (1 pint) hot vegetable stock
1 marinated red pepper, drained
    and chopped
2 tbsp chopped flat-leafed parsley,
    plus extra to garnish
ground black pepper

1 Heat the oil in a pan, add the onion and cook over a low heat for 15 minutes or until soft. Add the celery, carrot and bay leaves and cook for 2 minutes.

2 Add the lentils with the hot stock and stir everything together. Half cover the pan with a lid and simmer over a low heat for 25–30 minutes.

3 Add the red pepper and parsley and season with pepper. Stir everything together well, spoon into a warmed serving dish, garnish with extra parsley and serve as an accompaniment.

Serves 2
Preparation Time 10 minutes
Cooking Time 32 minutes

Nutritional Information (Per Serving)
260 calories, 2g fat (of which 1g saturates), 45g carbohydrate, 0g salt
Gluten Free · Dairy Free · Easy

Lentil Casserole

V

1 Preheat the oven to 180°C (160°C fan oven) mark 4. Heat the oil in a flameproof casserole, add the onions, carrots and leeks and fry, stirring, for 5 minutes. Add the mushrooms, garlic, ginger and ground coriander and fry for 2–3 minutes.

2 Stir the lentils into the casserole with the hot stock. Season with salt and pepper and return to the boil. Cover and cook in the oven for 45–50 minutes until the vegetables and lentils are tender. Stir in the chopped coriander before serving.

2 tbsp olive oil
2 onions, sliced
4 carrots, sliced
3 leeks, trimmed and sliced
450g (1lb) button mushrooms
2 garlic cloves, crushed
2.5cm (1in) piece fresh root ginger, peeled and grated
1 tbsp ground coriander
225g (8oz) split red lentils, rinsed and drained
750ml (1¼ pints) hot vegetable stock
4 tbsp freshly chopped coriander
salt and ground black pepper

Nutritional Information (Per Serving)
239 calories, 6g fat (of which 1g saturates), 36g carbohydrate, 0.4g salt
Gluten Free • Dairy Free • Easy

Serves 6
Preparation Time 20 minutes
Cooking Time 1 hour

Lentil Chilli

oil-water spray (see Cook's Tip)
2 red onions, chopped
1½ tsp each ground coriander
    and ground cumin
½ tsp ground paprika
2 garlic cloves, crushed
2 sun-dried tomatoes, chopped
¼ tsp crushed dried chilli flakes
125ml (4fl oz) red wine
300ml (½ pint) hot vegetable stock
2 × 400g cans brown or green lentils,
    drained and rinsed
2 × 400g cans chopped tomatoes
sugar to taste
salt and ground black pepper
natural low-fat yogurt or soya yogurt
    and rice to serve

1 Spray a saucepan with the oil-water spray and cook the onions for 5 minutes or until softened. Add the coriander, cumin and paprika. Combine the garlic, sun-dried tomatoes, chilli, wine and hot stock and add to the pan. Cover and simmer for 5–7 minutes. Uncover and simmer until the onions are very tender and the liquid has almost gone.

2 Stir in the lentils and canned tomatoes and season with salt and pepper. Simmer, uncovered, for 15 minutes or until thick. Stir in sugar to taste. Remove from the heat.

3 Ladle out a quarter of the mixture and whiz in a food processor or blender. Combine the puréed and unpuréed portions. Serve with yogurt and rice.

Cook's Tip
Oil-water spray is far lower in calories than oil alone and, as it sprays on thinly and evenly, you'll use less. Fill one-eighth of a travel-sized spray bottle with oil such as sunflower, light olive or vegetable (rapeseed) oil, then top up with water. To use, shake well before spraying. Store in the fridge.

Serves 6
Preparation Time 10 minutes
Cooking Time 30 minutes

Nutritional Information (Per Serving)
195 calories, 2g fat (of which trace saturates), 32g carbohydrate, 0.1g salt
Gluten Free · Dairy Free · Easy

Warm Lentil and Egg Salad

1. Heat the oil in a large pan. Add the onion, carrot and celery and cook for 5 minutes. Add the peppers and mushrooms, cover and cook for a further 5 minutes. Stir in the lentils and hot stock and bring to the boil, then reduce the heat and simmer, covered, for 25–30 minutes.

2. Meanwhile, bring a large pan of water to the boil. Break the eggs into the water and cook for 3–4 minutes. Lift them out with a slotted spoon, drain on kitchen paper and keep warm.

3. A couple of minutes before the end of the lentil cooking time, add the spinach and cook until wilted. Stir in the vinegar. Spoon on to four plates or bowls and top each with a poached egg. Season with pepper and serve.

1 tbsp olive oil
1 onion, 1 carrot and 1 celery
 stick, finely chopped
2 red peppers, seeded and
 roughly chopped
200g (7oz) flat mushrooms, sliced
200g (7oz) lentils, rinsed and drained
600ml (1 pint) hot vegetable stock
4 medium eggs
100g (3½ oz) baby leaf spinach
2 tbsp balsamic vinegar
ground black pepper

Nutritional Information (Per Serving)
317 calories, 10g fat (of which 2g saturates), 37g carbohydrate, 0.7g salt
Gluten Free • Dairy Free • Easy

Serves 4
Preparation Time 15 minutes
Cooking Time 35–40 minutes

Spicy Vegetable Kebabs

12 baby onions
12 new potatoes
12 button mushrooms
2 courgettes
2 garlic cloves, crushed
1 tsp each ground coriander
    and turmeric
½ tsp ground cumin
1 tbsp sun-dried tomato paste
1 tsp chilli sauce
juice of ½ lemon
4 tbsp olive oil
275g (10oz) smoked tofu, cut into
    2.5cm (1in) cubes
salt and ground black pepper
Yogurt Sauce (see Cook's Tip) and
    lemon wedges to serve

1 Blanch the baby onions in a pan of lightly salted boiling water for 3 minutes, then drain, refresh in cold water and peel away the skins. Put the potatoes into a pan of lightly salted cold water, bring to the boil and parboil for 8 minutes, then drain and refresh under cold water. Blanch the mushrooms in boiling water for 1 minute, then drain and refresh under cold water. Cut each courgette into six chunky slices and blanch for 1 minute, then drain and refresh.

2 Mix the garlic, spices, tomato paste, chilli sauce, lemon juice, olive oil, salt and pepper together in a shallow dish. Add the well-drained vegetables and tofu and toss to coat. Cover and chill for several hours or overnight.

3 Preheat the barbecue or grill. Soak four wooden skewers in water for 20 minutes. Thread the vegetables and tofu on to the skewers. Cook the kebabs for 8–10 minutes until the vegetables are charred and tender, turning frequently and basting with the marinade. Serve with Yogurt Sauce and lemon wedges.

Cook's Tip
Yogurt Sauce
Mix 225g (8oz) Greek yogurt with 1 crushed garlic clove and 2 tbsp freshly chopped coriander. Season with salt and pepper. Chill until ready to serve.

Serves 4
Preparation Time 30 minutes,
    plus marinating
Cooking Time 25 minutes

Nutritional Information (Per Serving)
247 calories, 14g fat (of which 3g saturates), 22g carbohydrate, 0.1g salt
Gluten Free • Easy

Smoked Sesame Tofu

1 Put the sesame seeds into a bowl, add the tamari, sugar, vinegar and ½ tbsp sesame oil. Mix together, then add the smoked tofu and stir to coat. Set aside to marinate for 10 minutes.

2 Heat a large wok or non-stick frying pan, add the marinated tofu, reserving the marinade, and fry for 5 minutes or until golden all over. Remove from the wok with a slotted spoon and set aside.

3 Heat the remaining oil in the wok, add the cabbage and carrots and stir-fry for 5 minutes. Stir in the bean sprouts, peppers, spring onions, cooked tofu and reserved marinade and cook for a further 2 minutes. Serve with brown rice.

2 tbsp toasted sesame seeds
2 tbsp tamari (wheat-free Japanese soy sauce)
1 tsp light muscovado sugar
1 tsp rice wine vinegar
1 tbsp sesame oil
225g (8oz) smoked tofu, cubed
½ small white or green cabbage, shredded
2 carrots, peeled and cut into strips
200g (7oz) bean sprouts
4 roasted red peppers, roughly chopped
2 spring onions, shredded
brown rice to serve

Nutritional Information (Per Serving)
208 calories, 11g fat (of which 2g saturates), 19g carbohydrate, 1.4g salt
Gluten Free • Dairy Free • Easy

Serves 4
Preparation Time 20 minutes, plus marinating
Cooking Time 12 minutes

Curried Tofu Burgers

1 tbsp sunflower oil, plus
   extra to fry
1 large carrot, finely grated
1 large onion, finely grated
2 tsp coriander seeds, finely crushed
   (optional)
1 garlic clove, crushed
1 tsp curry paste (see Cook's Tip,
   page 96)
1 tsp tomato purée
225g pack firm tofu
25g (1oz) fresh wholemeal
   breadcrumbs
25g (1oz) mixed nuts, finely chopped
plain flour to dust
salt and ground black pepper
rice and green vegetables to serve

1 Heat the oil in a large frying pan. Add the carrot and onion and fry for 3–4 minutes until the vegetables are softened, stirring all the time. Add the coriander seeds, if using, the garlic, curry paste and tomato purée. Increase the heat and cook for 2 minutes, stirring all the time.

2 Put the tofu into a bowl and mash with a potato masher. Stir in the vegetables, breadcrumbs and nuts and season with salt and pepper. Beat thoroughly until the mixture starts to stick together. With floured hands, shape the mixture into eight burgers.

3 Heat some oil in a frying pan and fry the burgers for 3–4 minutes on each side until golden brown. Alternatively, brush lightly with oil and cook under a hot grill for about 3 minutes on each side or until golden brown. Drain on kitchen paper and serve hot, with rice and green vegetables.

Serves 4
Preparation Time 20 minutes
Cooking Time 6–8 minutes

Nutritional Information (Per Serving)
253 calories, 18g fat (of which 3g saturates), 15g carbohydrate, 0.2g salt
Dairy Free · Easy

Sweet Chilli Tofu Stir-fry

1 Drain the tofu, pat it dry and cut it into large cubes. Put the tofu into a shallow container and pour 1 tbsp sweet chilli sauce and 1 tbsp light soy sauce over it. Cover and marinate for 10 minutes.

2 Meanwhile, toast the sesame seeds in a hot wok or large frying pan until golden. Tip on to a plate.

3 Return the wok or frying pan to the heat and add 1 tbsp sesame oil. Add the marinated tofu and stir-fry for 5 minutes until golden. Remove and set aside.

4 Heat the remaining 1 tbsp oil in the pan, add the vegetables and stir-fry for 3–4 minutes until just tender. Stir in the cooked tofu.

5 Pour the remaining sweet chilli sauce and soy sauce into the pan, toss well and cook for a further minute until heated through. Sprinkle with the toasted sesame seeds and pea shoots or salad leaves and serve immediately, with rice.

200g (7oz) firm tofu
4 tbsp sweet chilli sauce
2 tbsp light soy sauce
1 tbsp sesame seeds
2 tbsp toasted sesame oil
600g (1lb 5oz) ready-prepared mixed stir-fry vegetables, such as carrots, broccoli, mangetouts and bean sprouts
a handful of pea shoots or young salad leaves to garnish
rice to serve

Nutritional Information (Per Serving)
167 calories, 11g fat (of which 2g saturates), 5g carbohydrate, 1.6g salt
Dairy Free • Easy

Serves 4
Preparation Time 5 minutes, plus marinating
Cooking Time 12 minutes

Tofu Laksa Curry

2 tbsp light soy sauce
½ red chilli, seeded and chopped (see
    Cook's Tips, page 37)
5cm (2in) piece fresh root ginger,
    peeled and grated
250g pack fresh tofu
1 tbsp olive oil
1 onion, finely sliced
3 tbsp laksa paste
200ml (7fl oz) coconut milk
900ml (1½ pints) hot vegetable stock
200g (7oz) baby sweetcorn,
    halved lengthways
200g (7oz) fine green beans, trimmed
250g pack medium rice noodles
salt and ground black pepper
2 spring onions, sliced diagonally,
    2 tbsp chopped coriander and
    1 lime, cut into four wedges,
    to garnish

1 Put the soy sauce, chilli and ginger into a bowl, add the tofu and leave to marinate.

2 Heat the oil in a large pan. Add the onion and fry over a medium heat for 10 minutes, stirring, until golden. Add the laksa paste and cook for 2 minutes. Add the tofu, coconut milk, hot stock and sweetcorn and season. Bring to the boil, then add the green beans, reduce the heat and simmer for 8–10 minutes.

3 Meanwhile, put the noodles into a large bowl, pour boiling water over them and soak for 30 seconds. Drain, then stir into the curry. Pour into bowls and garnish with the spring onions, coriander and lime wedges. Serve immediately.

Serves 4
Preparation Time 15 minutes
Cooking Time 22 minutes

Nutritional Information (Per Serving)
349 calories, 7g fat (of which 1g saturates), 59g carbohydrate, 1.4g salt
Dairy Free · Easy

Chickpea and Butternut Pot

1 Put the butternut squash, peanut butter and hot stock into a large pan and simmer for 10 minutes until the squash is tender. Remove three-quarters of the squash with a slotted spoon and put to one side. Mash the remaining squash into the liquid, then put the reserved squash back into the pan.

2 Meanwhile, heat the oil in a pan over a low heat and fry the onions, chilli, curry paste and sweetcorn until the onions are soft and caramelised, then tip the contents of the pan into the squash.

3 Add the chickpeas and coriander to the squash and stir through. Season with salt and pepper and cook for 4–5 minutes until piping hot. Serve immediately.

1 large butternut squash, peeled, seeded and chopped
2 tbsp smooth peanut butter
900ml (1½ pints) hot vegetable stock
2 tbsp olive oil
2 large onions, finely chopped
1 small red chilli, seeded and finely chopped (see Cook's Tips, page 37)
2 tsp mild curry paste (see Cook's Tip, page 96)
225g (8oz) baby sweetcorn
2 x 400g cans chickpeas, drained and rinsed
a handful of freshly chopped coriander
salt and ground black pepper

PULSES

Nutritional Information (Per Serving)
307 calories, 14g fat (of which 2g saturates), 34g carbohydrate, 2.8g salt
Gluten Free • Dairy Free • Easy

Serves 4
Preparation Time 10 minutes
Cooking Time 15–20 minutes

Spiced Chickpeas
with Sweet Potatoes

3 sweet potatoes, chopped into chunks

½ tsp cumin seeds, roasted and ground

1 tsp olive oil

3 tbsp extra virgin olive oil

1 tbsp red wine vinegar

1 red chilli, seeded and chopped (see Cook's Tips, page 37)

4 spring onions, sliced

400g can chickpeas, drained and rinsed (see Cook's Tip)

a handful of spinach leaves

salt and ground black pepper

1 Preheat the oven to 200°C (180°C fan oven) mark 6. Put the sweet potatoes into a roasting tin and toss in the ground cumin and olive oil. Season with salt and pepper and roast for 20–30 minutes until tender.

2 Mix the extra virgin olive oil with the vinegar, chilli and spring onions. Stir into the sweet potatoes with the chickpeas, then check the seasoning. Stir in the spinach until it just wilts, then serve.

Cook's Tip

Allow half a can of chickpeas per person if you're serving them as a main meal, and a quarter of a can per person if they're part of a side dish. They are a rich source of protein and high in fibre too.

Serves 4
Preparation Time 10 minutes
Cooking Time 20–30 minutes

Nutritional Information (Per Serving)
306 calories, 12g fat (of which 2g saturates), 45g carbohydrate, 0.7g salt
Gluten Free · Dairy Free · Easy

Chickpeas with Spinach

1 Heat the oil in a large heavy-based pan, add the ginger, garlic and spices and cook for 2 minutes, stirring. Stir in the chickpeas.

2 Add the tomatoes to the pan with the coriander leaves and spinach and cook gently for 10 minutes. Season to taste with salt and pepper and serve immediately, with rice and a salad of grated carrots tossed in a little lemon juice.

3 tbsp olive oil
2.5cm (1in) piece fresh root ginger, peeled and finely chopped
3 garlic cloves, chopped
2 tsp each ground coriander and paprika
1 tsp ground cumin
2 × 400g cans chickpeas, drained and rinsed
4 tomatoes, roughly chopped
a handful of coriander leaves
450g (1lb) fresh spinach
salt and ground black pepper
rice and grated carrots with lemon juice to serve

Nutritional Information (Per Serving)
204 calories, 10g fat (of which 1g saturates), 21g carbohydrate, 0.8g salt
Gluten Free · Dairy Free · Easy

Serves 6
Preparation Time 10 minutes
Cooking Time 12–15 minutes

Moroccan Chickpea Stew

1 red pepper, halved and seeded
1 green pepper, halved and seeded
1 yellow pepper, halved and seeded
2 tbsp olive oil
1 onion, finely sliced
2 garlic cloves, crushed
1 tbsp harissa paste
2 tbsp tomato purée
½ tsp ground cumin
1 aubergine, diced
400g can chickpeas, drained
    and rinsed
450ml (¾ pint) vegetable stock
4 tbsp roughly chopped flat-leafed
    parsley, plus a few sprigs
    to garnish
salt and ground black pepper
crusty bread to serve

1 Preheat the grill and lay the peppers, skin side up, on a baking sheet. Grill for around 5 minutes or until the skin begins to blister and char. Put the peppers into a plastic bag, seal and put to one side for a few minutes. When cooled a little, peel off the skins and discard, then slice the peppers and put to one side.

2 Heat the oil in a large heavy-based frying pan over a low heat, add the onion and cook for 5–10 minutes until soft. Add the garlic, harissa, tomato purée and cumin and cook for 2 minutes.

3 Add the peppers to the pan with the aubergine. Stir everything to coat evenly with the spices and cook for 2 minutes. Add the chickpeas and stock, season well with salt and pepper and bring to the boil. Reduce the heat and simmer for 20 minutes.

4 Just before serving, stir the chopped parsley through the chickpea stew. Garnish with parsley sprigs and serve with crusty bread.

Serves 4
Preparation Time 10 minutes
Cooking Time 40 minutes

Nutritional Information (Per Serving)
232 calories, 9g fat (of which 1g saturates), 29g carbohydrate, 0.6g salt
Gluten Free · Dairy Free · Easy

Chickpea Curry

1. Heat the oil in a pan and fry the onions for 10–15 minutes until golden – when they have a good colour they will add depth of flavour. Add the garlic, coriander, chilli, mustard seeds, tamarind paste and sun-dried tomato paste. Cook for 1–2 minutes until the aroma from the spices is released.

2. Add the potatoes and toss in the spices for 1–2 minutes. Add the tomatoes and hot stock and season with salt and pepper, then cover and bring to the boil. Reduce the heat and simmer, half covered, for 20 minutes or until the potatoes are just cooked.

3. Add the beans and chickpeas and continue to cook for 5 minutes or until the beans are tender and the chickpeas are warmed through. Stir in the garam masala and serve.

2 tbsp vegetable oil
2 onions, finely sliced
2 garlic cloves, crushed
1 tbsp ground coriander
1 tsp mild chilli powder
1 tbsp black mustard seeds
2 tbsp tamarind paste (see Cook's Tips)
2 tbsp sun-dried tomato paste
750g (1lb 10oz) new potatoes, quartered
400g can chopped tomatoes
1 litre (1¾ pints) hot vegetable stock
250g (9oz) green beans, trimmed
2 × 400g cans chickpeas, drained and rinsed
2 tsp garam masala (see Cook's Tips)
salt and ground black pepper

Cook's Tips

Garam Masala
Sold ready prepared, this Indian spice mix is aromatic rather than hot.

To make your own masala: Grind together 10 green cardamom pods, 1 tbsp black peppercorns and 2 tsp cumin seeds. Store in an airtight container and use within one month.

Tamarind Paste
This has a very sharp, sour flavour and is widely used in Asian and Southeast Asian cooking.

PULSES

Nutritional Information (Per Serving)
291 calories, 8g fat (of which 1g saturates), 46g carbohydrate, 1.3g salt
Gluten Free • Dairy Free • Easy

Serves 6
Preparation Time 20 minutes
Cooking Time 40–45 minutes

Chickpea and Chilli Stir-fry

2 tbsp olive oil
1 tsp ground cumin
1 red onion, sliced
2 garlic cloves, finely chopped
1 red chilli, seeded and finely
 chopped (see Cook's Tips,
 page 37)
2 × 400g cans chickpeas,
 drained and rinsed
400g (14oz) cherry tomatoes
125g (4oz) baby spinach leaves
salt and ground black pepper
rice or pasta to serve

1 Heat the oil in a wok or large frying pan. Add the cumin and fry for 1–2 minutes. Add the onion and stir-fry for 5–7 minutes.

2 Add the garlic and chilli and stir-fry for 2 minutes.

3 Add the chickpeas to the wok with the tomatoes. Reduce the heat and simmer until the chickpeas are hot. Season with salt and pepper. Add the spinach and cook for 1–2 minutes until the leaves have wilted. Serve with rice or pasta.

Serves 4
Preparation Time 10 minutes
Cooking Time 15–20 minutes

Nutritional Information (Per Serving)
258 calories, 11g fat (of which 1g saturates), 30g carbohydrate, 1g salt
Dairy Free · Easy

Black-eye Bean Chilli

1 Heat the oil in a frying pan. Add the onion and celery and cook for 10 minutes until softened.

2 Add the beans, tomatoes and Tabasco to the pan. Bring to the boil, then reduce the heat and simmer for 10 minutes.

3 Just before serving, stir in the coriander. Spoon the chilli on to the warm tortillas, roll up and serve with soured cream.

1 tbsp olive oil
1 onion, chopped
3 celery sticks, finely chopped
2 × 400g cans black-eye beans, drained and rinsed
2 × 400g cans chopped tomatoes
2 or 3 splashes of Tabasco sauce
3 tbsp freshly chopped coriander
4 warmed tortillas and soured cream to serve

Try Something Different
Replace half the black-eye beans with red kidney beans.

PULSES

Nutritional Information (Per Serving)
245 calories, 5g fat (of which 1g saturates), 39g carbohydrate, 1.8g salt
Easy

Serves 4
Preparation Time 10 minutes
Cooking Time 20 minutes

159

Chilli Bean Cake

3 tbsp olive oil
75g (3oz) wholemeal breadcrumbs
1 bunch of spring onions,
    finely chopped
1 orange pepper, seeded and chopped
1 small green chilli, seeded and
    finely chopped (see Cook's Tips,
    page 37)
1 garlic clove, crushed
1 tsp ground turmeric (optional)
400g can mixed beans, drained
    and rinsed
3 tbsp mayonnaise
a small handful of fresh basil, chopped
salt and ground black pepper

TO SERVE
soured cream
freshly chopped coriander
lime wedges (optional)

1 Heat 2 tbsp oil in a non-stick frying pan over a medium heat and fry the breadcrumbs until golden and beginning to crisp. Remove and put to one side.

2 Add the remaining oil to the pan and fry the spring onions until soft and golden. Add the orange pepper, chilli, garlic and turmeric, if using. Cook, stirring, for 5 minutes.

3 Tip in the beans, mayonnaise, two-thirds of the fried breadcrumbs and the basil. Season with salt and pepper, mash roughly with a fork, then press the mixture down to flatten and sprinkle with the remaining breadcrumbs. Fry the bean cake over a medium heat for 4–5 minutes until the base is golden. Remove from the heat, cut into wedges and serve with soured cream, coriander and the lime wedges, if you like.

Serves 4
Preparation Time 10 minutes
Cooking Time 20 minutes

Nutritional Information (Per Serving)
265 calories, 6g fat (of which 1g saturates), 41g carbohydrate, 2.1g salt
Dairy Free • Easy

Spiced Bean and
Vegetable Stew

V

1 Heat the oil in a large heavy pan over a very gentle heat. Add the onion and garlic and cook for 5 minutes. Stir in the paprika and chilli and cook for a further 2 minutes.

2 Add the sweet potatoes, pumpkin, okra, passata and 900ml (1½ pints) water and season generously with salt and pepper. Cover and bring to the boil, then reduce the heat and simmer for 20 minutes or until the vegetables are tender.

3 Add the haricot or cannellini beans and cook for 3 minutes to warm through. Serve immediately.

3 tbsp olive oil
2 small onions, sliced
2 garlic cloves, crushed
1 tbsp sweet paprika
1 small dried red chilli, seeded and finely chopped
700g (1½lb) sweet potatoes, peeled and cubed
700g (1½lb) pumpkin, peeled and cut into chunks
125g (4oz) okra, trimmed
500g (1lb 2oz) passata
400g can haricot or cannellini beans, drained and rinsed
salt and ground black pepper

PULSES

Nutritional Information (Per Serving)
262 calories, 7g fat (of which 1g saturates), 44g carbohydrate, 1.3g salt
Gluten Free · Dairy Free · Easy

Serves 6
Preparation Time 5 minutes
Cooking Time about 30 minutes

Mixed Beans with
Lemon Vinaigrette

400g can mixed beans, drained
    and rinsed
400g can chickpeas, drained
    and rinsed
2 shallots, finely chopped
fresh mint sprigs and lemon zest
    to garnish

FOR THE VINAIGRETTE
2 tbsp lemon juice
2 tsp clear honey
8 tbsp extra virgin olive oil
3 tbsp freshly chopped mint
4 tbsp freshly chopped flat-leafed
    parsley
salt and ground black pepper

1 Put the beans and chickpeas into a bowl and add the shallots.

2 To make the vinaigrette, whisk together the lemon juice, honey and salt and pepper to taste. Gradually whisk in the oil and stir in the chopped herbs. Just before serving, pour the dressing over the bean mixture and toss well.

3 Transfer the salad to a serving dish, garnish with mint sprigs and lemon zest and serve immediately.

Get Ahead
To prepare ahead Complete the recipe to the end of step 2 but don't add the herbs to the vinaigrette. Cover and chill for up to two days.

To use Remove from the fridge up to 1 hour before serving, stir in the herbs and complete the recipe.

Serves 6
Preparation Time 15 minutes

Nutritional Information (Per Serving)
285 calories, 19g fat (of which 3g saturates), 22g carbohydrate, 1g salt
Gluten Free · Dairy Free · Easy

Cannellini Bean and
Sunblush Tomato Salad

1 Put the onion into a small bowl, add the vinegar and toss. Leave to marinate for 30 minutes – this stage is important as it takes the astringency out of the onion.

2 Tip the onion and vinegar into a large bowl, add the remaining ingredients, season with salt and pepper and toss everything together.

½ red onion, very finely sliced
2 tbsp red wine vinegar
a small handful each of freshly chopped mint and flat-leafed parsley
2 × 400g cans cannellini beans, drained and rinsed
4 tbsp extra virgin olive oil
4 celery sticks, sliced
75g (3oz) sunblush tomatoes, snipped in half
salt and ground black pepper

PULSES

Nutritional Information (Per Serving)
163 calories, 8g fat (of which 1g saturates), 17g carbohydrate, 1.3g salt
Gluten Free · Dairy Free · Easy

Serves 6
Preparation Time 5 minutes, plus marinating

163

Simple Bean Salad

2 tbsp olive oil
2 garlic cloves, sliced
2 × 400g cans flageolet beans,
    drained and rinsed
extra virgin olive oil to drizzle
2 tbsp fresh pesto (see Cook's Tip,
    page 38)
lemon juice to taste
a small handful of basil leaves, bruised
salt and ground black pepper

1 Put the olive oil into a small pan and fry the garlic until golden. Stir in the flageolet beans, then leave to marinate in the oil for 10–15 minutes.

2 When ready to serve, drizzle a little extra virgin olive oil over the beans until generously coated. Add the pesto and lemon juice to taste and season with salt and pepper, then stir in the basil leaves.

Try Something Different
Instead of flageolet beans, use cannellini, haricot or borlotti beans.

Serves 6
Preparation Time 5 minutes,
    plus marinating
Cooking Time 5 minutes

Nutritional Information (Per Serving)
208 calories, 10g fat (of which 2g saturates), 21g carbohydrate, 1.2g salt
Gluten Free · Easy

Split Pea Roti

1 Drain the split peas and put into a small pan with the turmeric, cumin, garlic and 1 tsp salt. Add 200ml (7fl oz) cold water and bring to the boil, then reduce the heat and simmer for 30 minutes or until the peas are soft, adding a little more water if necessary. Take off the heat and leave to cool.

2 Sift the flour, baking powder and remaining salt into a large bowl. Make a well in the centre, add the oil and gradually mix in enough milk to form a soft dough. Transfer to a lightly floured surface and knead until smooth. Cover with a damp teatowel and leave to rest for 30 minutes.

3 Put the cooled peas in a food processor and blend until smooth, adding 1 tbsp water.

4 Divide the dough into eight. Roll out each piece on a lightly floured surface, to make a 20cm (8in) round. Divide the pea mixture between four of the rounds, placing it in the centre, then top with the other rounds and press the edges together to seal.

5 Heat a large heavy-based frying pan until really hot. Brush each roti with a little oil and fry (one or two at a time) for 1 minute on each side or until lightly brown. Keep warm while you cook the rest. Serve with a vegetable curry.

125g (4oz) yellow split peas, soaked in cold water overnight
¼ tsp ground turmeric
1 tsp ground cumin
1 garlic clove, finely sliced
1½ tsp salt
225g (8oz) plain flour, plus extra to dust
1½ tsp baking powder
1 tbsp vegetable oil, plus extra to fry
125–150ml (4–5fl oz) full-fat milk
vegetable curry to serve

Nutritional Information (Per Serving)
429 calories, 13.7g fat (of which 2g saturates), 65.5g carbohydrate, 1.3g salt
Easy

Serves 4
Preparation Time 25 minutes, plus soaking and resting
Cooking Time 40 minutes

Rice and grains

Roasted Tomato Bulgur Salad

Asparagus, Pea and Mint Rice Salad

One-pot Vegetable Rice

Curried Coconut and Vegetable Rice

Oven-baked Chilli Rice

Vegetable Fried Rice

Wild Mushroom Risotto

Asparagus Risotto

Tomato Risotto

Pumpkin Risotto with Hazelnut Butter

Aubergine and Chickpea Pilau

Spiced Egg Pilau

Polenta with Mixed Mushrooms

Cheesy Polenta with Tomato Sauce

Griddled Polenta with Gorgonzola Salad

Summer Couscous

Roasted Tomato Bulgur Salad

175g (6oz) bulgur wheat
700g (1½lb) cherry tomatoes
  or baby plum tomatoes
8 tbsp extra virgin olive oil
a handful each of mint and basil,
  roughly chopped, plus fresh basil
  sprigs to garnish
3–4 tbsp balsamic vinegar
1 bunch of spring onions, sliced
salt and ground black pepper

1 Put the bulgur wheat into a bowl and add boiling water to cover by 1cm (½in). Leave to soak for 30 minutes.

2 Preheat the oven to 220°C (200°C fan oven) mark 7. Put the tomatoes into a small roasting tin, drizzle with half the oil and add half the mint. Season with salt and pepper and roast for 10–15 minutes until beginning to soften.

3 Put the remaining oil and the vinegar into a large bowl. Add the warm pan juices from the roasted tomatoes and the soaked bulgur wheat.

4 Stir in the remaining chopped herbs and the spring onions and check the seasoning. You may need a little more vinegar depending on the sweetness of the tomatoes.

5 Add the tomatoes and carefully toss to combine, then serve garnished with basil sprigs.

Cook's Tip
Bulgur wheat is widely used in Middle Eastern cooking and has a light, nutty flavour and texture. It is available in several different sizes – from coarse to fine.

Serves 6
Preparation Time 10 minutes,
  plus soaking
Cooking Time 10–15 minutes

Nutritional Information (Per Serving)
225 calories, 15g fat (of which 2g saturates), 19g carbohydrate, 0g salt
Dairy Free · Easy

Asparagus, Pea and
Mint Rice Salad

1 Put the rice into a pan with twice its volume of water and a pinch of salt. Cover and bring to the boil. Reduce the heat to very low and cook according to the pack instructions. Once cooked, tip the rice on to a baking sheet and spread out to cool quickly. When cool, spoon into a large bowl.

2 In a small bowl, mix the shallot with the lemon zest and juice, oil and chopped mint, then stir into the rice. Season with salt and pepper.

3 Bring a large pan of lightly salted water to the boil. Add the asparagus and peas and cook for 3–4 minutes until tender. Drain and refresh in a bowl of cold water. Drain well and stir into the rice. Put into a serving dish and garnish with mint sprigs.

175g (6oz) mixed basmati and
   wild rice
1 large shallot, finely sliced
grated zest and juice of 1 small lemon
2 tbsp sunflower oil
12 fresh mint leaves, roughly
   chopped, plus extra sprigs
   to garnish
150g (5oz) asparagus tips
75g (3oz) fresh or frozen peas
salt and ground black pepper

RICE AND GRAINS

Nutritional Information (Per Serving)
157 calories, 4g fat (of which trace saturates), 26g carbohydrate, trace salt
Gluten Free · Dairy Free · Easy

Serves 6
Preparation Time 10 minutes
Cooking Time 20 minutes

One-pot Vegetable Rice

1 tbsp sunflower oil
1 large onion, thinly sliced
200g (7oz) basmati rice
1 tbsp curry paste, mild, medium
    or hot (see Cook's Tip, page 96)
800ml (1 pint 7fl oz) hot
    vegetable stock
400g can green lentils, drained
550g (1¼lb) vegetables, such as
    diced carrots, courgettes, fennel
    and red pepper
mango chutney and mini
    poppadums to serve

1 Heat the oil in a large pan and fry the onion for 10 minutes, stirring, or until golden. Set half the onion aside. Add the rice to the pan and stir into the onion, then cook for 1 minute to coat with the oil. Stir in the curry paste and fry for another minute.

2 Pour in the hot stock, lentils and vegetables and bring to the boil. Reduce the heat, cover the pan and simmer for 20 minutes or until the stock has been absorbed and the rice is tender.

3 Leave to stand for 5 minutes, then fluff up with a fork. Garnish with the reserved onion and serve with mango chutney and mini poppadums.

Serves 4
Preparation Time 15 minutes
Cooking Time about 30 minutes

Nutritional Information (Per Serving)
572 calories, 6g fat (of which 1g saturates), 103g carbohydrate, 0.2g salt
Gluten Free · Dairy Free · Easy

Curried Coconut
and Vegetable Rice

1 Cut the aubergine and butternut squash into 2cm (¾in) cubes. Slice the green beans into 2cm (¾in) pieces.

2 Heat the oil in a large pan. Add the onion and cook for about 5 minutes until a light golden colour. Add the mustard seeds and cook, stirring, until they begin to pop. Stir in the korma paste and cook for 1 minute.

3 Add the aubergine and cook, stirring, for 5 minutes. Add the butternut squash, beans, rice and 2 tsp salt, mixing well. Pour in the coconut milk and add 600ml (1pint) water. Bring to the boil, then reduce the heat, cover and simmer for 15–18 minutes.

4 When the rice and vegetables are cooked, remove the lid and put the spinach leaves on top. Cover and leave, off the heat, for 5 minutes. Gently stir the wilted spinach through the rice, check the seasoning and serve immediately.

1 large aubergine, about 300g (11oz), trimmed
1 large butternut squash, about 500g (1lb 2oz), peeled and seeded
250g (9oz) dwarf green beans, trimmed
100ml (3½fl oz) vegetable oil
1 large onion, chopped
1 tbsp black mustard seeds
3 tbsp korma paste (see Cook's Tip)
350g (12oz) basmati rice
400ml can coconut milk
200g (7oz) baby spinach leaves
salt and ground black pepper

Cook's Tip
Korma Paste
Sold ready prepared, this is a mild Indian curry paste.

To make your own korma paste: Put 3 tbsp ground cinnamon, seeds from 36 green cardamom pods, 30 cloves, 18 bay leaves, 1 tbsp fennel seeds and 1 tsp salt into a food processor and whiz to a powder. Tip the powder into a bowl and add 4 tbsp water, stirring well to make a paste. Divide into three equal portions, then freeze for up to three months. To use, thaw at cool room temperature for 1 hour.

RICE AND GRAINS

Nutritional Information (Per Serving)
413 calories, 17g fat (of which 2g saturates), 57g carbohydrate, 0.4g salt
Gluten Free · Dairy Free · Easy

Serves 6
Preparation Time 15 minutes
Cooking Time 30 minutes, plus standing

Oven-baked Chilli Rice

3 tbsp olive oil
1 large red onion, thinly sliced
1 red chilli, seeded and thinly sliced
   (see Cook's Tips, page 37)
1 tbsp tamarind paste
1 tbsp light muscovado sugar
350g (12oz) mixed basmati and
   wild rice
a little oil or butter to grease
20g pack fresh mint, roughly chopped
100g bag baby leaf spinach
50g (2oz) flaked almonds, toasted
salt and ground black pepper

1 Heat the oil in a frying pan and fry the onion for 7–10 minutes over a medium heat until golden and soft. Add the chilli, tamarind paste and sugar. Cool, cover and chill.

2 Meanwhile, put the rice into a large pan. Add 800ml (1 pint 7fl oz) boiling water. Cover and bring to the boil, then reduce the heat to its lowest setting and cook according to the pack instructions. Spread on a baking sheet and leave to cool, then chill.

3 When ready to serve, preheat the oven to 200°C (180°C fan oven) mark 6. Tip the rice into a lightly greased, shallow ovenproof dish. Stir in the onion mixture and season with salt and pepper.

4 Reheat the rice in the oven for 20 minutes until piping hot. Stir in the mint, spinach and almonds and serve immediately.

Get Ahead

To prepare ahead Complete the recipe to the end of step 2, up to one day ahead. Cover and chill the rice and onions separately.

To serve Complete the recipe.

Serves 8
Preparation Time 15 minutes,
   plus chilling
Cooking Time 40 minutes

Nutritional Information (Per Serving)
265 calories, 8g fat (of which 1g saturates), 42g carbohydrate, 0.1g salt
Gluten Free • Dairy Free • Easy

Vegetable Fried Rice

1. Put the rice into a pan and cover with enough cold water to come 2.5cm (1in) above the rice. Bring to the boil, then reduce the heat, cover tightly and simmer very gently for 20 minutes. Do not stir.

2. Remove the pan from the heat and leave to cool for 20 minutes, then cover with clingfilm and chill for 2–3 hours or overnight.

3. When ready to fry the rice, soak the dried mushrooms, if using, in warm water for about 30 minutes.

4. Drain the mushrooms, squeeze out excess moisture, then thinly slice.

5. Heat the oil in a wok or large frying pan over a high heat. Add the mushrooms, spring onions, bamboo shoots, bean sprouts and peas and stir-fry for 2–3 minutes. Add the soy sauce and cook briefly, stirring.

6. Fork up the rice, add it to the pan and stir-fry for 2 minutes. Pour in the eggs and continue to stir-fry for 2–3 minutes until the egg has scrambled and the rice is heated through. Serve immediately, garnished with coriander, with lime halves to squeeze over.

200g (7oz) long-grain rice
3 Chinese dried mushrooms, or 125g (4oz) button mushrooms, sliced
2 tbsp vegetable oil
4 spring onions, sliced diagonally into 2.5cm (1in) lengths
125g (4oz) canned bamboo shoots, drained and cut into 2.5cm (1in) strips
125g (4oz) bean sprouts
125g (4oz) frozen peas
2 tbsp soy sauce
3 medium eggs, beaten
fresh coriander sprigs to garnish
lime halves to serve

Nutritional Information (Per Serving)
464 calories, 11g fat (of which 2g saturates), 76g carbohydrate, 1.5g salt
Dairy Free · Easy

Serves 4
Preparation Time 10 minutes, plus soaking and chilling
Cooking Time about 30 minutes

Wild Mushroom Risotto

900ml (1½ pints) vegetable stock
6 tbsp olive oil
2 shallots, finely chopped
2 garlic cloves, finely chopped
2 tsp freshly chopped thyme, plus
    sprigs to garnish
1 tsp grated lemon zest
350g (12oz) risotto (arborio) rice
150ml (¼ pint) dry white wine
450g (1lb) mixed fresh mushrooms,
    such as oyster, shiitake and cep,
    sliced if large
1 tbsp freshly chopped flat-leafed
    parsley
salt and ground black pepper

1 Heat the stock in a pan to a steady, low simmer.

2 Meanwhile, heat half the oil in a heavy-based pan. Add the shallots, garlic, chopped thyme and lemon zest and fry gently for 5 minutes or until the shallots are softened. Add the rice and stir for 1 minute or until the grains are glossy. Add the wine, bring to the boil and let bubble until almost totally evaporated.

3 Gradually add the stock to the rice, a ladleful at a time, stirring with each addition and allowing it to be absorbed before adding more. Continue adding the stock slowly until the rice is tender. This should take about 25 minutes.

4 About 5 minutes before the rice is ready, heat the remaining oil in a large frying pan and stir-fry the mushrooms over a high heat for 4–5 minutes. Add to the rice with the parsley. The risotto should still be moist: if necessary add a little more stock. Check the seasoning and serve at once, garnished with thyme sprigs.

Dos and Don'ts For the Perfect Risotto

Always use risotto (arborio) rice: the grains are thicker and shorter than long-grain rice and have a high starch content. They absorb more liquid slowly, producing a creamy-textured risotto.

Stock should be hot when added: this swells the grains, yet keeps them firm. Keep stock simmering in a pan. Add it ladle by ladle to the risotto, allowing it to be absorbed by the rice after each addition.

The correct heat is vital. If the risotto gets too hot, the liquid evaporates too quickly and the rice won't cook evenly. If the heat is too low, the risotto will go gluey. Over a medium heat, the rice should cook in about 25 minutes.

Don't leave risotto – stir constantly to loosen the rice from the bottom of the pan.

The quantity of liquid given is approximate – adjust it so that, when cooked, the rice is tender but firm to the bite. It should be creamily bound together, neither runny nor dry.

Serves 6
Preparation Time 10 minutes
Cooking Time 30 minutes

Nutritional Information (Per Serving)
341 calories, 12g fat (of which 2g saturates), 48g carbohydrate, 0g salt
Gluten Free · Dairy Free · Easy

Asparagus Risotto

1 Melt the butter in a heavy-based pan, add the shallots and garlic and sauté over a gentle heat until soft.

2 Stir in the rice, cook for 1–2 minutes, then add the hot stock. Bring to the boil, then reduce the heat and simmer for 15–20 minutes, stirring occasionally to ensure that the rice isn't sticking, until almost all the stock has been absorbed and the rice is tender.

3 Add the mascarpone, half the Parmesan and half the parsley to the pan. Stir in the asparagus and the remaining parsley and Parmesan. Divide among four plates, garnish with shavings of Parmesan and serve.

50g (2oz) butter
2 shallots, diced
2 garlic cloves, crushed
225g (8oz) risotto (arborio) rice
500ml (18fl oz) hot vegetable stock
2 tbsp mascarpone cheese
50g (2oz) Parmesan, finely grated, plus shavings to garnish (see Cook's Tip, page 35)
2 tbsp freshly chopped parsley
400g (14oz) asparagus spears, blanched and halved

Nutritional Information (Per Serving)
374 calories, 16g fat (of which 10g saturates), 47g carbohydrate, 1.1g salt
Gluten Free · Easy

Serves 4
Preparation Time 10 minutes
Cooking Time 25 minutes

Tomato Risotto

1 large rosemary sprig
2 tbsp olive oil
1 small onion, finely chopped
350g (12oz) risotto (arborio) rice
4 tbsp dry white wine
750ml (1¼ pints) hot vegetable stock
300g (11oz) cherry tomatoes, halved
salt and ground black pepper
shavings of Parmesan (optional, see
    Cook's Tip, page 35), green salad
    and extra virgin olive oil to serve

1 Pull the leaves from the rosemary and chop roughly. Set aside.

2 Heat the oil in a flameproof casserole, add the onion and cook for 8–10 minutes until beginning to soften. Add the rice and stir to coat in the oil and onion. Pour in the wine, then the hot stock, stirring well to mix.

3 Bring to the boil, stirring, then reduce the heat, cover and simmer for 5 minutes. Stir in the tomatoes and chopped rosemary. Simmer, covered, for a further 10–15 minutes until the rice is tender and most of the liquid has been absorbed. Season to taste.

4 Serve immediately with shavings of Parmesan, if you like, a large green salad and extra virgin olive oil to drizzle over.

RICE AND GRAINS

Serves 6
Preparation Time 10 minutes
Cooking Time 25–30 minutes

Nutritional Information (Per Serving)
264 calories, 4g fat (of which 1g saturates), 49g carbohydrate, 0.5g salt
Gluten Free · Easy

Pumpkin Risotto
with Hazelnut Butter

1 To make the hazelnut butter, spread the hazelnuts on a baking sheet and toast under a hot grill until golden brown, turning frequently. Put the nuts in a clean teatowel and rub off the skins, then chop finely. Put the nuts, butter and parsley on a piece of non-stick baking parchment. Season with pepper and mix together. Mould into a sausage shape, twist the baking parchment at both ends and chill.

2 To make the risotto, melt the butter in a large pan and fry the onion until soft but not coloured. Add the pumpkin and sauté over a low heat for 5–8 minutes until just beginning to soften. Add the garlic and rice and stir until well mixed. Increase the heat to medium and add the hot stock a little at a time, allowing the liquid to be absorbed after each addition. This will take about 25 minutes.

3 Stir in the orange zest and Parmesan and season with salt and pepper. Serve the risotto with a slice of the hazelnut butter melting on top.

50g (2oz) butter
175g (6oz) onion, finely chopped
900g (2lb) pumpkin, halved, peeled, seeded and cut into small cubes
2 garlic cloves, crushed
225g (8oz) risotto (arborio) rice
600ml (1 pint) hot vegetable stock
grated zest of ½ orange
40g (1½oz) Parmesan, shaved (see Cook's Tip, page 35)
salt and ground black pepper

FOR THE HAZELNUT BUTTER
50g (2oz) hazelnuts
125g (4oz) butter, softened
2 tbsp freshly chopped flat-leafed parsley

Cook's Tip
If you can't find pumpkin, use butternut squash.

Nutritional Information (Per Serving)
706 calories, 50g fat (of which 27g saturates), 51g carbohydrate, 1.1g salt
Gluten Free • Easy

Serves 4
Preparation Time 15 minutes
Cooking Time 40 minutes

Aubergine and Chickpea Pilau

4–6 tbsp olive oil
275g (10oz) aubergine,
    roughly chopped
225g (8oz) onions, finely chopped
25g (1oz) butter
½ tsp cumin seeds
175g (6oz) long-grain rice
600ml (1 pint) vegetable stock
400g can chickpeas, drained
    and rinsed
225g (8oz) baby spinach leaves
salt and ground black pepper

1 Heat half the oil in a large pan or flameproof casserole over a medium heat. Fry the aubergine for 4–5 minutes, in batches, until deep golden brown. Remove from the pan with a slotted spoon and put to one side. Add the remaining oil to the pan, then add the onions and cook for 5 minutes or until golden and soft.

2 Add the butter, then stir in the cumin seeds and rice. Fry for 1–2 minutes. Pour in the stock, season with salt and pepper and bring to the boil. Reduce the heat, then simmer, uncovered, for 10–12 minutes until most of the liquid has evaporated and the rice is tender.

3 Remove the pan from the heat. Stir in the chickpeas, spinach and reserved aubergine. Cover with a tight-fitting lid and leave to stand for 5 minutes until the spinach has wilted and the chickpeas are heated through. Adjust the seasoning to taste. Fork through the rice grains to separate and make the rice fluffy before serving.

Get Ahead

To prepare ahead Fry the aubergine and onion as in step 1. Cover and keep in a cool place for 1½ hours.

To use Complete the recipe.

Serves 4
Preparation Time 10 minutes
Cooking Time 20 minutes, plus standing

Nutritional Information (Per Serving)
462 calories, 20g fat (of which 5g saturates), 58g carbohydrate, 0.9g salt
Gluten Free • Easy

Spiced Egg Pilau

1 Put the rice into a pan with 450ml (¾ pint) boiling water over a low heat and cook for 15 minutes or until just tender. Add the peas for the last 5 minutes of cooking time.

2 Meanwhile, put the eggs into a large pan of boiling water, then reduce the heat and simmer for 6 minutes. Drain and shell.

3 Put the coconut cream, curry paste, chilli sauce and peanut butter into a small pan and whisk together. Heat the sauce gently, stirring, without allowing it to boil.

4 Drain the rice and stir in the chopped coriander and 2 tbsp of the sauce.

5 Divide the rice among four bowls. Cut the eggs into halves and serve on the rice, spooning the remaining coconut sauce over the top. Serve with poppadums and chutney.

200g (7oz) basmati or wild rice
150g (5oz) frozen peas
4 medium eggs
200ml (7fl oz) coconut cream
1 tsp mild curry paste (see Cook's Tip, page 96)
1 tbsp sweet chilli sauce
1 tbsp smooth peanut butter
1 large bunch of fresh coriander, roughly chopped
mini poppadums and mango chutney to serve

Nutritional Information (Per Serving)
331 calories, 9g fat (of which 12g saturates), 50g carbohydrate, 0.6g salt
Gluten Free · Dairy Free · Easy

Serves 4
Preparation Time 5 minutes
Cooking Time 15 minutes

Polenta with Mixed Mushrooms

50g (2oz) butter
1.1kg (2½lb) mixed mushrooms
1 red chilli, seeded and finely
    chopped (see Cook's Tips,
    page 37)
3 garlic cloves, sliced
100g (3½oz) sun-dried tomatoes,
    roughly chopped
1 tsp freshly chopped thyme, plus
    thyme sprigs to garnish
1kg (2¼lb) ready-made polenta
3 tbsp olive oil
truffle oil (optional)
salt and ground black pepper

1 Melt half the butter in a deep-sided frying pan or wok. Add half the mushrooms and cook over a high heat until all the liquid has evaporated, then set aside. Repeat with the remaining butter and mushrooms. Add the chilli and garlic to the pan and fry for 2 minutes, then add to the mushrooms, together with the sun-dried tomatoes and thyme. Mix well and season with salt and pepper.

2 Slice the polenta into 12 pieces, about 1cm (½ in) thick. Heat the oil in a non-stick frying pan. Add the polenta in batches and fry for 3–4 minutes on each side until golden.

3 To serve, arrange two slices of polenta per person on a plate, top with the mushroom mixture and drizzle with a little truffle oil, if using. Garnish with thyme sprigs.

RICE AND GRAINS

Serves 6
Preparation Time 10 minutes
Cooking Time 20 minutes

Nutritional Information (Per Serving)
383 calories, 13g fat (of which 4g saturates), 56g carbohydrate, 0.1g salt
Gluten Free · Easy

Cheesy Polenta
with Tomato Sauce

1 Lightly oil a 25.5 × 18cm (10 × 7in) dish. Bring 1.1 litres (2 pints) water and ¼ tsp salt to the boil in a large pan. Sprinkle in the polenta, whisking constantly. Reduce the heat and simmer, stirring frequently, for 10–15 minutes until the mixture leaves the sides of the pan.

2 Stir in the herbs and Parmesan and season to taste with salt and pepper. Turn into the prepared dish and leave to cool.

3 Next, make the tomato and basil sauce. Heat the oil in a pan and fry the garlic for 30 seconds (do not brown). Add the creamed tomatoes or passata, the bay leaf, thyme and a large pinch of sugar. Season with salt and pepper and bring to the boil, then reduce the heat and simmer, uncovered, for 5–10 minutes. Remove the bay leaf and thyme sprig and add the chopped basil.

4 To serve, cut the polenta into pieces and lightly brush with oil. Preheat a griddle and fry for 3–4 minutes on each side, or grill under a preheated grill for 7–8 minutes on each side. Serve with the tomato and basil sauce, fresh Parmesan shavings and chopped basil.

Get Ahead

To prepare ahead Complete the recipe to the end of step 3. Cover and chill separately for up to two days.

To use Complete the recipe.

oil to grease
225g (8oz) polenta
4 tbsp freshly chopped herbs,
   such as oregano, chives and
   flat-leafed parsley
100g (3½oz) freshly grated Parmesan
   (see Cook's Tip, page 35), plus
   fresh Parmesan shavings to serve
salt and ground black pepper

FOR THE TOMATO AND
BASIL SAUCE
1 tbsp vegetable oil
3 garlic cloves, crushed
500g carton creamed tomatoes
   or passata
1 bay leaf
1 fresh thyme sprig
caster sugar
3 tbsp freshly chopped basil,
   plus extra to garnish

Nutritional Information (Per Serving)
249 calories, 9g fat (of which 4g saturates), 31g carbohydrate, 0.9g salt
Gluten Free · Easy

Serves 6
Preparation Time 15 minutes,
   plus cooling
Cooking Time 45 minutes

Griddled Polenta
with Gorgonzola Salad

2 tbsp olive oil, plus extra to grease
300ml (½ pint) semi-skimmed milk
10 sage leaves, roughly chopped
125g (4oz) quick-cook polenta
2 garlic cloves, crushed
25g (1oz) butter
100g (3½oz) salad leaves
125g (4oz) Gorgonzola, cut
   into cubes (see Cook's Tip,
   page 35)
125g (4oz) each sunblush tomatoes
   and roasted red peppers
salt and ground black pepper

1 Lightly oil a 450g (1lb) loaf tin. Pour the milk into a pan, then add the sage, 1 scant tsp salt and 300ml (½ pint) water and bring to the boil. Add the polenta to the pan in a thin steady stream, stirring, to make a smooth paste.

2 Reduce the heat, add the garlic and cook for about 8 minutes, stirring occasionally. Add the oil, then season with pepper and stir well. Press into the prepared loaf tin, smooth the top and leave to cool for 45 minutes.

3 Once the polenta is cool, turn out on to a board and cut into eight slices.

4 Melt the butter in a griddle pan and fry the polenta slices on each side until golden. Divide among four plates. Add the salad leaves, Gorgonzola, sunblush tomatoes and peppers and serve.

Serves 4
Preparation Time 20 minutes,
   plus cooling
Cooking Time 20 minutes

Nutritional Information (Per Serving)
362 calories, 22g fat (of which 11g saturates), 28g carbohydrate, 1.1g salt
Gluten Free · Easy

Summer Couscous

1. Preheat the oven to 230°C (210°C fan oven) mark 8. Put the vegetables and garlic into a large roasting tin, drizzle 3 tbsp oil over them and season with salt and pepper. Toss to coat. Roast for 20 minutes or until tender.

2. Meanwhile, put the couscous into a separate roasting tin and add 300ml (½ pint) cold water. Leave to soak for 5 minutes. Stir in the tomatoes and harissa and drizzle with the remaining oil. Pop in the oven next to the vegetables for 4–5 minutes to warm through.

3. Stir the pumpkin seeds, if you like, and the coriander into the couscous and season. Add the vegetables and stir through.

175g (6oz) baby plum tomatoes, halved
2 small aubergines, thickly sliced
2 large yellow peppers, seeded and roughly chopped
2 red onions, cut into thin wedges
2 fat garlic cloves, crushed
5 tbsp olive oil
250g (9oz) couscous
400g can chopped tomatoes
2 tbsp harissa paste
25g (1oz) toasted pumpkin seeds (optional)
1 large bunch of coriander, roughly chopped
salt and ground black pepper

Nutritional Information (Per Serving)
405 calories, 21g fat (of which 3g saturates), 49g carbohydrate, 0g salt
Dairy Free · Easy

Serves 4
Preparation Time 10 minutes
Cooking Time 20 minutes

Pasta

Spinach and Cheese Lasagne

Artichoke and Mushroom Lasagne

Mixed Mushroom Cannelloni

Butternut Squash and Spinach Lasagne

Fast Macaroni Cheese

Pasta Shells Stuffed with Spinach and Ricotta

Pasta with Vegetables, Pinenuts and Pesto

Pappardelle with Spinach

Tomato and Artichoke Pasta

Pasta with Pesto and Beans

Pea, Mint and Ricotta Pasta

Fusilli with Chilli and Tomatoes

Roast Tomato Pasta

Pasta with Goat's Cheese and Sunblush Tomatoes

Pesto Gnocchi

Very Easy Four-cheese Gnocchi

Spinach and Cheese
Lasagne

125g (4oz) fresh or frozen leaf
  spinach, thawed
40g (1½oz) fresh basil,
  roughly chopped
250g (9oz) ricotta cheese (see Cook's
  Tip, page 35)
5 pieces marinated artichokes,
  drained and chopped
350g carton cheese sauce (see
  as above)
175g (6oz) Dolcelatte cheese,
  roughly diced (see Cook's Tip
  as above, and below)
9 sheets fresh egg lasagne
25g (1oz) pinenuts, toasted
tomato salad to serve

1 Preheat the oven to 180°C (160°C fan oven) mark 4. Chop the spinach finely (if it was frozen, squeeze out the excess liquid first). Put into a bowl with the basil, ricotta cheese, artichokes and 6 tbsp cheese sauce. Mix well.

2 Beat the Dolcelatte into the remaining cheese sauce. Layer the ricotta mixture, lasagne, then cheese sauce into a 23 × 23cm (9 × 9in) ovenproof dish. Repeat to use up the remainder.

3 Cook the lasagne for 40 minutes. Sprinkle the pinenuts over the top and put back in the oven for a further 10–15 minutes until golden. Serve with a tomato salad.

Cook's Tip
Italian Dolcelatte cheese has a much milder flavour than Stilton or Roquefort; it also has a deliciously rich creamy texture.

Serves 6
Preparation Time 30 minutes
Cooking Time 50–55 minutes

Nutritional Information (Per Serving)
442 calories, 27g fat (of which 14g saturates), 32g carbohydrate, 1.6g salt
Easy

Artichoke and Mushroom
Lasagne

1 Heat the oil in a large pan and fry the onions gently for 10 minutes until soft. Add the garlic and walnuts and fry for 3–4 minutes until pale golden. Stir in the mushrooms and cook for 10 minutes. Let the mixture bubble briskly for a further 10 minutes or until all the liquid has evaporated. Add the tomatoes to the pan, then remove from the heat and set aside.

2 Preheat the oven to 200°C (180°C fan oven) mark 6. Melt the butter in a pan, add the flour and stir over a gentle heat for 1 minute. Slowly whisk in the milk until you have a smooth mixture. Bring to the boil, add the bay leaves, then stir over a gentle heat for 10 minutes or until thickened and smooth. Add the lemon juice and season to taste with salt and pepper. Discard the bay leaves.

3 Grease a shallow ovenproof dish and layer lasagne sheets over the bottom. Spoon half the mushroom mixture over, then half the artichokes. Cover with a layer of lasagne and half the sauce. Spoon the remaining mushroom mixture over, then the remaining artichokes. Top with the remaining lasagne sheets. Stir the Parmesan into the remaining sauce and spoon evenly over the top of the lasagne.

4 Cook in the oven for 40–50 minutes until golden and bubbling. Garnish with oregano sprigs, if using, and serve.

Get Ahead

To prepare ahead Complete the recipe to the end of step 3, then cool, cover and chill for up to three hours.

To use Remove from the refrigerator about 30 minutes before cooking, then complete the recipe.

3 tbsp olive oil
225g (8oz) onions, roughly chopped
3 garlic cloves, crushed
25g (1oz) walnuts
1.1kg (2½lb) mixed mushrooms, such as brown-cap and button, roughly chopped
125g (4oz) cherry tomatoes
50g (2oz) butter, plus extra to grease
50g (2oz) plain flour
1.1 litres (2 pints) whole milk
2 bay leaves
2 tbsp lemon juice
200g pack fresh chilled lasagne
400g can artichoke hearts in water, drained and halved
75g (3oz) freshly grated Parmesan (see Cook's Tip, page 35)
salt and ground black pepper
fresh oregano sprigs to garnish (optional)

Nutritional Information (Per Serving)
322 calories, 21g fat (of which 11g saturates), 19g carbohydrate, 0.7g salt
Easy

Serves 6
Preparation Time 25 minutes
Cooking Time about 1½ hours

Mixed Mushroom Cannelloni

1. Preheat the oven to 180°C (160°C fan oven) mark 4. Cook the lasagne in boiling water until just tender. Drain well and run it under cold water to cool. Keep covered with cold water until ready to use.

2. Heat the oil in a large pan and add the onion. Cook over a medium heat for 7–10 minutes until the onion is soft. Add the garlic and fry for 1–2 minutes. Keep a few slices of garlic to one side. Keep a little thyme for sprinkling later, then add the rest to the pan with the mushrooms. Cook for a further 5 minutes or until the mushrooms are golden brown and there is no excess liquid in the pan. Season, remove from the heat and put to one side.

3. Crumble one of the goat's cheese logs into the cooled mushroom mixture and stir together. Drain the lasagne sheets and pat dry with kitchen paper. Spoon 2–3 tbsp of the mushroom mixture along the long edge of each lasagne sheet, leaving a 1cm (½in) border. Roll up the pasta sheets and cut each roll in half. Put the pasta into a shallow ovenproof dish and spoon the cheese sauce over it. Slice the remaining goat's cheese into thick rounds and arrange across the middle of the pasta rolls. Sprinkle the reserved garlic and thyme on top. Cook in the oven for 30–35 minutes until golden and bubbling. Serve with a green salad.

Cook's Tip
Fresh lasagne sheets wrapped around a filling are used here to make cannelloni, but you can also buy cannelloni tubes, which can easily be filled using a teaspoon.

6 sheets fresh lasagne
3 tbsp olive oil
1 small onion, finely sliced
3 garlic cloves, sliced
20g pack fresh thyme, finely chopped
225g (8oz) chestnut or brown-cap
   mushrooms, roughly chopped
125g (4oz) flat-cap mushrooms,
   roughly chopped
2 × 125g goat's cheese logs, with rind
   (see Cook's Tip, page 35)
350g carton cheese sauce (see as
   above)
salt and ground black pepper
green salad to serve

Serves 4
Preparation Time 15 minutes
Cooking Time 50–55 minutes

Nutritional Information (Per Serving)
631 calories, 37g fat (of which 18g saturates), 50g carbohydrate, 1.9g salt
A Little Effort

Butternut Squash and
Spinach Lasagne

1. Preheat the oven to 200°C (180°C fan oven) mark 6. Put the squash into a roasting tin with the oil, onion and 1 tbsp water. Mix well and season with salt and pepper. Roast for 25 minutes, tossing halfway through.

2. To make the sauce, melt the butter in a pan, then stir in the flour and cook over a medium heat for 1–2 minutes. Gradually add the milk, stirring constantly. Reduce the heat to a simmer and cook, stirring, for 5 minutes or until the sauce has thickened. Crumble the ricotta into the sauce and add the nutmeg. Mix together thoroughly and season with salt and pepper.

3. Heat 1 tbsp water in a pan. Add the spinach, cover and cook until just wilted. Season generously.

4. Spoon the squash mixture into a 1.7 litre (3 pint) ovenproof dish. Layer the spinach on top, then cover with a third of the sauce, then the lasagne. Spoon the remaining sauce on top, season and sprinkle with the grated cheese. Cook for 30–35 minutes until the cheese topping is golden and the pasta is cooked.

1 butternut squash, peeled, halved, seeded and cut into 3cm (1¼in) cubes
2 tbsp olive oil
1 onion, sliced
25g (1oz) butter
25g (1oz) plain flour
600ml (1 pint) milk
250g (9oz) ricotta cheese (see Cook's Tip, page 35)
1 tsp freshly grated nutmeg
225g bag baby leaf spinach
6 'no need to pre-cook' lasagne sheets
50g (2oz) pecorino cheese or Parmesan, freshly grated (see as above)
salt and ground black pepper

PASTA

Nutritional Information (Per Serving)
273 calories, 17g fat (of which 7g saturates), 18g carbohydrate, 0.6g salt
Easy

Serves 6
Preparation Time 30 minutes
Cooking Time about 1 hour

189

Fast Macaroni Cheese

500g (1lb 2oz) macaroni
500ml (18fl oz) crème fraîche
200g (7oz) freshly grated Parmesan
   (see Cook's Tip, page 35)
2 tbsp ready-made English or
   Dijon mustard
5 tbsp freshly chopped flat-leafed
   parsley
ground black pepper
green salad to serve

1 Cook the macaroni in a large pan of lightly salted boiling water according to the pack instructions. Drain and keep to one side.

2 Preheat the grill to high. Put the crème fraîche into a pan and heat gently. Stir in 175g (6oz) Parmesan, the mustard and parsley and season well with black pepper. Stir the pasta into the sauce, spoon into bowls and sprinkle with the remaining cheese. Grill until golden and serve immediately with salad.

Serves 4
Preparation Time 5 minutes
Cooking Time 15 minutes

Nutritional Information (Per Serving)
1137 calories, 69g fat (of which 44g saturates), 96g carbohydrate, 2g salt
Easy

Pasta Shells Stuffed with
Spinach and Ricotta

1. Put the spinach into a large pan. Cover and cook over a low to medium heat for 2–3 minutes until wilted. Drain, squeeze out the excess liquid and chop finely.

2. Put the spinach into a large bowl with the ricotta and beat in the egg. Stir in the grated nutmeg, lemon zest and 25g (1oz) grated Parmesan and season.

3. Preheat the oven to 200°C (180°C fan oven) mark 6. Meanwhile, cook the pasta according to the pack instructions for oven-baked dishes. Drain well.

4. Spread the Classic Tomato Sauce in the bottom of an 18 × 23cm (7 × 9in) ovenproof dish. Fill the shells with spinach mixture and arrange on top of the sauce. Sprinkle with 25g (1oz) grated Parmesan and the pinenuts. Cook in the oven for 20–25 minutes until golden.

450g (1lb) fresh spinach, washed
125g (4oz) ricotta cheese (see Cook's Tip, page 35)
1 medium egg
a pinch of freshly grated nutmeg
grated zest of ½ lemon
50g (2oz) freshly grated Parmesan (see as above)
225g (8oz) conchiglione pasta shells
½ quantity of Classic Tomato Sauce (see Cook's Tip)
25g (1oz) pinenuts
salt and ground black pepper

Cook's Tip
Classic Tomato Sauce
Heat 1 tbsp olive oil in a pan. Add 1 small chopped onion, 1 grated carrot and 1 chopped celery stick, then fry gently for 20 minutes until softened. Add 1 crushed garlic clove and ½ tbsp tomato purée and fry for 1 minute. Stir in 2 × 400g cans plum tomatoes, add 1 bay leaf, ½ tsp oregano and 2 tsp caster sugar and simmer for 30 minutes until thickened. Serves 4.

PASTA

Nutritional Information (Per Serving)
430 calories, 17g fat (of which 7g saturates), 50g carbohydrate, 1.6g salt
Easy

Serves 4
Preparation Time 10 minutes
Cooking Time about 45 minutes

Pasta with Vegetables,
Pinenuts and Pesto

300g (11oz) penne pasta
50g (2oz) pinenuts
1 tbsp olive oil
1 garlic clove, crushed
250g (9oz) closed-cup
　　mushrooms, sliced
2 courgettes, sliced
250g (9oz) cherry tomatoes
6 tbsp fresh Pesto (see Cook's Tip,
　　page 38)
25g (1oz) Parmesan shavings (see
　　Cook's Tip, page 35)

1 Cook the pasta in a large pan of lightly salted boiling water according to the pack instructions until al dente.

2 Meanwhile, gently toast the pinenuts in a dry frying pan, tossing them around until golden, then remove from the pan and set aside. Add the oil to the pan, followed by the garlic, mushrooms and courgettes. Add a splash of water to the pan, then cover and cook for 4–5 minutes.

3 Uncover the pan and add the tomatoes, then cook for a further 1–2 minutes.

4 Drain the pasta and return to the pan. Add the vegetables, pinenuts and pesto to the drained pasta. Toss well to combine and serve immediately, topped with the Parmesan shavings.

Serves 4
Preparation Time 5 minutes
Cooking Time 15 minutes

Nutritional Information (Per Serving)
556 calories, 27g fat (of which 6g saturates), 60g carbohydrate, 0.5g salt
Easy

Pappardelle with Spinach

1 Cook the pappardelle in a large pan of lightly salted boiling water according to the pack instructions until al dente.

2 Drain the pasta well, return to the pan and add the spinach, oil and ricotta, tossing for 10–15 seconds until the spinach has wilted. Season with a little nutmeg, salt and pepper and serve immediately.

350g (12oz) pappardelle pasta
350g (12oz) baby leaf spinach, roughly chopped
2 tbsp olive oil
75g (3oz) ricotta cheese (see Cook's Tip, page 35)
freshly grated nutmeg
salt and ground black pepper

Nutritional Information (Per Serving)
404 calories, 11g fat (of which 3g saturates), 67g carbohydrate, 0.3g salt
Easy

Serves 4
Preparation Time 5 minutes
Cooking Time 12 minutes

Tomato and Artichoke Pasta

300g (11oz) penne pasta
6 pieces sunblush tomatoes in oil
1 red onion, sliced
about 10 pieces roasted artichoke
    hearts in oil, drained and
    roughly chopped
50g (2oz) pitted black olives,
    roughly chopped
50g (2oz) pecorino cheese, grated
    (see Cook's Tip, page 35)
100g (3½oz) rocket

1 Cook the pasta in a large pan of lightly salted boiling water according to the pack instructions until al dente. Drain well.

2 Meanwhile, drain the sunblush tomatoes, reserving the oil, and roughly chop. Heat 1 tbsp oil from the tomatoes in a large frying pan, add the onion and fry for 5–6 minutes until softened and turning golden. Add the tomatoes, artichokes and olives to the pan and heat for 3–4 minutes until hot.

3 Add half the pecorino cheese and stir through. Remove from the heat and stir in the rocket and pasta. Divide the pasta among four bowls and sprinkle the remaining pecorino over the top to serve.

PASTA

Serves 4
Preparation Time 10 minutes
Cooking Time 10–12 minutes

Nutritional Information (Per Serving)
380 calories, 11g fat (of which 4g saturates), 59g carbohydrate, 1.3g salt
Easy

Pasta with Pesto and Beans

1 Cook the pasta in a large pan of lightly salted boiling water according to the pack instructions for 5 minutes.

2 Add the beans and potatoes to the pan and continue to boil for a further 7–8 minutes until the potatoes are just tender.

3 Drain the pasta, beans and potatoes in a colander, then tip everything back into the pan and stir in the pesto. Serve scattered with Parmesan shavings.

350g (12oz) pasta shapes
175g (6oz) fine green beans, roughly chopped
175g (6oz) small salad potatoes, such as Anya, thickly sliced
250g (9oz) fresh Pesto (see Cook's Tip, page 38)
Parmesan shavings to serve (see Cook's Tip, page 35)

Cook's Tip
Use leftover cooked pasta, beans or potatoes: tip the pasta into a pan of boiling water and bring back to the boil for 30 seconds. Bring the beans or potatoes to room temperature, but there's no need to re-boil them.

Nutritional Information (Per Serving)
738 calories, 38g fat (of which 10g saturates), 74g carbohydrate, 1g salt
Easy

Serves 4
Preparation Time 5 minutes
Cooking Time 15 minutes

Pea, Mint and Ricotta Pasta

300g (11oz) farfalle pasta
200g (7oz) frozen peas
175g (6oz) ricotta cheese (see
    Cook's Tip, page 35)
3 tbsp freshly chopped mint
2 tbsp extra virgin olive oil
salt and ground black pepper

1 Cook the pasta in a large pan of lightly salted boiling water according to the pack instructions until al dente. Add the frozen peas for the last 4 minutes of cooking.

2 Drain the pasta and peas, reserving a ladleful of pasta cooking water, then return to the pan. Stir in the ricotta and mint with the pasta water. Season well, drizzle with the oil and serve at once.

Serves 4
Preparation Time 5 minutes
Cooking Time 10 minutes

Nutritional Information (Per Serving)
431 calories, 14g fat (of which 5g saturates), 63g carbohydrate, trace salt
Easy

Fusilli with Chilli and Tomatoes

1 Cook the pasta in a large pan of lightly salted boiling water according to the pack instructions until al dente. Drain.

2 Meanwhile, heat the oil in a large frying pan over a high heat. Add the chilli and garlic and cook for 30 seconds. Add the tomatoes, season with salt and pepper and cook over a high heat for 3 minutes or until the skins begin to split.

3 Add the basil and drained pasta and toss together. Transfer to a serving dish, sprinkle the Parmesan shavings over the top and serve immediately.

350g (12oz) fusilli or other
    short pasta
4 tbsp olive oil
1 large red chilli, seeded and
    finely chopped (see Cook's Tips,
    page 37)
1 garlic clove, crushed
500g (1lb 2oz) cherry tomatoes
2 tbsp freshly chopped basil
50g (2oz) Parmesan shavings (see
    Cook's Tip, page 35)
salt and ground black pepper

Nutritional Information (Per Serving)
738 calories, 38g fat (of which 10g saturates), 74g carbohydrate, 1g salt
Easy

Serves 4
Preparation Time 5 minutes
Cooking Time 15 minutes

Roast Tomato Pasta

400g (14oz) rigatoni pasta
700g (1½lb) cherry tomatoes
olive oil to drizzle
50g (2oz) pinenuts
a large handful of fresh basil
    leaves, torn
salt and ground black pepper
Parmesan shavings to serve (see
    Cook's Tip, page 35)

1 Preheat the oven to 240°C (220°C fan oven) mark 9. Cook the pasta in a large pan of lightly salted boiling water according to the pack instructions until al dente.

2 Meanwhile, cut half the tomatoes in two and arrange them in a large roasting tin, cut side up. Add the remaining whole tomatoes and drizzle all with oil, then season with salt and pepper. Put the pinenuts on a separate roasting tray and roast both in the oven for 15 minutes until the tomatoes are softened and lightly caramelised. Watch carefully to make sure the pinenuts don't scorch and remove from the oven earlier if necessary.

3 Drain the pasta well and add to the roasting tin when the tomatoes are done. Scatter on the basil and pinenuts, then stir thoroughly to coat the pasta in the juices. Adjust the seasoning and stir in a little more oil, if you like. Sprinkle with the Parmesan shavings and serve.

Serves 4
Preparation Time 5 minutes
Cooking Time 15 minutes

Nutritional Information (Per Serving)
507 calories, 16g fat (of which 2g saturates), 80g carbohydrate, 0g salt
Easy

Pasta with Goat's Cheese
and Sunblush Tomatoes

1 Cook the pasta in a large pan of lightly salted boiling water according to the pack instructions until al dente.

2 Meanwhile, heat the oil in a pan and fry the red and yellow peppers for 5–7 minutes until softened and just beginning to brown. Add the tomato paste and cook for a further minute. Add a ladleful of pasta cooking water to the pan and simmer for 1–2 minutes to make a sauce.

3 Drain the pasta and return to the pan. Pour the sauce on top, then add the tomatoes, goat's cheese and parsley. Toss together until the cheese begins to melt, then season with pepper and serve.

300g (11oz) conchiglie pasta
2 tbsp olive oil
1 red pepper, seeded and chopped
1 yellow pepper, seeded and chopped
½ tbsp sun-dried tomato paste
75g (3oz) sunblush tomatoes
75g (3oz) soft goat's cheese (see
  Cook's Tip, page 35)
2 tbsp freshly chopped parsley
salt and ground black pepper

Nutritional Information (Per Serving)
409 calories, 12g fat (of which 4g saturates), 64g carbohydrate, 0.4g salt
Easy

Serves 4
Preparation Time 5 minutes
Cooking Time 10 minutes

Pesto Gnocchi

800g (1lb 12oz) fresh gnocchi
200g (7oz) green beans, trimmed
    and chopped
125g (4oz) fresh Pesto (see Cook's
    Tip, page 38)
10 sunblush tomatoes, roughly chopped

1 Cook the gnocchi in a large pan of lightly salted boiling water according to the pack instructions or until all the gnocchi have floated to the surface. Add the beans to the water for the last 3 minutes of cooking time.

2 Drain the gnocchi and beans and put back into the pan. Add the pesto and tomatoes and toss well. Serve immediately.

Serves 4
Preparation Time 10 minutes
Cooking Time 10 minutes

Nutritional Information (Per Serving)
481 calories, 24g fat (of which 6g saturates), 56g carbohydrate, 0.4g salt
Easy

Very Easy Four-cheese Gnocchi

1 Cook the gnocchi in a large pan of lightly salted boiling water according to the pack instructions or until all the gnocchi have floated to the surface. Drain well and put the gnocchi back into the pan.

2 Preheat the grill. Add the four-cheese sauce and tomatoes to the gnocchi and heat gently, stirring, for 2 minutes.

3 Season with salt and pepper, then add the basil and stir again. Spoon into individual heatproof bowls, sprinkle a little Parmesan over each one and dot with butter.

4 Cook under the grill for 3–5 minutes until golden and bubbling. Garnish with basil sprigs and serve with salad.

350g pack fresh gnocchi
300g tub fresh four-cheese sauce (see Cook's Tip, page 35)
240g pack sunblush tomatoes
2 tbsp freshly torn basil leaves, plus basil sprigs to garnish
1 tbsp freshly grated Parmesan (see as above)
15g (½oz) butter, chopped
salt and ground black pepper
salad to serve

Nutritional Information (Per Serving)
630 calories, 28g fat (of which 15g saturates), 77g carbohydrate, 0g salt
Gluten Free • Easy

Serves 2
Preparation Time 3 minutes
Cooking Time 10 minutes

Pies, pastry and pizza

Easy Leek Pie

Spinach and Feta Pie

Winter Roasted Vegetable Tart

Roasted Vegetable Tartlets

Caramelised Onion and Goat's Cheese Tart

Leek and Fennel Tart

Soured Cream and Onion Tarts

Country Tomato and Parmesan Tart

Sesame and Cabbage Rolls

Egg and Pepper Pizza

Garlic Cheese Pizza

Deli Pizza

Easy Leek Pie

275g (10oz) plain flour, plus
    extra to dust
1 tsp English mustard powder
175g (6oz) cold butter, cut into cubes
50g (2oz) mature Cheddar, grated
    (see Cook's Tip, page 35)
2 egg yolks, lightly beaten
900g (2lb) leeks, cut into 1cm (½in)
    slices, washed and drained
2 medium red onions, each cut into
    8 wedges
juice of ½ lemon
leaves of 5 thyme sprigs
4 tbsp olive oil
1 small egg, lightly beaten
salt and ground black pepper
seasonal vegetables to serve

1 Put the flour, mustard powder, butter and ½ tsp salt into a food processor. Pulse until the mixture forms crumbs, then add the cheese, egg yolks and 2–3 tbsp cold water. Process briefly until the mixture comes together, then form into a ball, wrap in clingfilm and put in the freezer for 10 minutes.

2 Preheat the oven to 200°C (180°C fan oven) mark 6. Cook the leeks with 3 tbsp water in a covered pan until softened. Drain and set aside. Gently cook the onions and lemon juice in a covered pan until softened.

3 Roll out the pastry on a large lightly floured sheet of baking parchment, to a 38cm (15in) round. Lift paper and pastry on to a baking sheet. Put the onions and leeks in the centre of the pastry, leaving a 7.5cm (3in) border. Sprinkle with the thyme, season with salt and pepper and drizzle with the oil. Fold the pastry edges over the filling. Brush the pastry rim with beaten egg. Bake for 50 minutes or until the vegetables are tender. Serve with vegetables.

204

Serves 6
Preparation Time 15 minutes
Cooking Time 1 hour

Nutritional Information (Per Serving)
571 calories, 39g fat (of which 20g saturates), 45g carbohydrate, 0.7g salt
Easy

Spinach and Feta Pie

1 Heat the oil in a large pan and cook the onion for 10 minutes until soft. Add the garlic and cumin and cook for 1–2 minutes. Add the spinach, cover and cook until the spinach has just wilted – 1–2 minutes. Tip into a bowl and allow to cool. Add the potatoes, cheese and eggs, then season and mix.

2 Preheat the oven to 200°C (180°C fan oven) mark 6. Lightly butter a 28cm (11in) tart tin. Unroll the pastry and cut the sheets lengthways into three. Work with one-third of the strips at a time and cover the remainder with clingfilm. Lay a strip on the tin, starting from the middle so that half covers the tin and half hangs over the edge. Brush with melted butter, then lay another strip next to it, slightly overlapping, and brush again. Repeat, working quickly around the tin in a cartwheel shape.

3 Add the filling and level the surface. Fold in the overhanging pastry to cover the mixture, filling any gaps with leftover pastry. Drizzle with the remaining melted butter, then cook for 45 minutes or until golden.

1 tbsp vegetable oil
1 onion, finely chopped
1 garlic clove, crushed
1 tbsp cumin seeds
400g (14oz) baby leaf spinach
1.1kg (2½lb) waxy potatoes, such as Desirée, boiled until tender, cooled, peeled and sliced
2 × 200g packs feta cheese, crumbled (see Cook's Tip, page 35)
2 medium eggs, beaten
200g pack filo pastry, thawed if frozen
50g (2oz) butter, melted
salt and ground black pepper

Nutritional Information (Per Serving)
311 calories, 15g fat (of which 9g saturates), 33g carbohydrate, 1.7g salt
Easy

Serves 10
Preparation Time 40 minutes, plus cooling
Cooking Time 45 minutes

Winter Roasted Vegetable Tart

250g pack ready-rolled shortcrust
  pastry, removed from refrigerator
  5 minutes before using
1 small red onion, cut into six wedges
1 raw baby beetroot, peeled and
  thickly sliced
1 baby aubergine, quartered
1 small red apple, quartered, cored
  and cut into chunky slices
1 garlic clove, crushed
juice of ½ lemon
1 tsp freshly chopped thyme
1 tbsp olive oil
125g (4oz) Cranberry and Red Onion
  Marmalade (see Cook's Tip)
25g (1oz) chestnut mushrooms, sliced
50g (2oz) cooked and peeled (or
  vacuum-packed) chestnuts, chopped
1 tbsp redcurrant jelly, warmed
salt and ground black pepper

1 Preheat the oven to 200°C (180°C fan oven) mark 6. Put an 11.5 × 20.5cm (4½ × 8in) loose-based rectangular tart tin on a baking sheet. Line the tin with pastry, then line the pastry case with greaseproof paper, fill with baking beans and bake blind for 15–20 minutes. Remove the paper and beans, prick the pastry base all over with a fork and bake for a further 5–10 minutes until golden. Cool and remove from the tin.

2 Put the onion, beetroot, aubergine, apple and garlic into a roasting tin. Squeeze the lemon juice over, scatter the thyme over and drizzle with oil, then roast for 20 minutes. Tip into a bowl and leave to cool.

3 Put the cooked pastry case on a baking sheet. Spoon the Cranberry and Red Onion Marmalade over the base. Arrange the roasted vegetables and mushrooms on top of the tart. Sprinkle the chestnuts on top, then season. Brush warmed redcurrant jelly over the vegetables and cook for 20 minutes. Serve hot.

Cook's Tip
Cranberry and Red Onion Marmalade
Heat 2 tbsp olive oil in a pan and gently fry 500g (1lb 2oz) sliced red onions for 5 minutes. Add the juice of 1 orange, 1 tbsp pickling spice, 150g (5oz) dark muscovado sugar and 150ml (¼ pint) ruby port, and simmer gently for 40 minutes. Add 450g (1lb) fresh cranberries and cook over a medium heat for 20 minutes. Cool and chill for up to two days.

Serves 6
Preparation Time including marmalade
  30 minutes
Cooking Time (as above) 2 hours

Nutritional Information (Per Serving)
540 calories, 24g fat (of which 1g saturates), 85g carbohydrate, 0.5g salt
Easy

Roasted Vegetable Tartlets

1 Preheat the oven to 220°C (200°C fan oven) mark 7. Unroll the puff pastry on a lightly floured surface and cut it into six squares. Put the pastry squares on a large baking sheet and prick each one all over with a fork. Brush the surface with beaten egg and sprinkle the edges with sea salt. Bake for 5–7 minutes until the pastry is golden brown and cooked through. Press down the centre of each tartlet slightly with the back of a fish slice.

2 Make the dressing. Pour 4 tbsp oil from the jar of antipasti into a bowl (top it up with a little more olive oil if there's not enough in the antipasti jar). Add the vinegar, season with salt and pepper and mix well, then set aside.

3 To serve, spread some hummus over the central part of each tartlet. Put the tartlets on individual plates and spoon on the antipasti – there's no need to be neat. Whisk the balsamic vinegar dressing. Add the rocket leaves and toss to coat, then pile a small handful of leaves on top of each tartlet. Serve immediately.

375g pack ready-rolled puff pastry, thawed if frozen
plain flour to dust
1 medium egg, beaten
2 tbsp coarse sea salt
300g (11oz) vegetable antipasti in olive oil
olive oil, if needed
2 tbsp balsamic vinegar
190g tub red pepper hummus
50g (2oz) wild rocket
salt and ground black pepper

Get Ahead

To prepare ahead Complete the recipe to the end of step 1. Leave the tartlets to cool on a wire rack, then store in an airtight container. It will keep for up to two days.

To use Complete the recipe.

Nutritional Information (Per Tartlet)
356 calories, 24g fat (of which 1g saturates), 30g carbohydrate, 1.1g salt
Easy

Makes 6
Preparation Time 15 minutes
Cooking Time about 7 minutes

Caramelised Onion
and Goat's Cheese Tart

230g ready-made shortcrust
    pastry case
275g jar onion confit
300g (11oz) mild soft goat's cheese
    (see Cook's Tip, page 35)
1 medium egg, beaten
25g (1oz) freshly grated Parmesan
    (see as above)
50g (2oz) wild rocket
balsamic vinegar and extra virgin
    olive oil to drizzle
salt and ground black pepper

1 Preheat the oven to 200°C (180°C fan oven) mark 6. Line the pastry case with greaseproof paper, fill with baking beans and bake blind for 10 minutes. Remove the paper and beans, prick the pastry base all over with a fork and bake for a further 15–20 minutes until golden.

2 Spoon the onion confit into the pastry case. Beat the goat's cheese and egg together in a bowl until smooth, season with salt and pepper, then spoon on top of the onions. Level the surface with a knife and sprinkle the Parmesan all over. Cook the tart for 25–30 minutes until the filling is set and just beginning to turn golden.

3 Leave to cool for 15 minutes, then cut away the sides of the foil case and carefully slide the tart on to a plate. Just before serving, arrange the rocket on top of the tart and drizzle with vinegar and oil. Serve warm.

Serves 6
Preparation Time 10 minutes
Cooking Time 1 hour

Nutritional Information (Per Serving)
480 calories, 28g fat (of which 14g saturates), 44g carbohydrate, 1.5g salt
Easy

Leek and Fennel Tart

1 Pulse the flour and butter in a processor until they resemble breadcrumbs. Tip into a bowl and stir in 40g (1½oz) Parmesan, then 75ml (3fl oz) cold water until the dough comes together. Knead lightly, form into a ball, wrap in clingfilm and chill for 30 minutes.

2 Heat the oil in a large pan, add the leeks and fennel, then cover and cook over a low heat for 15–20 minutes until soft. Strain off any liquid and leave the vegetables to cool.

3 Preheat the oven to 200°C (180°C fan oven) mark 6. Roll out the pastry and line a 30.5cm (12in) loose-bottomed fluted tart tin. Prick the base, cover with greaseproof paper and fill with baking beans. Chill for 10 minutes. Bake blind for 12–15 minutes. Remove the paper and beans and bake for a further 8–10 minutes. If pastry puffs up, push it down. Reduce the oven temperature to 170°C (150°C fan oven) mark 3. Mix the eggs, yolks, milk, cream, poppy seeds and remaining Parmesan and season. Spoon the leek mixture into the pastry case. Pour in the egg mixture, sprinkle with thyme and cook for 40–45 minutes until set. Remove the outside of the tin but leave the tart on the base to cool.

Freezing Tip

To freeze Complete the recipe and leave to cool. Return the tart to the tin, wrap well and freeze for up to one month.

To use Thaw at cool room temperature, then warm through for 15 minutes in an oven preheated to 200°C (180°C fan oven) mark 6.

275g (10oz) plain flour
125g (4oz) butter, chilled and cut
    into cubes
75g (3oz) Parmesan, finely grated
    (see Cook's Tip, page 35)
1 tbsp sunflower oil
2 large leeks – about 200g (7oz) –
    trimmed and chopped
525g (1lb 3oz) fennel, chopped
3 medium eggs, plus 2 yolks
200ml (7fl oz) each milk and
    double cream
1½ tbsp poppy seeds
a few thyme sprigs, leaves stripped
    and stalks discarded
salt and ground black pepper

Nutritional Information (Per Serving)
319 calories, 24g fat (of which 13g saturates), 20g carbohydrate, 0.5g salt
Easy

Serves 12
Preparation Time 35 minutes,
    plus chilling
Cooking Time 1¼–1½ hours

Soured Cream and Onion Tarts

700g (1½lb) tomatoes, halved
1 tbsp freshly chopped thyme or
   1 tsp dried thyme
2 tbsp olive oil
200g (7oz) chilled butter
175g (6oz) plain flour, plus extra
   to dust
6–7 tbsp soured cream
900g (2lb) onions, finely sliced
125g (4oz) Roquefort cheese (see
   Cook's Tip, page 35)
salt and ground black pepper

1 Preheat the oven to 170°C (150°C fan oven) mark 3. Put the tomatoes on a baking sheet. Season, then sprinkle with thyme, drizzle with oil and cook, uncovered, for 40 minutes until slightly shrivelled. Leave to cool.

2 Meanwhile, cut 150g (5oz) butter into small dice and put into a food processor with the flour. Pulse until the butter is roughly cut up through the flour (you should still be able to see pieces of butter), then add the soured cream and pulse again for 2–3 seconds until just mixed. (Alternatively, rub the fat into the flour in a large bowl by hand or using a pastry cutter. Stir in the cream using a fork.)

3 On a lightly floured surface, cut the pastry into six and thinly roll each into a 12.5cm (5in) round. Put on two baking sheets, cover and chill for 30 minutes.

4 Meanwhile, melt the remaining butter in a pan, add the onions and cook over a low heat for 15 minutes until very soft. Increase the heat for 3–4 minutes until the onions are well browned. Cool.

5 Spoon the onions into the centre of the pastries, leaving a 1cm (½in) edge. Crumble the cheese on top and add the tomatoes. Season, then roughly fold up the pastry edge. Chill for 20 minutes. Preheat the oven to 200°C (180°C fan oven) mark 6. Cook the tarts for 30 minutes until golden. Serve immediately.

Try Something Different
Other cheeses to try with this pie are feta, crumbly goat's cheese, Red Leicester or other blue cheese.

PIES, PASTRY AND PIZZA

Serves 6
Preparation Time 20 minutes,
   plus chilling
Cooking Time 1½ hours, plus cooling

Nutritional Information (Per Serving)
556 calories, 41g fat (of which 24g saturates), 39g carbohydrate, 1.2g salt
Easy

Country Tomato
and Parmesan Tart

1 Preheat the oven to 180°C (160°C fan oven) mark 4. Put the flour, butter, 75g (3oz) grated Parmesan, ½ tsp salt and the cayenne pepper into a food processor and whiz until the mixture looks like rough breadcrumbs. Set aside one-third of the mixture, cover and chill. Press the remaining crumb mixture into the base of a 20.5cm (8in) square, loose-based flan tin, using the back of a spoon to spread it out to the edges. Chill for 10 minutes. Cook the crumb base for 15–20 minutes until light golden brown. Cool.

2 Spread the tomato paste over the cooled crumb base, then sprinkle with half the breadcrumbs. Layer the tomato slices and thyme on top and sprinkle with the remaining breadcrumbs, the remaining Parmesan and the reserved crumb mixture. Season with salt and black pepper.

3 Cook the tart in the oven for a further 15–20 minutes until golden brown. Allow it to cool slightly, then cut into portions and garnish with fresh thyme.

75g (3oz) plain flour
75g (3oz) butter
150g (5oz) Parmesan, finely grated (see Cook's Tip, page 35)
¼ tsp cayenne pepper
4 tbsp sun-dried tomato paste
15g (½oz) fresh breadcrumbs
900g (2lb) tomatoes, preferably plum, thickly sliced
1 tbsp freshly chopped thyme, plus extra sprigs to garnish
salt and ground black pepper

Cook's Tip
The same mixture can be cooked in a 23cm (9in) round tin.

Nutritional Information (Per Serving)
274 calories, 19g fat (of which 12g saturates), 37g carbohydrate, 0.9g salt
Easy

Serves 4
Preparation Time 40 minutes, plus chilling
Cooking Time 40 minutes

Sesame and Cabbage Rolls

50g (2oz) dried shiitake mushrooms
3 tbsp sesame oil
4 garlic cloves, crushed
4 tbsp sesame seeds
450g (1lb) cabbage, finely shredded
1 bunch of spring onions, chopped
225g can bamboo shoots, drained
3 tbsp soy sauce
½ tsp caster sugar
2 × 270g packs filo pastry
1 large egg, beaten
vegetable oil for deep-frying
Spiced Plum Sauce or Thai Chilli
   Dipping Sauce to serve (see
   Cook's Tips)

1 Put the mushrooms into a heatproof bowl and cover with boiling water. Soak for 20 minutes.

2 Heat the sesame oil in a wok or large frying pan. Add the garlic and sesame seeds and fry gently until golden brown. Add the cabbage and spring onions and fry, stirring, for 3 minutes.

3 Drain and slice the mushrooms. Add them to the pan with the bamboo shoots, soy sauce and sugar and stir until well mixed. Remove the pan from the heat and leave to cool.

4 Cut the filo pastry into 24 x 18cm (7in) squares. Keep the filo squares covered with a damp teatowel as you work. Place one square of filo pastry on the worksurface and cover with a second square. Place a heaped tablespoon of the cabbage mixture across the centre of the top square to within 2.5cm (1in) of the ends. Fold the 2.5cm (1in) ends of pastry over the filling. Brush one unfolded edge of the pastry with a little beaten egg, then roll up to make a thick parcel shape. Shape the remaining pastry and filling in the same way to make 12 parcels.

5 Heat a 5cm (2in) depth of vegetable oil in a deep-fryer or large heavy-based saucepan to 180°C (test by frying a small cube of bread: it should brown in 30 seconds). Fry the rolls in batches for about 3 minutes or until crisp and golden. Remove with a slotted spoon and drain on kitchen paper; keep them warm while you fry the remainder. Serve hot with a sauce for dipping.

Cook's Tips

Spiced Plum Sauce
Slice 2 spring onions as thinly as possible. Put them into a small pan with 6 tbsp plum sauce, the juice of 1 lime, ½ tsp Chinese five-spice powder and 2 tbsp water. Heat gently for 2 minutes.

Thai Chilli Dipping Sauce
Put 200ml (7fl oz) white wine vinegar and 6 tbsp caster sugar into a small pan. Bring to the boil, then reduce the heat and simmer for 2 minutes. Add 1 finely chopped red chilli and 50g (2oz) each finely chopped cucumber, onion and pineapple.

Makes 12
Preparation Time 30 minutes,
   plus soaking and cooling
Cooking Time about 15 minutes

Nutritional Information (Per Roll)
224 calories, 13g fat (of which 2g saturates), 23g carbohydrate, 0.7g salt
Dairy Free • A Little Effort

Egg and Pepper Pizza

1 Preheat the oven to 220°C (200°C fan oven) mark 7. Put two large baking sheets, big enough to hold two pizzas each, into the oven to heat up.

2 Chop the peppers into thin strips. Spoon 2 tbsp passata over each pizza base and scatter strips of pepper around the edges. Make a dip in the passata in the middle of each pizza and break an egg into it. Carefully slide the pizzas on to the preheated baking sheets. Place in the oven and cook for 12 minutes or until the egg is thoroughly cooked.

3 Top the pizzas with the watercress, drizzle with a little of the reserved oil from the peppers and serve.

150g (5oz) red and yellow marinated peppers in oil, drained and oil reserved
8 tbsp passata
4 small pizza bases
4 medium eggs
125g (4oz) watercress, washed and stalks removed

Cook's Tip

Watercress is the salad superfood par excellence. It is a good source of iron, and vitamins C and E.

Nutritional Information (Per Serving)
403 calories, 13g fat (of which 2g saturates), 61g carbohydrate, 1g salt
Gluten Free · Easy

Serves 4
Preparation Time 15 minutes
Cooking Time 12 minutes

Garlic Cheese Pizza

280g pack pizza base mix
plain flour to dust
2 × 150g packs garlic and herb
   cheese (see Cook's Tip, page 35)
12 whole sun-dried tomatoes, drained
   of oil and cut into rough pieces
40g (1½oz) pinenuts
12 fresh basil leaves
3 tbsp olive oil
green salad to serve

1 Preheat the oven to 220°C (200°C fan oven) mark 7. Put a pizza stone or large baking sheet in the oven to heat up.

2 Mix the pizza base dough according to the pack instructions. Turn out on to a lightly floured worksurface and knead for a few minutes or until smooth. Roll out to a 33cm (13in) round. Transfer the dough to the preheated pizza stone or baking sheet. Pinch a lip around the edge.

3 Crumble the cheese over the dough and flatten with a palette knife, then sprinkle on the sun-dried tomatoes, pinenuts and basil leaves.

4 Drizzle with the oil and bake for 20–30 minutes until pale golden and cooked to the centre. Serve with a green salad.

Try Something Different
Use goat's cheese instead of the garlic and herb cheese.

214

Serves 4
Preparation Time 20 minutes
Cooking Time 30 minutes

Nutritional Information (Per Serving)
536 calories, 30g fat (of which 9g saturates), 54g carbohydrate, 0.6g salt
Easy

Deli Pizza

1 Preheat the oven to 220°C (200°C fan oven) mark 7. Put a large baking sheet on the top shelf to heat up.

2 Spread a thin layer of the tomato sauce over each of the pizza bases, leaving a 2.5cm (1in) border around the edge. Top with dollops of goat's cheese, then scatter the red onion, tomatoes and olives over it.

3 Slide one of the pizzas on to the hot baking sheet and bake for 15 minutes or until golden and crisp. Repeat with the second pizza base. Scatter the torn basil over each pizza and serve immediately with a green salad.

6 tbsp tomato pizza sauce
2 pizzeria-style pizza bases
100g (3½oz) soft goat's cheese (see Cook's Tip, page 35)
1 red onion, finely sliced
100g (3½oz) sunblush tomatoes
100g (3½oz) pitted black olives
a handful of fresh basil, roughly torn
green salad to serve

Try Something Different
Try marinated peppers, artichokes or chargrilled aubergines instead of the olives and sunblush tomatoes.

Nutritional Information (Per Serving)
440 calories, 15g fat (of which 5g saturates), 64g carbohydrate, 2.8g salt
Easy

Serves 4
Preparation Time 5 minutes
Cooking Time 15 minutes

Special suppers

Chestnut and Butternut Filo Parcels

Leek, Artichoke and Mushroom Croute

Aubergine, Feta and Tomato Stacks

Baked Stuffed Pumpkin

Couscous-stuffed Mushrooms

Wild Mushroom Pithiviers

Stuffed Aubergines

Red Cabbage Timbales with Mushroom Stuffing

Vegetable Moussaka

Mushroom and Roasted Potato Bake

Aubergine Parmigiana

Red Onion Tarte Tatin

Nut and Cranberry Terrine

White Nut Roast

Chestnut and Butternut
Filo Parcels

½ tbsp olive oil
75g (3oz) butter
½ onion, finely chopped
5 fresh rosemary sprigs
½ small butternut squash, peeled
   and finely chopped
1 celery stalk, finely chopped
½ firm pear, finely chopped
100g (3½oz) peeled, cooked (or
   vacuum-packed) chestnuts,
   roughly chopped
1 slice walnut bread, about 50g (2oz),
   cut into small cubes
8 sheets filo pastry, about 30.5 ×
   20.5cm (12 × 8in) each
50g (2oz) cream cheese (see Cook's
   Tip, page 35)
salt and ground black pepper

1 Heat the oil and 15g (½oz) butter in a medium pan, add the onion and fry gently for 10 minutes. Finely chop one rosemary sprig and add to the pan, along with the squash. Continue to cook for 5 minutes or until everything is soft and golden. Add the celery and pear and cook for 1–2 minutes. Add the chestnuts, season and mix well. Add the bread to the pan, mix everything together, then set aside to cool.

2 Preheat the oven to 200°C (180°C fan oven) mark 6. Melt the remaining butter in a pan. Brush one sheet of filo pastry with the melted butter and layer another sheet of pastry on top, diagonally. Put a quarter of the chestnut mixture in the centre of the pastry and dot with a quarter of the cream cheese. Brush the edges of the pastry with a little more butter, bring the edges up and over the filling and pinch together tightly to make a parcel. Repeat to make three more parcels.

3 Put the parcels on a lightly greased baking sheet and cook for 25–30 minutes until the pastry is golden and the filling is piping hot; 5 minutes before the end of the cooking time, put a rosemary sprig into the top of each parcel. Serve hot.

Freezing Tip
To freeze Complete the recipe to the end of step 2, put the parcels in a freezerproof container and freeze for up to one month.

To use Cook from frozen in a preheated oven at 200°C (180°C fan oven) mark 6 for 30 minutes or until the pastry is golden. Complete the recipe.

Serves 4
Preparation Time 40 minutes
Cooking Time 45–50 minutes

Nutritional Information (Per Serving)
408 calories, 22g fat (of which 13g saturates), 49g carbohydrate, 0.5g salt
Easy

Leek, Artichoke and
Mushroom Croûte

1 Heat 2 tbsp olive oil in a large pan and fry the garlic for 1 minute. Add the mushrooms and cook over a low heat for 3 minutes to soften. Add the vinegar, chestnuts, ½ tsp thyme leaves and the artichokes, then cook for 1 minute. In a separate pan, soften the leeks in the remaining 1 tbsp oil for 4 minutes. Tip into a bowl and cool for 5 minutes.

2 Unroll the pastry, sprinkle with the remaining thyme and roll it lightly into the pastry. Flip the pastry over so that the herbs are on the underside, then lightly roll out to a 38 × 25.5cm (15 × 10in) rectangle. Using a sharp knife, cut the pastry in half to create two long thin rectangles. Spoon half the mushroom mixture down the centre of each. Top with the leeks and season. Brush the pastry edges with water, then fold each side of the pastry up over the filling and seal. Cut both rolls in half and put on to a greased baking sheet. Cover and chill overnight.

3 Preheat the oven to 200°C (180°C fan oven) mark 6. Brush the pastry with egg to glaze. Cook for 20 minutes until the pastry is golden. Slice each croûte into six and serve three slices per person, with cranberry sauce and a light drizzle of extra virgin olive oil.

Freezing Tip

To freeze Complete the recipe to the end of step 2, then wrap and freeze for up to one month.

To use Cook from frozen in a preheated oven at 200°C (180°C fan oven) mark 6 for 25 minutes until the pastry is golden. Complete the recipe.

3 tbsp olive oil
2 garlic cloves, crushed
125g (4oz) shiitake mushrooms, sliced
1 tbsp balsamic vinegar
50g (2oz) peeled cooked (or vacuum-packed) chestnuts, roughly chopped
1½ tsp fresh thyme leaves
400g can artichoke hearts, drained and quartered
350g (12oz) leeks, sliced
375g pack ready-rolled puff pastry
butter to grease
1 medium egg, lightly beaten
salt and ground black pepper
cranberry sauce and a little extra virgin olive oil to serve

Nutritional Information (Per Serving)
236 calories, 17g fat (of which 1g saturates), 20g carbohydrate, 0.4g salt
Easy

Serves 8
Preparation Time 30 minutes, plus cooling and chilling overnight
Cooking Time 30–35 minutes

Aubergine, Feta and
Tomato Stacks

200g (7oz) feta cheese, crumbled (see
    Cook's Tip, page 35)
2 tbsp olive oil, plus extra to brush
1 garlic clove, crushed, plus 1 garlic
    clove for rubbing
2 plump aubergines, cut into 1cm
    (½in) thick slices
a handful of fresh basil leaves, torn
3 large vine-ripened tomatoes, each
    sliced into four
salt and ground black pepper
rocket and toasted ciabatta to serve

1 Preheat the barbecue or grill. Put the feta into a bowl, stir in the oil and garlic, season with salt and pepper and set aside.

2 Brush each aubergine slice with a little oil and barbecue or grill for about 6 minutes, turning occasionally, or until softened and golden. Remove from the heat.

3 Sprinkle a little of the feta mixture on six of the aubergine slices and put some torn basil leaves on top, then a slice of tomato on each. Season well. Repeat with the feta mixture, basil leaves, aubergine and tomato. Finish with a third aubergine slice and press down firmly.

4 Secure each stack with a cocktail stick. Either use a hinged grill rack, well oiled, or wrap the stacks in foil and barbecue for 2–3 minutes on each side. Serve with rocket leaves and toasted ciabatta rubbed with a garlic clove.

Serves 4
Preparation Time 10 minutes
Cooking Time 12 minutes

Nutritional Information (Per Serving)
138 calories, 11g fat (of which 5g saturates), 4g carbohydrate, 1.2g salt
Gluten Free • Easy

Baked Stuffed Pumpkin

1 Cut a 5cm (2in) slice from the top of the pumpkin and put to one side for the lid. Scoop out and discard the seeds. Using a knife and a spoon, cut out most of the pumpkin flesh, leaving a thin shell. Cut the pumpkin flesh into small pieces and put to one side.

2 Heat the oil in a large pan, add the leeks, garlic, thyme, paprika and turmeric and fry for 10 minutes. Add the chopped pumpkin flesh and fry for a further 10 minutes or until golden, stirring frequently to prevent sticking. Transfer the mixture to a bowl. Preheat the oven to 180°C (160°C fan oven) mark 4.

3 Add the pumpkin mixture to the cooked rice along with the tomatoes, cashews and cheese. Fork through to mix and season with salt and pepper.

4 Spoon the stuffing mixture into the pumpkin shell, top with the lid and bake for 1¼–1½ hours until the pumpkin is softened and the skin is browned. Remove from the oven and leave to stand for 10 minutes. Cut into wedges to serve.

1 pumpkin, about 1.4–1.8kg (3–4lb)
2 tbsp olive oil
2 leeks, trimmed and chopped
2 garlic cloves, crushed
2 tbsp freshly chopped thyme leaves
2 tsp paprika
1 tsp turmeric
125g (4oz) long-grain rice, cooked
2 tomatoes, peeled, seeded and diced
50g (2oz) cashew nuts, toasted and
    roughly chopped
125g (4oz) Cheddar, grated (see
    Cook's Tip, page 35)
salt and ground black pepper

Nutritional Information (Per Serving)
438 calories, 24g fat (of which 9g saturates), 38g carbohydrate, 0.7g salt
Easy

Serves 4
Preparation Time about 40 minutes
Cooking Time 1½ hours–1 hour
    50 minutes, plus standing

Couscous-stuffed Mushrooms

125g (4oz) couscous

20g pack fresh flat-leafed parsley, roughly chopped

280g jar mixed antipasti in oil, drained and oil put to one side

8 large flat portabellini mushrooms

25g (1oz) butter

25g (1oz) plain flour

300ml (½ pint) skimmed milk

75g (3oz) mature Cheddar, grated, plus extra to sprinkle (see Cook's Tip, page 35)

green salad to serve

1 Preheat the oven to 220°C (200°C fan oven) mark 7. Put the couscous into a bowl with 200ml (7fl oz) boiling water, the parsley, antipasti and 1 tbsp of the reserved oil. Stir well.

2 Put the mushrooms on a non-stick baking tray and spoon a little of the couscous mixture into the centre of each. Cook in the oven while you make the sauce.

3 Whisk together the butter, flour and milk in a small pan over a high heat until the mixture comes to the boil. Reduce the heat as soon as it starts to thicken, then whisk constantly until smooth. Take the pan off the heat and stir in the cheese.

4 Spoon the sauce over the mushrooms and sprinkle with the remaining cheese. Put back into the oven for a further 7–10 minutes until golden. Serve with a green salad.

Serves 4
Preparation Time 3 minutes
Cooking Time about 12 minutes

Nutritional Information (Per Serving)
373 calories, 25g fat (of which 10g saturates), 25g carbohydrate, 0.6g salt
Easy

Wild Mushroom Pithiviers

1. Rinse the mushrooms in cold running water to remove any grit, then pat dry with kitchen paper. Roughly slice.

2. Put the milk and cream into a large heavy-based pan with the garlic. Bring to the boil, then add the potatoes. Bring back to the boil and simmer gently, stirring occasionally, for 15–20 minutes until the potatoes are tender. Season with salt, pepper and nutmeg. Leave to cool.

3. Melt the butter in a large frying pan. When it's sizzling, add the mushrooms and cook over a high heat, stirring all the time, for 5–10 minutes until the mushrooms are cooked and the juices have evaporated completely. Season. Stir in the chopped thyme, then set aside to cool.

4. On a lightly floured surface, roll out the pastry thinly. Cut into eight rounds, approximately 12.5cm (5in) in diameter, for the tops and eight rounds, approximately 11.5cm (4½in) in diameter, for the bases. Put the smaller pastry rounds on baking sheets and brush the edges with beaten egg. Put a large spoonful of the cooled potato mixture in the centre of each round, leaving a 1cm (½in) border around the edge. Top with a spoonful of the mushroom mixture, then cover with the pastry tops. Press the edges together well to seal. Chill for 30 minutes–1 hour.

5. Meanwhile, preheat the oven to 220°C (200°C fan oven) mark 7 and put two baking trays in to heat up. Use the back of a knife to scallop the edges of the pastry and brush the top with the remaining beaten egg. If you like, use a knife to decorate the tops of the pithiviers.

6. Put the pithiviers, on their baking sheets, on the preheated baking trays. Cook for 15–20 minutes until deep golden brown, swapping the trays around in the oven halfway through cooking. Serve immediately, garnished with thyme sprigs.

450g (1lb) wild mushrooms
300ml (½ pint) milk
200ml (7fl oz) double cream
2 garlic cloves, crushed
450g (1lb) floury potatoes, peeled and thinly sliced
freshly grated nutmeg
50g (2oz) butter
2 tsp freshly chopped thyme, plus fresh sprigs to garnish
2 x 500g packs puff pastry, thawed if frozen
flour to dust
1 large egg, beaten
salt and ground black pepper

Get Ahead
Complete the recipe to the end of step 4, then cover and chill overnight until ready to cook.

Nutritional Information (Per Serving)
710 calories, 51g fat (of which 12g saturates), 58g carbohydrate, 1.2g salt
Easy

Serves 8
Preparation Time 1 hour, plus 1 hour chilling and cooling
Cooking Time about 1 hour

Stuffed Aubergines

4 small aubergines
2 tbsp olive oil
25g (1oz) butter
1 small onion, very finely chopped
4 small ripe tomatoes, peeled and
    roughly chopped
2 tsp chopped fresh basil or 1 tsp
    dried basil
2 medium eggs, hard-boiled and
    roughly chopped
1 tbsp capers
225g (8oz) fontina or Gruyère cheese,
    sliced (see Cook's Tip, page 35)
salt and ground black pepper
herby couscous to serve

1 Cut the aubergines in half lengthways and scoop out the flesh. Put the aubergine shells to one side.

2 Chop the aubergine flesh finely, then spread out on a plate and sprinkle with salt. Leave to stand for 20 minutes (this removes the bitter flavour), then turn into a colander. Rinse, drain and dry. Preheat the oven to 180°C (160°C fan oven) mark 4.

3 Heat half the oil in a frying pan with the butter, add the onion and fry gently for 5 minutes until soft but not coloured. Add the tomatoes, basil and salt and pepper to taste.

4 Meanwhile, put the aubergine shells in a single layer in an oiled ovenproof dish. Brush the insides with the remaining oil, then bake in the oven for 10 minutes.

5 Spoon half the tomato mixture into the aubergine shells. Cover with a layer of egg, capers, then a layer of cheese. Spoon the remaining tomato mixture over the top. Bake for a further 15 minutes and serve sizzling hot with couscous.

Serves 4
Preparation Time 10 minutes,
    plus standing
Cooking Time 30 minutes

Nutritional Information (Per Serving)
367 calories, 28g fat (of which 14g saturates), 8g carbohydrate, 1.7g salt
Easy

Red Cabbage Timbales
with Mushroom Stuffing

1 Put the cabbage into a large pan of boiling water and bring to the boil, then reduce the heat and simmer until the outside leaves have softened enough to be eased away. Lift the cabbage out of the pan, and keep the water. Remove three outer leaves and boil them for a further 3–4 minutes, then place in a bowl of cold water. Quarter the whole cabbage and remove the core. Take 700g (1½lb) of the cabbage, remove and discard any thick central vein, then shred the leaves very finely, cover and set aside. Preheat the oven to 190°C (170°C fan oven) mark 5. Line six 150ml (¼ pint) moulds with clingfilm. Drain the whole cabbage leaves and cut in half; discard the central vein. Use the leaves to line the moulds. Fill with stuffing and cover with foil. Place in a large roasting tin and pour in enough warm water to come halfway up the sides of the moulds. Cook for 30 minutes or until just set to the centre.

2 Meanwhile, melt the butter in a pan, add the onions and cook until soft. Mix in the shredded cabbage, vinegar, 3 tbsp water and season. Cook, stirring from time to time, for 15–20 minutes until just tender.

3 To make the sauce, put the sugar and vinegar into a small pan. Cook over a low heat until the sugar has dissolved, then bring to the boil and cook to a rich caramel. Pour in the wine and allow to reduce by half, then add lemon juice to taste and season. Cool.

4 Turn out the timbales, spoon shredded cabbage on top and around, drizzle the sauce over and garnish with thyme, if you like. Serve with green vegetables.

Cook's Tip
Mushroom and Cashew Nut Stuffing
Melt 50g (2oz) butter in a pan, add 200g (7oz) finely chopped onions and cook until soft and golden. Add 450g (1lb) roughly chopped chestnut mushrooms and fry over a moderate heat or until the moisture has evaporated. Stir in 75g (3oz) roughly chopped salted cashew nuts, 4 tbsp freshly chopped flat-leafed parsley and 125g (4oz) fresh breadcrumbs. Leave to cool, then stir in 2 large eggs, beaten, and season with salt and pepper. Mix well, then cover and set aside.

1 medium red cabbage, about
   1.4kg (3lb)
Mushroom and Cashew Nut Stuffing
   (see Cook's Tip)
40g (1½oz) butter
375g (12oz) onions, finely chopped
3 tbsp balsamic vinegar
salt and ground black pepper
small thyme sprigs to garnish
   (optional)
green vegetables to serve

FOR THE SAUCE
4 tbsp caster sugar
4 tbsp red wine vinegar
150ml (¼ pint) red wine
1 tbsp lemon juice

Nutritional Information (Per Serving)
454 calories, 22g fat (of which 10g saturates), 49g carbohydrate, 0.8g salt
A Little Effort

Serves 6
Preparation Time 1 hour, plus cooling
Cooking Time 1 hour

Vegetable Moussaka

450g (1lb) potatoes, peeled and cut
   lengthways into 5mm (¼in) slices
1 aubergine, sliced into rounds
1 large red onion, cut into wedges
2 red peppers, seeded and sliced
4 tbsp olive oil
2 tbsp chopped thyme
225g (8oz) tomatoes, thickly sliced
2 garlic cloves, sliced
250g (9oz) passata
250g (9oz) soft goat's cheese (see
   Cook's Tip, page 35)
300g (11oz) natural yogurt
3 medium eggs
25g (1oz) Parmesan, grated (see as
   above)
salt and ground black pepper
green salad to serve

1 Preheat the oven to 230°C (210°C fan oven) mark 8. Boil the potatoes in a pan of lightly salted water for 5 minutes. Drain and put into a large roasting tin with the aubergine, onion and peppers. Drizzle with oil, add the thyme, toss and season with salt and pepper. Roast for 30 minutes, stirring occasionally.

2 Add the tomatoes and garlic and roast for 15 minutes, then take out of the oven. Reduce the oven temperature to 200°C (180°C fan oven) mark 6.

3 Put half the vegetables into a 1.7 litre (3 pint) ovenproof dish, then spoon half the passata over them and spread the goat's cheese on top. Repeat with the rest of the vegetables and passata. Mix together the yogurt, eggs and Parmesan. Season and then pour over the top. Cook in the oven for 45 minutes or until heated through. Serve with a green salad.

Try Something Different
Use sliced sweet potatoes, or butternut squash, seeded and cut into chunks, instead of the potatoes.

Serves 6
Preparation Time 45 minutes
Cooking Time about 1½ hours

Nutritional Information (Per Serving)
399 calories, 24g fat (of which 11g saturates), 29g carbohydrate, 1.2g salt
Gluten Free • Easy

Mushroom and
Roasted Potato Bake

1. Preheat the oven to 200°C (180°C fan oven) mark 6. Toss the potatoes with 4 tbsp oil in a roasting tin and cook for 40 minutes or until tender.

2. Heat the remaining oil in a large heavy-based pan. Add the onions and cook for 10 minutes or until soft, then add the fresh mushrooms and garlic and cook over a high heat for 5 minutes. Stir in the tomato purée and tomato paste, the porcini mushrooms, if using, and the thyme and wine. Bring to the boil and simmer for 2 minutes. Add the stock and cream and bring to the boil, then bubble for 20 minutes or until well reduced and syrupy.

3. Pour into a 2.4 litre (4¼ pint) ovenproof dish. Stir in the potatoes, spinach, Gruyère and half the Parmesan. Season well with salt and pepper.

4. Combine the yogurt with the eggs and season. Spoon over the vegetable mixture and sprinkle with the remaining Parmesan.

5. Cook in the oven for 30–35 minutes until golden and bubbling. Serve hot.

Freezing Tip

To freeze Complete the recipe to the end of step 4, then cool and freeze for up to one month.

To use Thaw overnight at cool room temperature. Preheat the oven to 200°C (180°C fan oven) mark 6. Bake for 40–45 minutes until golden and bubbling.

900g (2lb) small potatoes, quartered
6 tbsp olive oil
225g (8oz) onions, roughly chopped
450g (1lb) mixed fresh mushrooms, such as shiitake and brown-cap, roughly chopped
2 garlic cloves, crushed
2 tbsp tomato purée
4 tbsp sun-dried tomato paste
25g (1oz) dried porcini mushrooms, rinsed (optional)
2 tsp freshly chopped thyme
300ml (½ pint) each of dry white wine and vegetable stock
300ml (½ pint) double cream
400g (14oz) large fresh spinach leaves, roughly chopped
175g (6oz) Gruyère cheese (see Cook's Tip, page 35)
125g (4oz) freshly grated Parmesan (see as above)
300g (11oz) Greek yogurt
2 medium eggs, beaten
salt and ground black pepper

Nutritional Information (Per Serving)
809 calories, 63g fat (of which 31g saturates), 33g carbohydrate, 1.7g salt
Gluten Free · Easy

Serves 6
Preparation Time 15 minutes
Cooking Time 1¼ hours

227

Aubergine Parmigiana

2 large aubergines, thinly
   sliced lengthways
2 tbsp olive oil, plus extra to brush
3 fat garlic cloves, sliced
2 × 200ml tubs fresh Napoletana sauce
4 ready-roasted red peppers,
   roughly chopped
20g (¾oz) fresh basil, roughly
   chopped (see Cook's Tip)
150g (5oz) Taleggio or fontina
   cheese, coarsely grated (see Cook's
   Tip, page 35)
50g (2oz) Parmesan, coarsely grated
   (see as above)
salt and ground black pepper
green salad to serve

1 Preheat the oven to 200°C (180°C fan oven) mark 6 and preheat the grill until hot. Put the aubergines on an oiled baking sheet, brush with oil, scatter with the garlic and season with salt and pepper. Grill for 5–6 minutes until golden.

2 Spread a little Napoletana sauce over the bottom of an oiled ovenproof dish, then cover with a layer of aubergine and peppers, packing the layers together as tightly as you can. Sprinkle a little basil and some of each cheese over the top. Repeat the layers, finishing with a layer of cheese. Season with pepper. Cook in the oven for 20 minutes or until golden. Serve hot with a green salad.

Cook's Tip
Choose bags or bunches of fresh basil, as the larger leaves have a stronger, more peppery flavour than those of the plants sold in pots.

Serves 4
Preparation Time 10 minutes
Cooking Time about 25 minutes

Nutritional Information (Per Serving)
432 calories, 28g fat (of which 11g saturates), 25g carbohydrate, 2.4g salt
Gluten Free • Easy

Red Onion Tarte Tatin

1 Lightly grease two 23cm (9in) non-stick sandwich tins with a little of the butter and set aside.

2 Melt the remaining butter with the oil in a large non-stick frying pan. Add the onions and sugar and fry for 10–15 minutes until golden, keeping the onions in their rounds.

3 Preheat the oven to 220°C (200°C fan) mark 7. Add the wine, vinegar and thyme to the pan. Bring to the boil and let it bubble until the liquid has evaporated. Season with salt and pepper, then divide the mixture between the tins and leave to cool.

4 Halve the pastry. On a lightly floured surface, roll out each piece thinly into a round shape just larger than the sandwich tin. Put one pastry round over the onion mixture in each tin and tuck in the edges. Prick the pastry dough all over with a fork.

5 Cook the tarts for 15–20 minutes until the pastry is risen and golden. Take out of the oven and put a large warm plate over the pastry. Turn the whole thing over and shake gently to release the tart, then remove the tin. Scatter with thyme, if you like, and cut into wedges to serve.

Get Ahead
To prepare ahead Complete the recipe to the end of step 4. Cover and keep in the fridge for up to 24 hours.

To use Complete the recipe.

50g (2oz) butter
2 tbsp olive oil
1.1kg (2½lb) red onions, sliced
   into rounds
1 tbsp light muscovado sugar
175ml (6fl oz) white wine
4 tsp white wine vinegar
1 tbsp freshly chopped thyme,
   plus extra to garnish (optional)
450g (1lb) puff pastry
plain flour to dust
salt and ground black pepper

Nutritional Information (Per Serving)
235 calories, 15g fat (of which 3g saturates), 23g carbohydrate, 0.4g salt
Easy

Serves 12
Preparation Time 15 minutes
Cooking Time 35–40 minutes

Nut and Cranberry Terrine

125g (4oz) long-grain rice
4 tbsp olive oil
1 onion, finely chopped
1 leek, trimmed and thinly sliced
4 celery sticks, thinly sliced
4 tbsp chopped mixed fresh herbs,
 such as sage, parsley and thyme
40g (1½oz) walnuts, toasted and
 roughly ground
125g (4oz) dolcelatte cheese, crumbled
 (see Cook's Tip, page 35)
1 large egg, beaten
40g (1½oz) fresh white breadcrumbs
125g (4oz) fromage frais or
 crème fraîche
Hot Water Crust Pastry (see Cook's Tip)
salt and ground black pepper
bay leaves to garnish

FOR THE TOPPING

125g (4oz) redcurrant jelly
1 tsp lemon juice
125g (4oz) cranberries or
 redcurrants, thawed if frozen

1 Cook the rice for 10 minutes or until just tender. Refresh under cold water, drain thoroughly and set aside. Heat the oil in a frying pan, add the onion, leek, celery and herbs and fry gently for 10 minutes until softened. Transfer to a bowl. Add the rice, walnuts, cheese, egg, breadcrumbs and fromage frais or crème fraîche. Season well and stir until combined.

2 Preheat the oven to 220°C (200°C fan oven) mark 7. Roll out the pastry to a 25.5 × 20.5cm (10 × 8in) rectangle and use to line a 900g (2lb) loaf tin, pressing the dough into the corners. Trim the overhanging pastry and reserve.

3 Spoon the rice mixture into the pastry case and smooth the surface. Divide the pastry trimmings in half, roll each piece into a long thin rope and twist the two ropes together. Dampen the pastry edges and top with the pastry twist, pressing down gently. Cook the terrine in the oven for 45–50 minutes until golden and a skewer inserted into the centre comes out hot. Remove from the oven and leave to cool.

4 To make the topping, heat the redcurrant jelly in a small pan with the lemon juice and 1 tbsp water until melted, then simmer for 3 minutes. Remove from the heat and stir in the fruit.

5 To unmould the pie, turn the loaf tin upside-down and tap gently. Spoon the topping over and leave to set. When cold, garnish with bay leaves.

Cook's Tip
Hot Water Crust Pastry
Sift 225g (8oz) plain flour and a pinch of salt into a bowl and make a well in the middle. Heat 50g (2oz) white vegetable fat and 100ml (3½fl oz) water in a pan until it comes to the boil. Pour into the flour and work together, using a wooden spoon. When cool enough to handle, knead lightly until smooth; use while still warm and pliable.

Serves 8
Preparation Time 45 minutes,
 plus cooling
Cooking Time 1 hour 10 minutes

Nutritional Information (Per Serving)
495 calories, 28g fat (of which 12g saturates), 52g carbohydrate, 0.7g salt
A Little Effort

White Nut Roast

1 Preheat the oven to 200°C (180°C fan oven) mark 6. Melt the butter in a pan and cook the onion and garlic for 5 minutes or until soft. Put into a large bowl and set aside to cool.

2 Add the nuts, breadcrumbs, zest and juice of the lemon, cheese, chestnuts and artichokes. Season well and bind together with the egg. Stir in the chopped herbs.

3 Put the mixture on a large piece of buttered foil and shape into a fat sausage, packing tightly. Scatter with the extra herb sprigs and wrap in the foil.

4 Cook on a baking sheet for 35 minutes, then unwrap the foil slightly and cook for a further 15 minutes until turning golden.

40g (1½oz) butter
1 onion, finely chopped
1 garlic clove, crushed
225g (8oz) mixed white nuts, such as brazils, macadamias, pinenuts and whole almonds, ground in a food processor
125g (4oz) fresh white breadcrumbs
grated zest and juice of ½ lemon
75g (3oz) sage Derby cheese or Parmesan, grated (see Cook's Tip, page 35)
125g (4oz) cooked, peeled (or vacuum-packed) chestnuts, roughly chopped
½ x 400g can artichoke hearts, roughly chopped
1 medium egg, lightly beaten
2 tsp each freshly chopped parsley, sage and thyme, plus extra sprigs
salt and ground black pepper

Freezing Tip

To freeze Complete the recipe to the end of step 3, cool, cover and freeze for up to one month.

To use Cook from frozen for 45 minutes, then unwrap the foil slightly and cook for a further 15 minutes until turning golden.

Nutritional Information (Per Serving)
371 calories, 28g fat (of which 9g saturates), 20g carbohydrate, 0.8g salt
Easy

Serves 8
Preparation Time 20 minutes
Cooking Time about 1 hour

Breads, biscuits and cakes

Black Olive Bread

Walnut and Garlic Bread

Griddled Garlic Bread

Corn Bread

Apricot and Hazelnut Bread

Salt and Pepper Rolls

White and Dark Chocolate Cookies

Peanut and Raisin Cookies

Sultana and Pecan Cookies

Chocolate and Pistachio Biscotti

Almond Macaroons

Double-chocolate Brownies

Sticky Lemon Polenta Cake

Lamingtons

Mini Green Tea Cupcakes

Blackberry and Cinnamon Yogurt Loaf

Carrot Traybake

Fruity Teacake

Black Olive Bread

2 tsp traditional dried yeast
500g (1lb 2oz) strong white bread
    flour, plus extra to dust
2 tsp coarse salt, plus extra to sprinkle
6 tbsp extra virgin olive oil, plus extra
    to grease
100g (3½oz) black olives, pitted
    and chopped

1 Put 150ml (¼ pint) hand-hot water into a jug, stir in the yeast and leave for 10 minutes or until foamy. Put the flour into a bowl or a food processor, then add the salt, yeast mix, 200ml (7fl oz) warm water and 2 tbsp olive oil. Mix using a wooden spoon or the dough hook for 2–3 minutes to make a soft smooth dough. Put the dough into a lightly oiled bowl, cover with oiled clingfilm and leave in a warm place for 45 minutes or until doubled in size. Punch the dough to knock out the air, then knead on a lightly floured worksurface for 1 minute. Add the olives and knead until combined. Divide in half, shape into rectangles and put into two greased tins, each about 25.5 × 15cm (10 × 6in). Cover with clingfilm and leave in a warm place for 1 hour or until the dough is puffy.

2 Preheat the oven to 200°C (180°C fan oven) mark 6. Press your finger into the dough 12 times, drizzle 2 tbsp oil over the surface and sprinkle with salt. Bake for 30–35 minutes until golden. Drizzle with the remaining oil. Slice and serve warm.

Makes 2 loaves
Preparation Time 40 minutes,
    plus rising
Cooking Time 30–35 minutes

Nutritional Information (Per Loaf)
600 calories, 21g fat (of which 3g saturates), 97g carbohydrate, 3.8g salt
Dairy Free · Easy

Walnut and Garlic Bread

1 Lightly grease a 20.5cm (8in) springform tin. Put the flour, yeast and salt into a freestanding mixer with a dough hook. Add 300ml (½ pint) lukewarm water and the malt extract, then mix to a pliable dough. Increase the speed and machine-knead for 5 minutes.

2 On a lightly floured worksurface, roll the dough into a rectangle about 40.5 × 28cm (16 × 11in). Mix together the butter and garlic and spread over the dough. Scatter the walnuts over and, starting at one long edge, roll up the dough into a sausage. Cut into eight slices and put in the prepared tin. Cover with lightly oiled clingfilm and leave to rise in a warm place for 45 minutes or until doubled in size.

3 Preheat the oven to 220°C (200°C fan oven) mark 7 and put a baking sheet in to heat. Remove the clingfilm, cover the bread with foil and put on the hot baking sheet. Bake for 20 minutes. Reduce the oven temperature to 200°C (180°C fan oven) mark 6 and bake for 1 hour 10 minutes. Brush with the glaze and bake, uncovered, for a further 5 minutes or until golden brown. Leave in the tin to cool slightly. Serve warm.

Freezing Tip

To freeze Follow the recipe and cooking times in step 3, but don't glaze and bake for the final 5 minutes. Leave to cool in the tin. Wrap and freeze for up to two months.

To use Thaw, uncovered, at room temperature for 6 hours. Glaze the bread, put it on a hot baking sheet and bake at 220°C (200°C fan oven) mark 7 for 8–10 minutes until hot throughout.

oil to grease
500g (1lb 2oz) strong white bread
    flour with kibbled grains of rye
    and wheat, plus extra to dust
7g sachet fast-action dried yeast
2 tsp salt
1 tbsp malt extract
50g (2oz) butter, softened
3 garlic cloves, crushed
100g (3½oz) walnut pieces

FOR THE GLAZE
1 tbsp milk mixed with 1 tbsp
    malt extract

Nutritional Information (Per Serving)
359 calories, 15g fat (of which 4g saturates), 52g carbohydrate, 1.3g salt
Easy

Serves 8
Preparation Time 25 minutes,
    plus rising
Cooking Time about 1 hour 35 minutes

Griddled Garlic Bread

1 large crusty loaf
175g (6oz) butter, cubed
3 garlic cloves, crushed
a bunch of stiff-stemmed fresh
    thyme sprigs
salt and ground black pepper

1 Cut the bread into 2cm (¾in) thick slices.

2 Put the butter and garlic into a small metal or heatproof dish (a tin mug is ideal) and sit it on the barbecue grill. Leave to melt. Season with salt and pepper.

3 Dip the thyme into the melted butter and brush one side of each slice of bread. Put the slices, buttered side down, on the barbecue grill. Cook for 1–2 minutes until crisp and golden. Brush the uppermost sides with the remaining butter, turn over and cook the other side. Serve immediately.

Serves 8
Preparation Time 5 minutes
Cooking Time 5–6 minutes

Nutritional Information (Per Serving)
400 calories, 20g fat (of which 11g saturates), 50g carbohydrate, 1.6g salt
Easy

Corn Bread

1 Preheat the oven to 200°C (180°C fan oven) mark 6. Generously grease a 20.5cm (8in) square shallow tin.

2 Put the flour into a large bowl, then add the polenta or cornmeal, the baking powder, sugar and salt. Make a well in the centre and pour in the buttermilk or yogurt and milk mixture. Add the eggs and olive oil and stir together until evenly mixed.

3 Pour into the tin and bake for 25–30 minutes until firm to the touch. Insert a skewer into the centre – if it comes out clean, the cornbread is done.

4 Leave the cornbread to rest in the tin for 5 minutes, then turn out and cut into chunky triangles. Serve warm with butter.

oil to grease
125g (4oz) plain flour
175g (6oz) polenta (see Cook's Tip) or cornmeal
1 tbsp baking powder
1 tbsp caster sugar
½ tsp salt
300ml (½ pint) buttermilk, or equal quantities of natural yogurt and milk, mixed together
2 medium eggs
4 tbsp extra virgin olive oil

Cook's Tip
Use dried polenta grains for this recipe.

Nutritional Information (Per Serving)
229 calories, 8g fat (of which 1g saturates), 33g carbohydrate, 1.3g salt
Easy

Serves 8
Preparation Time 5 minutes
Cooking Time 25–30 minutes

Apricot and Hazelnut Bread

75g (3oz) hazelnuts
450g (1lb) strong Granary bread
   flour, plus extra to dust
1 tsp salt
25g (1oz) unsalted butter, diced,
   plus extra to grease
75g (3oz) ready-to-eat dried
   apricots, chopped
2 tsp fast-action dried yeast
2 tbsp molasses
milk to glaze

1 Spread the hazelnuts on a baking sheet. Toast under a hot grill until golden brown, turning frequently. Put the hazelnuts in a clean teatowel and rub off the skins. Leave to cool. Chop and put to one side.

2 Put the flour into a large bowl. Add the salt, then rub in the butter. Stir in the hazelnuts, apricots and yeast. Make a well in the middle and gradually work in the molasses and about 225ml (8fl oz) hand-hot water to form a soft dough, adding a little more water if the dough feels dry. Knead for 8–10 minutes until smooth, then transfer the dough to a greased bowl. Cover and leave to rise in a warm place for 1–1¼ hours until doubled in size.

3 Punch the dough to knock back, then divide in half. Shape each portion into a small, flattish round and put on a well-floured baking sheet. Cover loosely and leave to rise for a further 30 minutes.

4 Preheat the oven to 220°C (200°C fan oven) mark 7 and put a large baking sheet on the top shelf to heat up.

5 Using a sharp knife, cut several slashes on each round, brush with a little milk and transfer to the heated baking sheet. Bake for 15 minutes, then reduce the oven temperature to 190°C (170°C fan oven) mark 5 and bake for a further 15–20 minutes until the bread is risen and sounds hollow when tapped underneath. Turn out of the tin on to a wire rack to cool.

To Store
Store in an airtight container. It will keep for up to two days.

Try Something Different
Replace the hazelnuts with walnuts or pecan nuts and use sultanas instead of apricots.

BREADS, BISCUITS AND CAKES

Makes 2 loaves
Preparation Time 25 minutes, plus rising
Cooking Time 30–35 minutes,
   plus cooling

Nutritional Information (Per Serving)
94 calories, 3g fat (of which 1g saturates), 14g carbohydrate, 0g salt
Easy

Salt and Pepper Rolls

1 Sift the flour into a large warmed bowl. Stir in the yeast. Crush the salt and peppercorns in a pestle and mortar and stir into the flour. Make a well in the centre of the flour, then pour in the oil and enough lukewarm water to make a soft dough – about 500ml (almost 1 pint). Knead for 5 minutes or until smooth. (Alternatively, put the flour, yeast, salt, peppercorns, oil and water in a freestanding mixer and knead to a soft dough with a dough hook.)

2 Transfer the dough to a large oiled bowl, cover with oiled clingfilm and leave in a warm place until doubled in size.

3 Turn the dough out on to a lightly floured worksurface and knead for about 5 minutes. Return the dough to the oiled bowl, cover with oiled clingfilm and leave in a warm place until doubled in size.

4 Punch the dough to knock back, then knead for 1 minute. Divide into 16 pieces and shape each one into a roll. Put the rolls on greased baking sheets, spaced well apart, cover with oiled clingfilm and leave for 30 minutes or until spongy. Preheat the oven to 220°C (200°C fan oven) mark 7.

5 Brush the rolls with beaten egg, sprinkle with a little salt and bake for 30–35 minutes until golden. Serve warm.

700g (1½lb) strong white bread flour, plus extra to dust
7g sachet fast-action dried yeast
1 tsp sea salt flakes, plus extra to sprinkle
1 tsp red peppercorns
1 tsp green peppercorns
2 tbsp olive oil, plus extra to grease
1 medium egg, beaten

Freezing Tip

To freeze Complete the recipe, but only bake the rolls for 25 minutes, then cool, wrap and freeze for up to three months.

To use Bake from frozen in a preheated oven at 200°C (180°C fan oven) mark 6 for 12–15 minutes until golden and piping hot throughout.

Nutritional Information (Per Roll)
157 calories, 2g fat (of which trace saturates), 33g carbohydrate, 0.3g salt
Dairy Free · Easy

Makes 16
Preparation Time 40 minutes, plus rising
Cooking Time 30–35 minutes

White and Dark
Chocolate Cookies

125g (4oz) unsalted butter, softened, plus extra to grease
125g (4oz) golden caster sugar
2 medium eggs, beaten
2 tsp vanilla extract
250g (9oz) self-raising flour, sifted
finely grated zest of 1 orange
100g (3½oz) white chocolate, roughly chopped
100g (3½oz) plain chocolate (at least 70% cocoa solids), roughly chopped

1 Preheat the oven to 180°C (160°C fan oven) mark 4. Lightly grease three baking sheets.

2 Cream the butter and sugar together until the mixture is pale and fluffy. Gradually beat in the eggs and vanilla extract. Sift in the flour, then add the orange zest and sprinkle in the white and plain chocolate. Mix the dough together with your hands. Knead lightly, then wrap in clingfilm and chill for at least 30 minutes.

3 Divide the mixture into 26 pieces and roll each into a ball. Using a dampened palette knife, flatten each ball slightly to make a disc, then put on the prepared baking sheets, spaced well apart.

4 Bake for 10–12 minutes until golden. Leave on the baking sheets for 5 minutes, then transfer to a wire rack to cool completely.

To Store
Store in an airtight container.
They will keep for up to one week.

Makes 26
Preparation Time 15 minutes, plus chilling
Cooking Time 10–12 minutes, plus cooling

Nutritional Information (Per Cookie)
133 calories, 7g fat (of which 4g saturates), 17g carbohydrate, 0.1g salt
Easy

Peanut and Raisin Cookies

1 Preheat the oven to 190°C (170°C fan oven) mark 5 and grease two baking sheets. Beat together all the ingredients except the raisins, until well blended. Stir in the raisins.

2 Spoon large teaspoonfuls of the mixture, spaced well apart, on to the prepared baking sheets, leaving room for the mixture to spread.

3 Bake for about 15 minutes or until golden brown around the edges. Leave to cool slightly, then transfer to a wire rack to cool completely.

125g (4oz) unsalted butter, softened, plus extra to grease
150g (5oz) caster sugar
1 medium egg
150g (5oz) plain flour, sifted
½ tsp baking powder
½ tsp salt
125g (4oz) crunchy peanut butter
175g (6oz) raisins

To Store
Store in an airtight container.
They will keep for up to three days.

Try Something Different
Chocolate Nut Cookies
Omit the peanut butter and raisins and add 1 tsp vanilla extract. Stir in 175g (6oz) roughly chopped chocolate and 75g (3oz) roughly chopped walnuts.

Coconut and Cherry Cookies
Omit the peanut butter and raisins, reduce the sugar to 75g (3oz) and stir in 50g (2oz) desiccated coconut and 125g (4oz) rinsed, roughly chopped glacé cherries.

Oat and Cinnamon Cookies
Omit the peanut butter and raisins and add 1 tsp vanilla extract. Stir in 1 tsp ground cinnamon and 75g (3oz) rolled oats.

BREADS, BISCUITS AND CAKES

Nutritional Information (Per Cookie)
111 calories, 6g fat (of which 3g saturates), 14g carbohydrate, 0.2g salt
Easy

Makes 30
Preparation Time 10 minutes
Cooking Time 15 minutes, plus cooling

Sultana and Pecan Cookies

225g (8oz) unsalted butter, at room
  temperature, plus extra to grease
175g (6oz) light muscovado sugar
2 medium eggs, lightly beaten
225g (8oz) pecan nut halves
300g (11oz) self-raising flour, sifted
¼ tsp baking powder
125g (4oz) sultanas
2 tbsp maple syrup

1 Preheat the oven to 190°C (170°C fan oven) mark 5. Lightly grease four baking sheets.

2 Cream the butter and sugar together until the mixture is pale and fluffy. Gradually beat in the eggs until thoroughly combined.

3 Put 20 pecan nut halves to one side, then roughly chop the rest and fold into the mixture with the flour, baking powder, sultanas and syrup.

4 Roll the mixture into 20 balls and place them, spaced well apart, on to the prepared baking sheets. Using a dampened palette knife, flatten the cookies and top each with a piece of pecan nut.

5 Bake for 12–15 minutes until pale golden. Leave on the baking sheets for 5 minutes, then transfer to a wire rack to cool completely.

To Store
Store in an airtight container.
They will keep for up to one week.

Freezing Tip
To freeze Complete the recipe to the end of step 4, then open-freeze a tray of unbaked cookies. When frozen, pack into bags or containers.

To use Cook from frozen for 18–20 minutes.

Makes 20
Preparation Time 15 minutes
Cooking Time 12–15 minutes,
  plus cooling

Nutritional Information (Per Cookie)
276 calories, 18g fat (of which 7g saturates), 27g carbohydrate, 0.2g salt
Easy

Chocolate and Pistachio
Biscotti

1 Preheat the oven to 180°C (160°C fan oven) mark 4. Line a large baking sheet with baking parchment.

2 Mix the flour with the cocoa powder, baking powder, chocolate chips, pistachio nuts and salt. Using a hand-held electric whisk, beat the butter and granulated sugar together until light and fluffy. Gradually whisk in the beaten eggs.

3 Stir the dry ingredients into the mixture until it forms a stiff dough. With floured hands, shape the dough into two slightly flattened logs, each about 30.5 × 5cm (12 × 2in). Sprinkle with icing sugar. Put the logs on to the prepared baking sheet and bake for 40–45 minutes until they are slightly firm to the touch.

4 Leave the logs on the baking sheet for 10 minutes, then cut diagonally into 15 slices, 2cm (¾in) thick. Arrange them, cut side down, on the baking sheet and bake again for 15 minutes or until crisp. Cool on a wire rack.

300g (11oz) plain flour, sifted
75g (3oz) cocoa powder, sifted
1 tsp baking powder
150g (5oz) plain chocolate chips
150g (5oz) shelled pistachio nuts
a pinch of salt
75g (3oz) unsalted butter, softened
225g (8oz) granulated sugar
2 large eggs, beaten
1 tbsp icing sugar

To Store
Store in an airtight container. They will keep for up to one month.

Try Something Different
Cranberry, Hazelnut and Orange Biscotti
Increase the flour to 375g (13oz), omit the cocoa powder and add the grated zest of 1 orange. Replace the chocolate chips with dried cranberries and the pistachios with chopped blanched hazelnuts.

Nutritional Information (Per Biscuit)
152 calories, 7g fat (of which 3g saturates), 20g carbohydrate, 0.2g salt
Easy

Makes 30
Preparation Time 15 minutes
Cooking Time about 1 hour, plus cooling

Almond Macaroons

2 medium egg whites
125g (4oz) caster sugar
125g (4oz) ground almonds
¼ tsp almond extract
22 blanched almonds

1 Preheat the oven to 180°C (160°C fan oven) mark 4. Line baking trays with baking parchment. Whisk the egg whites in a clean, grease-free bowl until stiff peaks form. Gradually whisk in the caster sugar, a little at a time, until thick and glossy. Gently stir in the ground almonds and almond extract.

2 Spoon teaspoonfuls of the mixture on to the prepared baking trays, spacing them slightly apart. Press an almond into the centre of each one and bake in the oven for 12–15 minutes until just golden and firm to the touch.

3 Leave on the baking sheets for 10 minutes, then transfer to wire racks to cool completely. On cooling, these biscuits have a soft, chewy centre; they harden up after a few days.

To Store
Store in airtight containers. They will keep for up to one week.

Makes 22
Preparation Time 10 minutes
Cooking Time 12–15 minutes, plus cooling

Nutritional Information (Per Macaroon)
86 calories, 6g fat (of which 1g saturates), 7g carbohydrate, 0g salt
Gluten Free • Dairy Free • Easy

Double-chocolate Brownies

1 Preheat the oven to 200°C (180°C fan oven) mark 6. Grease a 20.5cm (8in) square shallow tin and baseline with baking parchment. Melt the butter and plain chocolate in a heatproof bowl set over a pan of gently simmering water, making sure the base of the bowl doesn't touch the water. Remove the bowl from the pan and put to one side.

2 In a separate bowl, melt the white chocolate over a pan of gently simmering water, making sure the base of the bowl doesn't touch the water. Remove the bowl from the pan and put to one side.

3 Put the eggs into a separate large bowl. Add the muscovado sugar and vanilla extract and whisk together until the mixture is pale and thick.

4 Add the flour, baking powder, cocoa powder, the pecan nuts and a pinch of salt to the bowl, then carefully pour in the dark chocolate mixture. Using a large metal spoon, gently fold the ingredients together to make a smooth batter – if you fold too roughly, the chocolate will seize up and become unusable.

5 Pour the brownie mixture into the prepared tin. Spoon dollops of the white chocolate over the brownie mix, then swirl a skewer through it several times to create a marbled effect.

6 Bake for 20–25 minutes. The brownie should be fudgy inside and the top should be cracked and crispy. Leave to cool in the tin.

7 Transfer the brownies to a board and cut into 16 individual brownies. To serve, dust with a little icing sugar and cocoa powder.

250g (9oz) butter, plus extra
  to grease
250g (9oz) plain chocolate (at
  least 50% cocoa solids), broken
  into pieces
100g (3½oz) white chocolate,
  broken into pieces
4 medium eggs
175g (6oz) light muscovado sugar
1 tsp vanilla extract
75g (3oz) plain flour, sifted
¼ tsp baking powder
1 tbsp cocoa powder, sifted, plus
  extra to dust
100g (3½oz) pecan nuts, chopped
a pinch of salt
a little icing sugar to dust

Try Something Different
Try making these brownies without butter – believe it or not, this recipe will still work. But you'll need to eat them within an hour of taking them out of the oven – fat is what makes cakes moist and allows them to be stored.

To Store
Complete the recipe to the end of step 6, then store in an airtight tin. It will keep for up to one week. Complete the recipe to serve.

BREADS, BISCUITS AND CAKES

Nutritional Information (Per Brownie)
352 calories, 25g fat (of which 13g saturates), 29g carbohydrate, 0.3g salt
Easy

Cuts into 16 brownies
Preparation Time 15 minutes
Cooking Time 20–25 minutes,
    plus cooling

Sticky Lemon Polenta Cake

50g (2oz) unsalted butter, softened,
    plus extra to grease
3 lemons
250g (9oz) golden caster sugar
250g (9oz) instant polenta
1 tsp wheat-free baking powder
2 large eggs
50ml (2fl oz) semi-skimmed milk
2 tbsp natural yogurt
2 tbsp poppy seeds

1 Preheat the oven to 180°C (160°C fan oven) mark 4. Lightly grease a 900g (2lb) loaf tin and baseline with greaseproof paper.

2 Grate the zest of 1 lemon and put into a food processor with the butter, 200g (7oz) sugar, the polenta, baking powder, eggs, milk, yogurt and poppy seeds, then whiz until smooth. Spoon the mixture into the prepared tin and level the surface. Bake for 55 minutes–1 hour until a skewer inserted into the centre comes out clean. Leave to cool in the tin for 10 minutes.

3 Next, make a syrup. Squeeze the juice from the zested lemon plus 1 more lemon. Thinly slice the third lemon. Put the lemon juice into a pan with the remaining sugar and 150ml (¼ pint) water. Add the lemon slices, bring to the boil and bubble for about 10 minutes or until syrupy. Take the pan off the heat and leave to cool for 5 minutes. Remove the lemon slices from the syrup and set aside.

4 Slide a knife around the edge of the cake and turn out on to a serving plate. Pierce the cake in several places with a skewer, spoon the syrup over it and decorate with the lemon slices.

To Store
Wrap in clingfilm and store in an airtight container. It will keep for up to three days.

Cuts into 12 slices
Preparation Time 10 minutes
Cooking Time 1 hour, plus cooling

Nutritional Information (Per Slice)
220 calories, 7g fat (of which 3g saturates), 37g carbohydrate, 0.1g salt
Gluten Free • A Little Effort

Lamingtons

1 Preheat the oven to 180°C (160°C fan oven) mark 4. Grease a 15cm (6in) square cake tin and baseline with baking parchment.

2 Put the butter, caster sugar, eggs, flour, baking powder and vanilla extract into a bowl and beat with a hand-held electric whisk until creamy. Turn the mixture into the prepared tin and level the surface. Bake for about 30 minutes or until just firm to the touch and a skewer inserted into the centre comes out clean. Transfer to a wire rack to cool completely. Wrap and store, preferably overnight, so that the cake is easier to slice.

3 To make the topping, sift the icing sugar and cocoa powder into a bowl. Put the butter and milk into a small pan and heat until the butter has just melted. Pour over the icing sugar and stir until smooth, adding 2–3 tbsp water if necessary, so that the icing thickly coats the back of a spoon.

4 Trim the side crusts from the cake and cut into 16 squares. Place a sheet of greaseproof paper under a wire rack to catch the drips. Scatter the coconut on to a large plate. Pierce a piece of cake through the top crust and dip into the icing until coated, turning the cake gently. Transfer to the wire rack. Once you've coated half the pieces, roll them in the coconut and transfer to a plate. Repeat with the remainder and leave to set for a couple of hours before serving.

To Store
Store in an airtight container. They will keep for up to 2 days.

Cook's Tip
If, towards the end of coating the cakes, the chocolate topping mixture has thickened, carefully stir in a drop of water to thin it down.

125g (4oz) unsalted butter, softened, plus extra to grease
125g (4oz) golden caster sugar
2 medium eggs
125g (4oz) self-raising flour, sifted
1 tsp baking powder
2 tsp vanilla extract

FOR THE COATING
200g (7oz) icing sugar
50g (2oz) cocoa powder
25g (1oz) unsalted butter, cubed
5 tbsp milk
200g (7oz) desiccated coconut

Nutritional Information (Per Square)
273 calories, 17g fat (of which 12g saturates), 29g carbohydrate, 0.4g salt
Easy

Cuts into 16 squares
Preparation Time 40 minutes
Cooking Time 30 minutes, plus cooling and setting

BREADS, BISCUITS AND CAKES

Mini Green Tea Cupcakes

100ml (3½fl oz) milk
2 tsp loose green tea leaves
100g (3½oz) unsalted butter, softened
125g (4oz) caster sugar
2 medium eggs
150g (5oz) self-raising flour, sifted
¼ tsp baking powder

FOR THE TOPPING AND DECORATION

3 tsp loose green tea leaves
about 75ml (2½fl oz) boiling water
75g (3oz) unsalted butter, softened
250g (9oz) icing sugar, sifted
ready-made sugar flowers

1 Preheat the oven to 190°C (170°C fan oven), mark 5. Line a 12-hole muffin tin with paper fairy cake or bun cases.

2 Put the milk into a small saucepan and bring to the boil. Add the green tea leaves and leave to infuse for 30 minutes.

3 Using a hand-held electric whisk, whisk the butter and caster sugar in a bowl, or beat with a wooden spoon, until pale and creamy. Gradually whisk in the eggs until just combined. Pass the green tea milk through a sieve into the bowl, then discard the tea. Using a metal spoon, fold in the flour and baking powder until combined. Divide the mixture equally between the paper cases.

4 Bake for 18–20 minutes until golden and risen. Leave to cool in the tin for 5 minutes, then transfer to a wire rack to cool completely.

5 For the topping, put the green tea leaves into a jug, add about 75ml (2½fl oz) boiling water and leave to infuse for 5 minutes. Put the butter into a bowl and whisk until fluffy. Gradually add the icing sugar and whisk until combined. Pass the green tea through a sieve into the bowl, then discard the tea. Continue to whisk until light and fluffy.

6 Insert a star nozzle into a piping bag, then fill the bag with the buttercream and pipe a swirl on to the top of each cake. Decorate each with a sugar flower.

To Store

Store in an airtight container. They will keep for 3–5 days.

Freezing Tip

To freeze Complete the recipe to the end of step 4. Open-freeze, then wrap and freeze.

To use Thaw for about 1 hour, then complete the recipe.

Makes 12
Preparation Time 40 minutes
Cooking Time 25 minutes, plus cooling and infusing

Nutritional Information (Per Cupcake)
282 calories, 13g fat (of which 8g saturates), 41g carbohydrate, 0.3g salt
Easy

Blackberry and Cinnamon
Yogurt Loaf

1 Preheat the oven to 190°C (170°C fan oven) mark 5. Grease a 900g (2lb) loaf tin and baseline with baking parchment.

2 Sift the flour, baking powder and cinnamon into a bowl, add the frozen berries and toss to coat. Make a well in the centre.

3 In another bowl, whisk the caster sugar, oil, lemon zest and juice, yogurt and eggs together. Pour into the well in the flour mixture and stir.

4 Spoon the mixture into the prepared tin, level the surface and bake for 55 minutes or until a skewer inserted into the centre comes out clean (cover lightly with foil, if necessary, to prevent over-browning). Leave to cool in the tin. Remove from the tin and dust with icing sugar to serve.

125ml (4fl oz) sunflower oil, plus extra to grease
175g (6oz) plain flour
1½ tsp baking powder
1½ tsp ground cinnamon
200g (7oz) frozen blackberries
125g (4oz) golden caster sugar
grated zest and juice of 1 lemon
125g (4oz) Greek yogurt
3 medium eggs, beaten
icing sugar to dust

To Store
Store in an airtight container. It will keep for up to two days.

Try Something Different
Apple and Cinnamon Yogurt Loaf
Replace the blackberries with 2 small Cox's or Braeburn apples, peeled, cored and chopped.

Raspberry and White Chocolate Yogurt Loaf
Omit the ground cinnamon. Replace the blackberries with 125g (4oz) frozen raspberries and 75g (3oz) chopped white chocolate, and use orange zest and juice instead of lemon.

BREADS, BISCUITS AND CAKES

Nutritional Information (Per Slice)
287 calories, 15g fat (of which 3g saturates), 35g carbohydrate, 0.1g salt
Easy

Cuts into 8 slices
Preparation Time 15 minutes
Cooking Time 55 minutes, plus cooling

Carrot Traybake

100g (3½oz) unsalted butter, chopped, plus extra to grease
140g (4½oz) carrots, grated
100g (3½oz) sultanas
100g (3½oz) chopped dried dates
50g (2oz) tenderised coconut
1 tsp ground cinnamon
½ tsp freshly grated nutmeg
330g bottle maple syrup
150ml (¼ pint) apple juice
zest and juice of 2 oranges
225g (8oz) wholemeal self-raising flour, sifted
2 tsp bicarbonate of soda
125g (4oz) walnut pieces

FOR THE TOPPING
pared zest from ½–1 orange
200g (7oz) cream cheese
200g (7oz) crème fraîche
2 tbsp icing sugar
1 tsp vanilla extract

To Store
Store in an airtight container. It will keep for up to 5 days.

1 Preheat the oven to 190°C (170°C fan oven) mark 5. Grease a 23 × 23cm (9 × 9in) cake tin and line with greaseproof paper.

2 Put the butter, carrots, sultanas, dates, coconut, spices, syrup, apple juice and orange zest and juice into a large pan. Cover and bring to the boil, then cook for 5 minutes. Tip into a bowl and leave to cool.

3 Put the flour, bicarbonate of soda and walnuts into a large bowl and stir together. Add the cooled carrot mixture and stir well. Spoon the mixture into the prepared tin and level the surface.

4 Bake for 45 minutes–1 hour until firm. Leave to cool in the tin for 10 minutes, then turn out on to a wire rack to cool completely.

5 To make the topping, finely slice the orange zest. Put the cream cheese, crème fraîche, icing sugar and vanilla into a bowl and stir with a spatula. Spread over the cake and top with the zest. Cut into 15 squares to serve.

250

Cuts into 15 squares
Preparation Time 30 minutes
Cooking Time 50 minutes–1 hour 5 minutes

Nutritional Information (Per Square)
399 calories, 25g fat (of which 13g saturates), 41g carbohydrate, 0.4g salt
Easy

Fruity Teacake

1 Pour the tea into a bowl and add all the dried fruit. Leave to soak for 30 minutes.

2 Preheat the oven to 190°C (170°C fan oven) mark 5. Oil a 900g (2lb) loaf tin and baseline with greaseproof paper.

3 Beat the sugar and eggs together until pale and slightly thickened. Add the flour, baking powder, mixed spice and soaked dried fruit and tea, then mix together well. Spoon the mixture into the prepared tin and level the surface.

4 Bake on the middle shelf of the oven for 45 minutes–1 hour. Leave to cool in the tin.

5 Serve sliced, with a little butter if you like.

150ml (¼ pint) hot black tea, made with 2 Earl Grey tea bags
200g (7oz) sultanas
75g (3oz) ready-to-eat dried figs, roughly chopped
75g (3oz) ready-to-eat dried prunes, roughly chopped
a little vegetable oil
125g (4oz) dark muscovado sugar
2 medium eggs, beaten
225g (8oz) gluten-free flour
2 tsp wheat-free baking powder
2 tsp ground mixed spice

To Store
Wrap the cake in clingfilm and store in an airtight container. It will keep for up to five days.

Nutritional Information (Per Slice)
185 calories, 1g fat (of which trace saturates), 42g carbohydrate, 0.1g salt
Gluten Free • Dairy Free • Easy

Cuts Into 12 slices
Preparation Time 20 minutes, plus soaking
Cooking Time 1 hour, plus cooling

Desserts and puddings

Almond Toffee Meringues

Baked Alaska

Italian Ice Cream Cake

Summer Pudding

Tropical Fruit and Coconut Trifle

Sticky Banoffee Pies

Pistachio Baklava

Fruity Rice Pudding

Exotic Fruit Salad

Strawberry Brûlée

Spiced Winter Fruit

Baked Raspberry Meringue Pie

Maple Pecan Pie

Pear and Blackberry Crumble

Quick Gooey Chocolate Puddings

Chocolate Crêpes with a Boozy Sauce

Cinnamon Pancakes

Baked Apples with Butterscotch Sauce

Griddled Peaches

Baked Apricots with Almonds

Almond Toffee Meringues

1. To make the marinated fruit, put the crème de cassis, orange juice and redcurrant jelly into a small pan. Heat gently to melt, then bubble for 2–3 minutes until syrupy. Pour into a large bowl to cool. Add the raspberries and nectarines and stir gently. Cover and chill.

2. Preheat the oven to 170°C (150°C fan oven) mark 3 and preheat the grill. Lightly oil a baking sheet and sprinkle the muscovado sugar over it. Grill for 2–3 minutes until the sugar begins to bubble and caramelise. Cool for about 15 minutes, then break the sugar into a food processor and whiz to a coarse powder.

3. Put the egg whites and caster sugar into a large, clean bowl set over a pan of gently simmering water. Stir until the sugar has dissolved and the egg white is warm (about 10 minutes). Remove from the heat and place on a teatowel. Beat with a hand-held electric whisk for at least 15 minutes or until cold and glossy and standing in stiff, shiny peaks when the whisk is lifted. Cover two baking sheets with baking parchment. Fold half the powdered sugar into the meringue mixture. Spoon four oval mounds on to the baking sheets, leaving plenty of space between each. Sprinkle with flaked almonds and the remaining powdered sugar. Bake for 20 minutes, then turn off the heat and leave in the oven to dry out overnight. Serve with the marinated fruit and lightly whipped cream.

oil to grease
25g (1oz) light muscovado sugar
100g (3½oz) egg whites (about 3 medium eggs)
225g (8oz) caster sugar
25g (1oz) flaked almonds
lightly whipped cream to serve

FOR THE MARINATED SUMMER FRUIT
125ml (4fl oz) crème de cassis
juice of 1 orange
2 tbsp redcurrant jelly
200g (7oz) raspberries
4 nectarines, halved, stoned and sliced

Cook's Tips

Make sure the bowl does not touch the hot water while you make the meringues.

The flavour of the marinated fruit will be even better if you chill it overnight. (If the syrup thickens during chilling, stir in 1–2 tbsp orange juice.)

DESSERTS AND PUDDINGS

Makes 4
Preparation Time 35 minutes
Cooking Time 22–25 minutes, plus cooling and drying

Nutritional Information (Per Meringue)
458 calories, 4g fat (of which trace saturates), 95g carbohydrate, 0.2g salt
Easy

Baked Alaska

1 Put the flan case on an ovenproof plate. Spoon the orange juice over the sponge, then spread the jam over. Scoop the ice cream on top of the jam, then put in the freezer for at least 30 minutes.

2 Put the egg whites into a large, clean, grease-free bowl and whisk until stiff. Beat in the cream of tartar and salt. Use a large spoon to fold in the sugar, 1 tbsp at a time, then whisk until very thick and shiny.

3 Spoon the meringue over the ice cream to cover, making sure that the meringue is sealed to the flan case edge all the way round. Freeze for at least 1 hour or overnight.

4 Preheat the oven to 230°C (210°C fan oven) mark 8. Bake for 3–4 minutes until the meringue is tinged golden brown. Serve immediately. If the Baked Alaska has been in the freezer overnight, bake and leave to stand for about 15 minutes before serving.

1 large sponge flan case, 25.5cm (10in) diameter
5 tbsp orange juice
7 tbsp jam – any kind
1.5 litre tub vanilla ice cream
6 large egg whites
a pinch of cream of tartar
a pinch of salt
275g (10oz) golden caster sugar

Try Something Different
Replace the jam with ginger conserve and use ginger ice cream instead of vanilla.

Nutritional Information (Per Serving)
659 calories, 30g fat (of which 17g saturates), 1g carbohydrate, 0.5g salt
Easy

Serves 8
Preparation Time 30 minutes, plus freezing
Cooking Time 3–4 minutes

Italian Ice Cream Cake

1. Put the cherries and Amaretto into a bowl, stir, cover with clingfilm and put to one side. Pour the crème de cacao into a shallow dish. Quickly dip a sponge finger into the liqueur on one side only, then cut in half lengthways to separate the sugary side from the base. Repeat with each biscuit.

2. Double-line a deep 24 × 4cm (9½ × 1½ in) round tin with clingfilm. Arrange the sugar-coated sponge finger halves, sugar side down, in the bottom of the tin. Drizzle with any remaining crème de cacao.

3. Put the egg yolks and caster sugar into a bowl and whisk until pale, light and fluffy. Fold in the cream, vanilla extract, nuts, chocolate and cherries with Amaretto. Spoon on top of the sponge fingers in the tin and cover with the remaining sponge finger halves, cut side down. Cover with clingfilm and freeze for at least 5 hours.

4. Upturn the cake on to a serving plate and remove the clingfilm. Sift cocoa powder and icing sugar over the cake and cut into wedges. Before serving, leave at room temperature for 20 minutes if the weather is warm, 40 minutes at cool room temperature, or 1 hour in the fridge, to allow the cherries to thaw and the ice cream to become mousse-like.

- 400g (14oz) fresh cherries, pitted and quartered
- 4 tbsp Amaretto liqueur
- 10 tbsp crème de cacao liqueur
- 200g (7oz) Savoiardi biscuits or sponge fingers
- 5 medium egg yolks
- 150g (5oz) golden caster sugar
- 450ml (¾ pint) double cream, lightly whipped
- 1 tbsp vanilla extract
- 75g (3oz) pistachio nuts or hazelnuts, roughly chopped
- 75g (3oz) plain chocolate (at least 70% cocoa solids), roughly chopped
- 2–3 tbsp cocoa powder
- 2–3 tbsp golden icing sugar

Cook's Tip

For a decorative top, use the tin to cut a template circle of greaseproof paper, then fold to make eight triangles. Cut these out. Put four on the cake and dust the uncovered cake with cocoa powder. Remove the triangles. Cover the cocoa with four triangles and dust the uncovered cake with icing sugar.

Cuts into 10 slices
Preparation Time 30 minutes, plus freezing and softening

Nutritional Information (Per Slice)
522 calories, 33g fat (of which 15g saturates), 46g carbohydrate, 0.2g salt
Easy

Summer Pudding

1 Put the redcurrants and blackcurrants into a medium pan. Add the sugar and cassis. Bring to a simmer and cook for 3–5 minutes until the sugar has dissolved. Add the raspberries and cook for 2 minutes. Once the fruit is cooked, taste it – there should be a good balance between tart and sweet.

2 Meanwhile, line a 1 litre (1¾ pint) bowl with clingfilm. Put the base of the bowl on one piece of bread and cut around it. Put the circle of bread in the bottom of the bowl.

3 Line the inside of the bowl with more slices of bread, slightly overlapping them to prevent any gaps. Spoon in the fruit, making sure the juice soaks into the bread. Keep back a few spoonfuls of juice in case the bread is unevenly soaked when you turn out the pudding.

4 Cut the remaining bread to fit the top of the pudding neatly, using a sharp knife to trim any excess bread from around the edges. Wrap in clingfilm, weigh down with a saucer and a can and chill overnight.

5 To serve, unwrap the outer clingfilm, upturn the pudding on to a plate and remove the inner clingfilm. Drizzle with the reserved juice and serve with crème fraîche or clotted cream, if you like.

800g (1lb 12oz) mixed summer berries, such as 250g (9oz) each redcurrants and blackcurrants and 300g (11oz) raspberries
125g (4oz) golden caster sugar
3 tbsp crème de cassis
9 thick slices slightly stale white bread, crusts removed
crème fraîche or clotted cream to serve (optional)

DESSERTS AND PUDDINGS

Nutritional Information (Per Serving)
173 calories, 1g fat (of which trace saturates), 38g carbohydrate, 0.4g salt
Easy

Serves 8
Preparation Time 10 minutes, plus overnight chilling
Cooking Time 10 minutes

257

Tropical Fruit and Coconut Trifle

1 small pineapple, roughly chopped

2 bananas, thickly sliced

2 × 400g cans mango slices in syrup, drained, syrup reserved

2 passion fruit, halved

175g (6oz) plain sponge, such as Madeira cake, roughly chopped

3 tbsp dark rum (optional)

200ml (7fl oz) coconut cream

500g carton fresh custard

500g carton Greek yogurt

600ml (1 pint) double cream

6 tbsp dark muscovado sugar

1 Put the pineapple pieces into a large trifle bowl, add the banana and mango slices and spoon the passion fruit pulp over them. Top with the chopped sponge, then pour on the rum, if using, and 6 tbsp of the reserved mango syrup.

2 Mix together the coconut cream and custard and pour the mixture over the sponge.

3 Put the Greek yogurt and cream into a bowl and whisk until thick. Spoon or pipe the mixture over the custard, then sprinkle with muscovado sugar. Cover and chill for at least 1 hour before serving.

Get Ahead

To prepare ahead Complete the recipe, cover and chill for up to two days.

Serves 16
Preparation Time 30 minutes, plus chilling

Nutritional Information (Per Serving)
404 calories, 29g fat (of which 18g saturates), 33g carbohydrate, 0.2g salt
Easy

Sticky Banoffee Pies

1 Put the biscuits into a food processor and whiz until they resemble fine crumbs. Alternatively, put them in a plastic bag and crush with a rolling pin. Transfer to a bowl. Add the melted butter and ginger, if using, then process, or stir well, for 1 minute to combine.

2 Butter six 10cm (4in) rings or tartlet tins and line with greaseproof paper. Press the biscuit mixture evenly into the bottom of each ring. Divide the toffee sauce equally among the rings and top with the bananas. Pipe or spoon on the cream, sprinkle with chocolate shavings and chill. Remove from the rings or tins to serve.

150g (5oz) digestive biscuits
75g (3oz) unsalted butter, melted, plus extra to grease
1 tsp ground ginger (optional)
450g (1lb) dulce de leche toffee sauce
4 bananas, peeled, sliced and tossed in the juice of 1 lemon
300ml (½ pint) double cream, lightly whipped
plain chocolate shavings

Cook's Tip
Slightly overripe bananas are ideal for this recipe.

DESSERTS AND PUDDINGS

Nutritional Information (Per Serving)
827 calories, 55g fat (of which 32g saturates), 84g carbohydrate, 1.2g salt
Easy

Serves 6
Preparation Time 15 minutes, plus chilling

259

Pistachio Baklava

175g (6oz) shelled, unsalted
  pistachio nuts
125g (4oz) pinenuts
1 tsp ground cinnamon
½ tsp ground cloves
a pinch of freshly grated nutmeg
2 tbsp caster sugar
225g (8oz) filo pastry, thawed
  if frozen
75g (3oz) unsalted butter, melted

FOR THE SYRUP
grated zest and juice of ½ lemon
225g (8oz) clear honey
2 cardamom pods, bruised
2 tbsp rosewater (optional)

1 Preheat the oven to 180°C (160°C fan oven) mark 4. Put the pistachio nuts, pinenuts, cinnamon, cloves and nutmeg into a food processor and pulse briefly until coarsely ground. Stir in the caster sugar.

2 Brush a sheet of filo pastry with melted butter and press into an 18 × 25.5cm (7 × 10in) baking tin. Continue to brush and layer half the filo. Scatter the nut mixture over, then top with the remaining filo sheets, brushing each with butter. Score through the pastry in a diamond pattern. Drizzle over any remaining butter and bake for 20 minutes. Reduce the oven temperature to 170°C (150°C fan oven) mark 3 and bake for a further 20–25 minutes until crisp and golden.

3 To make the syrup, put the lemon zest and juice, honey, cardamom pods and 150ml (¼ pint) water into a pan and simmer gently for 5 minutes. Remove from the heat and stir in the rosewater, if using. Pour half the honey syrup evenly over the hot baklava. Leave in the tin until completely cold. Cut into diamond shapes and drizzle with the remaining syrup.

Serves 8
Preparation Time 30 minutes
Cooking Time 40–45 minutes

Nutritional Information (Per Serving)
479 calories, 31g fat (of which 7g saturates), 45g carbohydrate, 0.4g salt
Easy

Fruity Rice Pudding

1. Put the rice into a pan with 600ml (1 pint) cold water and bring to the boil, then reduce the heat and simmer until the liquid has evaporated. Add the milk and bring to the boil, then reduce the heat and simmer for 45 minutes or until the rice is very soft and creamy. Leave to cool.

2. Add the vanilla extract and sugar to the rice. Lightly whip the cream and fold through the pudding. Chill for 1 hour.

3. Divide the rice mixture among six glass dishes and top with 1 tbsp lingonberry sauce.

125g (4oz) pudding rice
1.1 litres (2 pints) full-fat milk
1 tsp vanilla extract
3–4 tbsp caster sugar
200ml (7fl oz) whipping cream
6 tbsp wild lingonberry sauce

Try Something Different

Although wild lingonberry sauce is used here, a spoonful of any fruit sauce or compote, such as strawberry or blueberry, will taste delicious.

For an alternative presentation, serve in tumblers, layering the rice pudding with the fruit sauce; you will need to use double the amount of fruit sauce.

DESSERTS AND PUDDINGS

Nutritional Information (Per Serving)
323 calories, 17g fat (of which 10g saturates), 36g carbohydrate, 0.2g salt
Gluten Free · Easy

Serves 6
Preparation Time 10 minutes, plus cooling and chilling
Cooking Time 1 hour

Exotic Fruit Salad

2 oranges
1 mango, peeled, stoned and chopped
450g (1lb) peeled and diced fresh
   pineapple
200g (7oz) blueberries
½ Charentais melon, cubed
grated zest and juice of 1 lime

1 Using a sharp knife, peel the oranges, remove the pith
and cut the flesh into segments. Put into a bowl.

2 Add the mango, pineapple, blueberries and melon to the
bowl, then add the lime zest and juice. Gently mix together
and serve immediately.

Try Something Different

Use 2 papayas, peeled, seeded
and chopped, instead of the
pineapple.

Mix the seeds of 2 passion fruit
with the lime juice before adding
to the salad.

Serves 4
Preparation Time 10 minutes

Nutritional Information (Per Serving)
187 calories, 1g fat (of which 0g saturates), 47g carbohydrate, 0.1g salt
Gluten Free · Dairy Free · Easy

Strawberry Brûlée

1   Divide the strawberries among four ramekins and sprinkle with icing sugar.

2   Scrape the seeds from the vanilla pod and stir into the yogurt, then spread the mixture evenly over the fruit.

3   Preheat the grill to high. Sprinkle the caster sugar evenly over the yogurt until it's well covered.

4   Put the ramekins on a baking sheet or into the grill pan and grill until the sugar turns dark brown and caramelises. Leave for 15 minutes or until the caramel is cool enough to eat, or chill for up to 2 hours before serving.

250g (9oz) strawberries, hulled and sliced
2 tsp golden icing sugar
1 vanilla pod
400g (14oz) Greek yogurt
100g (3½ oz) golden caster sugar

Try Something Different
Use raspberries or blueberries instead of the strawberries.

Nutritional Information (Per Serving)
240 calories, 10g fat (of which 5g saturates), 35g carbohydrate, 0.2g salt
Gluten Free · Easy

Serves 4
Preparation Time 15 minutes, plus chilling
Cooking Time 5 minutes

Spiced Winter Fruit

150ml (¼ pint) port
150ml (¼ pint) freshly
squeezed orange juice
75g (3oz) light muscovado sugar
1 cinnamon stick
6 whole cardamom pods,
lightly crushed
5cm (2in) piece fresh root ginger,
peeled and thinly sliced
50g (2oz) large muscatel raisins
or dried blueberries
1 small pineapple, peeled,
cored and thinly sliced
1 mango, peeled, stoned
and thickly sliced
3 tangerines, peeled and
halved horizontally
3 fresh figs, halved

1 First, make the syrup. Pour the port and orange juice into a small pan, then add the sugar and 300ml (½ pint) water. Bring to the boil, stirring all the time. Add the cinnamon stick, cardamom pods and ginger, then bubble gently for 15 minutes.

2 Put all the fruit into a serving bowl. Remove the cinnamon stick and cardamom pods from the syrup, then pour the syrup over the fruit. Serve warm or cold.

Freezing Tip

To freeze Tip the fruit and syrup into a freezerproof container, leave to cool, then cover with a tight-fitting lid. Freeze for up to three months.

To use Thaw overnight in the fridge and serve cold.

Cook's Tips

It might sound odd freezing a fruit salad, but it saves all the last-minute chopping and slicing.

Not suitable for children due to the alcohol content.

DESSERTS AND PUDDINGS

Serves 6
Preparation Time 20 minutes
Cooking Time about 20 minutes

Nutritional Information (Per Serving)
222 calories, 0g fat, 48g carbohydrate, 0g salt
Gluten Free · Dairy Free · Easy

Baked Raspberry Meringue Pie

1 Preheat the oven to 230°C (210°C fan oven) mark 8. Put the trifle sponges in the bottom of a 2 litre (3½ pint) ovenproof dish. Spread the raspberries on top and drizzle with the raspberry liqueur.

2 Whisk the egg whites in a clean, grease-free bowl until stiff peaks form. Gradually whisk in the sugar until the mixture is smooth and glossy. Spoon the meringue mixture over the raspberries and bake for 6–8 minutes until golden.

8 trifle sponges
450g (1lb) raspberries, lightly crushed
2–3 tbsp raspberry liqueur
3 medium egg whites
150g (5oz) golden caster sugar

Cook's Tip
If you don't have any raspberry liqueur, you can use another fruit-based liqueur such as Grand Marnier instead.

Nutritional Information (Per Serving)
176 calories, 2g fat (of which 1g saturates), 37g carbohydrate, 0.1g salt
Easy

Serves 8
Preparation Time 15 minutes
Cooking Time 8 minutes

Maple Pecan Pie

250g (9oz) plain flour, sifted
a large pinch of salt
225g (8oz) unsalted butter, cubed
  and chilled
100g (3½oz) light muscovado sugar
125g (4oz) dates, stoned and
  roughly chopped
grated zest and juice of ½ lemon
100ml (3½fl oz) maple syrup, plus
  6 tbsp extra
1 tsp vanilla extract
4 medium eggs
300g (11oz) pecan nut halves
300ml (½ pint) double cream
2 tbsp bourbon whiskey

1 Put the flour and salt into a food processor. Add 125g (4oz) butter and whiz to fine crumbs; add 2 tbsp water and whiz until the mixture just comes together. Wrap in clingfilm and chill for 30 minutes. Use to line a 28 × 4cm (11 × 1½in) loose-bottomed tart tin, then cover and chill for 30 minutes. Preheat the oven to 200°C (180°C fan oven) mark 6.

2 Prick the pastry all over, cover with greaseproof paper and fill with baking beans. Bake for 25 minutes, then remove the paper and beans and bake for a further 5 minutes or until the base is dry and light golden.

3 Meanwhile, whiz the rest of the butter in a food processor to soften. Add the sugar and dates and whiz to cream together. Add the lemon zest and juice, 100ml (3½fl oz) maple syrup, the vanilla extract, eggs and 200g (7oz) nuts. Whiz until the nuts are finely chopped – the mixture will look curdled. Pour into the pastry case and top with the rest of the nuts.

4 Bake for 40–45 minutes until almost set in the middle. Cover with greaseproof paper for the last 10 minutes if the nuts turn very dark. Cool slightly before removing from the tin, then brush with 4 tbsp maple syrup. Lightly whip the cream with the whiskey and 2 tbsp maple syrup, then serve with the pie.

Try Something Different
Replace the lemon with orange, the pecans with walnut halves and the whiskey with Cointreau.

Serves 10
Preparation Time 40 minutes,
  plus chilling
Cooking Time 1¼ hours

Nutritional Information (Per Serving)
748 calories, 57g fat (of which 24g saturates), 51g carbohydrate, 0.6g salt
Easy

Pear and Blackberry Crumble

1. Put the pears and lemon juice into a bowl, add 100g (3½oz) sugar and the mixed spice, then add the blackberries and toss thoroughly to coat.

2. Preheat the oven to 200°C (180°C fan oven) mark 6. Lightly butter a 1.8 litre (3¼ pint) shallow ovenproof dish, then carefully tip the fruit into the dish in an even layer.

3. To make the topping, put the butter, flour, ground almonds and the remaining sugar into a food processor and pulse until the mixture begins to resemble breadcrumbs. Tip into a bowl. (Alternatively, rub the butter into the flour in a large bowl by hand or using a pastry cutter. Stir in the ground almonds and the remaining sugar.) Bring parts of the mixture together with your hands to make lumps.

4. Spoon the crumble topping evenly over the fruit, then bake for 35–45 minutes until the fruit is tender and the crumble is golden and bubbling. Serve with cream, custard or ice cream.

450g (1lb) pears, peeled, cored
   and chopped, tossed with the
   juice of 1 lemon
225g (8oz) golden caster sugar
1 tsp mixed spice
450g (1lb) blackberries
cream, vanilla custard or ice cream
   to serve

FOR THE CRUMBLE TOPPING
100g (3½oz) butter, chopped,
   plus extra to grease
225g (8oz) plain flour
75g (3oz) ground almonds

Cook's Tips

A versatile recipe that can be popped in the oven while you whip up your main course.

Make double the amount of crumble topping and freeze half for an easy pudding another day.

Try Something Different

Crumble is a great way to use leftover, slightly overripe fruit. Replace the pears with apples, or omit the blackberries and use 700g (1½lb) plums or rhubarb instead. You could also use gooseberries (omit the spice), or try 450g (1lb) rhubarb with 450g (1lb) strawberries.

DESSERTS AND PUDDINGS

Nutritional Information (Per Serving)
525 calories, 21g fat (of which 9g saturates), 81g carbohydrate, 0.3g salt
Easy

Serves 6
Preparation Time 20 minutes
Cooking Time 35–45 minutes

Quick Gooey
Chocolate Puddings

100g (3½oz) unsalted butter,
   plus extra to grease
100g (3½oz) golden caster sugar,
   plus extra to dust
100g (3½oz) plain chocolate
   (at least 70% cocoa solids),
   broken into pieces
2 large eggs
20g (¾oz) plain flour
icing sugar to dust

1 Preheat the oven to 200°C (180°C fan oven) mark 6. Butter four 200ml (7fl oz) ramekins and dust with sugar. Melt the chocolate and butter in a heatproof bowl set over a pan of gently simmering water, making sure the base of the bowl doesn't touch the water. Take the bowl off the pan and leave to cool for 5 minutes.

2 Whisk the eggs, caster sugar and flour together in a bowl until smooth. Fold in the chocolate mixture and pour into the ramekins.

3 Stand the dishes on a baking tray and bake for 12–15 minutes until the puddings are puffed and set on the outside, but still runny inside.

4 Turn out, dust with icing sugar and serve immediately.

Serves 4
Preparation Time 15 minutes
Cooking Time 12–15 minutes

Nutritional Information (Per Serving)
468 calories, 31g fat (of which 19g saturates), 46g carbohydrate, 0.6g salt
Easy

Chocolate Crêpes
with a Boozy Sauce

1 Put the flour and salt into a bowl, make a well in the centre and add the egg. Use a balloon whisk to mix the egg with a little of the flour, then gradually add the milk to make a smooth batter. Cover and leave to stand for about 20 minutes.

2 Pour the batter into a jug. Heat 1 tsp oil in a 23cm (9in) frying pan, then pour in 100ml (3½fl oz) batter, tilting the pan so that the mixture coats the bottom, and fry for 1–2 minutes until golden underneath. Turn carefully and fry the other side. Tip on to a plate, cover with greaseproof paper and repeat with the remaining batter, using more oil as needed.

3 Divide the chocolate among the crêpes. Fold each crêpe in half, and then in half again.

4 Put the butter and sugar into a heavy-based frying pan over a low heat. Add the brandy and stir. Slide the crêpes into the pan and cook for 3–4 minutes to melt the chocolate. Serve drizzled with sauce and sprinkled with sugar.

100g (3½oz) plain flour, sifted
a pinch of salt
1 medium egg
300ml (½ pint) semi-skimmed milk
sunflower oil for frying
50g (2oz) plain chocolate (at least 70% cocoa solids), roughly chopped
100g (3½oz) unsalted butter
100g (3½oz) light muscovado sugar, plus extra to sprinkle
4 tbsp brandy

Try Something Different
Replace the brandy with Grand Marnier and use orange-flavoured plain chocolate.

Nutritional Information (Per Serving)
594 calories, 35g fat (of which 17g saturates), 57g carbohydrate, 0.5g salt
Easy

Serves 4
Preparation Time 5 minutes, plus standing
Cooking Time 10–15 minutes

Cinnamon Pancakes

150g (5oz) plain flour
½ tsp ground cinnamon
1 medium egg
300ml (½ pint) skimmed milk
olive oil to fry
fruit compote or sugar and Greek
    yogurt to serve

1 In a large bowl, whisk together the flour, cinnamon, egg and milk to make a smooth batter. Leave to stand for 20 minutes.

2 Heat a heavy-based frying pan over a medium heat. When the pan is really hot, add 1 tsp oil, pour in a ladleful of batter and tilt the pan to coat the bottom with an even layer. Cook for 1 minute or until golden. Flip over and cook for 1 minute. Repeat with the remaining batter, adding more oil if necessary, to make six pancakes. Serve with a fruit compote or a sprinkling of sugar, and a dollop of yogurt.

Try Something Different
Serve with sliced bananas and vanilla ice cream instead of the fruit compote and yogurt.

Serves 6
Preparation Time 5 minutes
Cooking Time 20 minutes

Nutritional Information (Per Serving)
141 calories, 5g fat (of which 1g saturates), 20g carbohydrate, 0.1g salt
Easy

Baked Apples
with Butterscotch Sauce

1 Soak the sultanas in the brandy and set aside for 10 minutes, then stuff each apple with equal amounts.

2 Preheat the oven to 220°C (200°C fan oven) mark 7. Put the apples into a roasting tin and sprinkle with the brown sugar and apple juice. Bake for 15–20 minutes until soft.

3 Meanwhile, make the sauce. Melt the butter, brown sugar, golden syrup and treacle in a heavy-based pan, stirring continuously. When the sugar has dissolved and the mixture is bubbling, stir in the brandy and cream. Bring back to the boil and set aside.

4 Remove the apples from the oven. Serve the apples with the butterscotch sauce, hazelnuts and a dollop of ricotta cheese.

125g (4oz) sultanas
2 tbsp brandy
6 large Bramley apples, cored
4 tbsp soft brown sugar
2 tbsp apple juice
125g (4oz) hazelnuts, chopped
 and toasted
ricotta cheese to serve (see Cook's Tip,
 page 35)

**FOR THE BUTTERSCOTCH
 SAUCE**
125g (4oz) butter
125g (4oz) soft brown sugar
2 tbsp golden syrup
2 tbsp black treacle
4 tbsp brandy
300ml (½ pint) double cream

Get ahead

To prepare ahead Complete step 1 up to 4 hours in advance. Make the sauce (step 3), then cool, cover and chill for up to one day.

To use Complete the recipe and bring the sauce back to the boil to serve.

DESSERTS AND PUDDINGS

Nutritional Information (Per Serving)
821 calories, 56g fat (of which 28g saturates), 70g carbohydrate, 0.4g salt
Gluten Free · Easy

Serves 6
Preparation Time 5 minutes, plus
 soaking
Cooking Time 15–20 minutes

Griddled Peaches

4 ripe but firm peaches,
    halved and stoned
1 tbsp maple syrup
1 tsp light olive oil
25g (1oz) pecan nuts, toasted

1 Cut the peaches into thick slices, then put into a bowl with the maple syrup and toss to coat.

2 Heat the oil in a griddle or large frying pan, add the peaches and cook for 3–4 minutes on each side until starting to char and caramelise. Sprinkle with the toasted pecan nuts and serve at once.

Try Something Different
Use nectarines instead of peaches, or 8 plump plums.

Serves 4
Preparation Time 15 minutes
Cooking Time 6–8 minutes

Nutritional Information (Per Serving)
94 calories, 5g fat (of which 1g saturates), 11g carbohydrate, 0g salt
Gluten Free • Dairy Free • Easy

Baked Apricots with Almonds

1 Preheat the oven to 200°C (180°C fan oven) mark 6. Put the apricot halves, cut side up, into an ovenproof dish. Sprinkle with the sugar, drizzle with the liqueur, then dot each apricot half with a little butter. Scatter the flaked almonds over them.

2 Bake in the oven for 20–25 minutes until the apricots are soft and the juices are syrupy. Serve warm, with crème fraîche.

12 apricots, halved and stoned
3 tbsp golden caster sugar
2 tbsp Amaretto liqueur
25g (1oz) unsalted butter
25g (1oz) flaked almonds
crème fraîche to serve

Try Something Different
Use nectarines or peaches instead of apricots.

DESSERTS AND PUDDINGS

Nutritional Information (Per Serving)
124 calories, 6g fat (of which 2g saturates), 16g carbohydrate, 0.1g salt
Gluten Free · Easy

Serves 6
Preparation Time 5 minutes
Cooking Time 20–25 minutes

The Vegetarian Storecupboard

Cooking vegetarian food is a great chance to be creative and inventive, especially with the huge variety of fresh vegetables, fruits, nuts, seeds, spices and herbs available these days. Many products suitable for vegetarians are now clearly labelled and easy to identify – including invaluable ingredients such as vegetarian cheeses and stocks. Certain foods are particularly significant in a vegetarian diet, either because they contribute large amounts of a particular nutrient or because they require some explanation.

CHEESE

The traditional rennet used to separate milk into firm curds and liquid whey comes from the stomach lining of a young calf. Cheeses suitable for vegetarians are made using a non-animal rennet substitute, from either the bacteria *Bacillus subtilis* or *Bacillus prodigiosum*, the fungus *Mucor miehei*, or certain plants. Some traditional cheeses have always been made using natural rennets, including fig juice, melon, wild thistle and safflower.

Other cheeses, such as Parmesan, for example, are always made using animal rennet, because of European Union regulations for their production and labelling. However, a 'Parmesan-style hard cheese' is suitable for vegetarians and a wide variety of cheeses now made with non-animal rennet are labelled as suitable for vegetarians. There is no particular type of cheese that is exclusively vegetarian and soft cheeses are as likely to be non-vegetarian as hard cheese. Always check the label.

NON-DAIRY PRODUCTS

There are many alternatives to dairy products. Some contain very little protein, but provide carbohydrates and may be enriched with extra calcium and essential vitamins. Check the list of ingredients carefully, particularly for butter substitutes, as they may contain lactose, whey or casein, which are all animal products. The most common alternatives are:

MILKS

Rice milk Free of lactose, dairy, nuts, eggs, wheat and gluten, rice milk has a translucent appearance. It is sold plain or flavoured with chocolate or vanilla and is not recommended for savoury dishes. Rice milk has less protein than soya or almond milk. Shake well before using.

Almond milk Thick and creamy, with a smooth consistency and nutty taste, almond milk is not widely available, but you can make your own by blending blanched almonds with a little water, vanilla extract and raw honey. Beaten to a smooth consistency, it can be used as a butter substitute. Shake well before using.

Almond milk should be avoided by anyone with a nut allergy.

Oat milk Smooth and mild, oat milk has a less pronounced flavour than soya milk and no aftertaste, but has a hint of oat flakes or porridge. Darker than cow's milk, reflecting the colour of the oats, it is a versatile, low fat alternative. Chill well before serving and shake well just before using.

See also Soya milk (page 281).

NON-DAIRY SPREADS

There are many branded spreads available, made from milk alternatives or various oils – sunflower and olive being the most popular. Dairyfree spreads or coconut oil can be used to replace butter when making cakes or pastry, although the flavour will not be as good. Substitute olive or nut oil for butter when frying and sautéing.

As a substitute for buttermilk, add 1 tablespoon of white vinegar or lemon juice to a cup of soya milk and mix well. It has a similar flavour and will work well in recipes where buttermilk is called for, such as scones.

BUTTER SUBSTITUTES

Spreads made using a single oil or blend of oils, including sunflower, olive, vegetable and/or soya bean, are often labelled 'low-fat spread'. Some are manufactured to look and taste like butter. Spreads will keep in the fridge for several weeks.

UNUSUAL VEGETABLES

SWEET POTATO

Native to South America, the sweet potato is not related to the 'common potato'. It is usually elongated in shape, but there are also rounder varieties; the skin can be brown or red and the flesh can be deep orange or pale yellow. Sweet potatoes have a sweet, chestnut flavour and become tender and creamy when cooked; some may also have a somewhat fibrous texture. They are in season during the autumn and winter; look for smaller, firm potatoes, as these will have a better texture. To use, bake in its skin. Peel then boil, mash, roast, fry or add to stews and soups. Can be used to thicken soups.

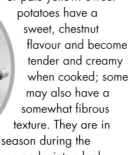

JERUSALEM ARTICHOKE

This small knobbly tuber is not a relative of the globe artichoke and is actually related to the sunflower. (The name Jerusalem is a corruption of *girasole*, the French word for sunflower.) Either pale brown or purplish-red, Jerusalem artichokes have firm, creamy white flesh with a distinctive, nutty taste. They are in season in winter. Look for firm artichokes with as few knobbles as possible, as this will make peeling easier and produce less waste. If the artichokes are young and very clean, they can be cooked with their skins on, but usually they are peeled before cooking. To use, boil, mash, sauté, fry or roast and use as an accompaniment. The flesh discolours when exposed to air, so drop the peeled and/or cut artichokes into acidulated water (1 tbsp lemon juice dissolved in 1 litre (1¾ pints) of water) as you prepare them.

YAM

There are many varieties of this starchy tuber and they vary in size and shape. They can grow to more than 2m (6½ft) long, but they are best for cooking when they are much smaller. Yams are usually cylindrical or sausage-shaped with a dark brown skin that may be tinged with pink and is often coarse and bark-like. The flesh may be white or yellow. The flavour is bland, but it goes well with spicy foods. When buying, look for hard yams with unblemished, unbroken skins. Store in a cool, dark place. To use, peel, then cook in the same way as potatoes.

KOHLRABI

This tasty vegetable is the swollen root of a member of the cabbage family; only the root is eaten, and not the scant, small leaves attached to it. The root is round, pale green or purple, with a tough, thick skin. The flesh is tender, sweet and juicy. It can be eaten raw, sliced or grated in salads, or cooked – sliced or cut into strips and stir-fried, or cut into larger chunks and braised with tomatoes and spices, or added to hearty vegetable stews. Kohlrabi is in season during summer, autumn and winter. Look for small bulbs, which are young and tender. Avoid larger bulbs, which may be tough. To use, peel off the skin with a knife, then slice, chop or grate. Eat raw; stir-fry or braise.

OKRA

Okra, also known as ladies' finger, is a green, velvety, ridged pod, which is at its best at about 7.5cm (3in) long. When the flesh is cut open, the pods release a slimy liquid that seeps out into the cooking liquid and gives it its distinctive 'gloopy' texture; this works well in stews. In other dishes such as curries, or as an accompaniment, it may be better just to trim the pod and cook whole. Okra is in season during the summer, although in some places it is available all year round. Look for firm green pods with no brown marks. Store in the fridge and use within a few days. To cook okra whole, wash and remove any wispy black 'hair' on the pods. Trim the end of the caps, taking care not to pierce the pods. If you want to use the gelatinous liquid inside the pod for thickening a stew, okra should be split. Wash and trim, then cut in half lengthways, from tip to cap.

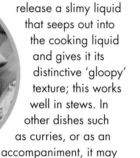

CASSAVA

Widely used in the Caribbean and Africa, cassava (also known as manioc) is served in the same way as potatoes. The long, thick, tapering tuber has a tough, dark brown skin and hard white or yellow flesh. There are two varieties: bitter and sweet. The bitter variety contains a natural poison and needs to be processed to make it safe to eat. When buying, look for firm roots with a smooth skin. Both sweet and bitter cassava are processed to make cassava flour, cassava meal and tapioca. To use, peel and boil in the same way as potatoes.

PULSES

The term pulse is used to describe all the various beans, peas and lentils, the edible seeds of various leguminous plants, which have been preserved by drying. They are highly nutritious, especially when eaten with grains, such as couscous, pasta, rice or bread, and are a good source of vegetarian protein. However, it should be noted that despite being a rich source of protein, most do not constitute a whole protein (containing all eight amino acids) and need to be combined with grains or cereals to make up full protein. They are a good source of fibre, B vitamins, potassium and iron.

HOW TO BUY AND STORE

Beans, pulses and lentils have a long shelf life and can be stored in an airtight container in a cool, dark and dry place for many months. However, they tend to become harder with prolonged storage and age and may require much longer cooking to achieve tender results. Buy from stores with a relatively high turnover of stock and use within six to nine months.

HOW TO PREPARE AND COOK

Always pick through beans, peas and lentils carefully and remove any tiny stones or grit, then rinse well. Some require fast boiling for 10–15 minutes to remove any toxins contained in the bean (see chart). They should then be drained and boiled in fresh unsalted water. Others can be brought to the boil and cooked without changing the water. A pressure cooker is a quick and economical way to cook soaked beans (see opposite). Beans must be cooked without salt – salt toughens the skin and stops the inside from becoming tender. Season when cooked.

CANNED PULSES

Canned pulses are an invaluable storecupboard item when you don't have a lot of time. Most types are available ready-cooked in cans and are relatively inexpensive, although of course they are more expensive than home-cooked ones. They tend to be softer than homecooked pulses, which makes them ideal for making purées and dips. They can also be served as an accompaniment with just brief heating, preferably with added garlic, onion or lemon juice to

TYPE	APPEARANCE	COOKING TIME AFTER SOAKING	PRESSURE COOKING TIME**
Aduki beans*	Round, red, very small	30–60 minutes	12 minutes
Black beans*	Kidney-shaped, black, shiny	1½ hours	20 minutes
Black-eye beans*	Small, kidney-shaped, pale cream with black spot, or 'eye'	1½ hours	12 minutes
Butter beans	Large, flattish, kidney-shaped pale cream	1½ hours	17 minutes
Cannellini beans	White, like long haricots	1 hour	25 minutes
Chickpeas	Round with pointed top, ivory	1½–2 hours	20 minutes
Flageolet beans	Kidney-shaped, pale green	1 hour	15 minutes
Haricot beans	Kidney-shaped, pale cream	1–1½ hours	20 minutes
Lentils (no soaking required)	Small and red or green, or larger and greenish-brown, round, flattish	1 hour	15 minutes
Mung beans (no soaking required)	Round, green, very small	40 minutes	12 minutes
Red kidney beans*	Kidney shaped, crimson red	1–1½ hours	20 minutes
Rose cocoa or borlotti beans*	Long, pink with dark flecks	1 hour	17 minutes
Soya beans*	Small, round, ivory	3–4 hours	30 minutes
Split peas	Small, green or yellow, round	45–60 minutes	15 minutes

The cooking times given above are approximate and depend on the age of the beans and the soaking time.

* For these beans, it is essential to cover them with fresh cold water after soaking, bring to the boil and boil rapidly for 10 minutes (15 minutes for soya beans) to destroy any toxins present in their skins. Then reduce the heat and cook at a steady simmer.

** High (15lb) pressure.

boost the flavour. Look for beans canned in water rather than brine, as many varieties can be high in salt. Drain and rinse well in cold water before using. A 400g can (drained weight about 235g) is roughly equivalent to 100g (3½oz) dried beans. The dried beans double in weight after soaking.

LENTILS

Green lentil One of the largest of the lentils, flat grey-green lentils have a mild flavour and soft, slightly 'dry' texture. They retain their shape well (unless overcooked) and are a good addition to soups and stews. They can be used to stuff vegetables or added to salads. (See page 277.)

Brown lentil Very similar to green lentils, brown lentils can be used in the same way in soups, stews and rice dishes. Their colour is sadly unexciting, but they have good flavour and a solid skin that holds up well to cooking. (See page 277.)

Puy lentil These small, speckled, dark green gems are highly prized for their excellent taste and texture. They can be served as an accompaniment, tossed in salads, or used in soups and stews. Puy lentils hold their shape better than any other lentil, even when fully cooked. (See page 277.)

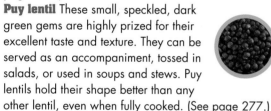

Red split lentil These tiny pink-orange split lentils disintegrate as they cook, producing a thick purée with a slightly dry texture. They benefit from the addition of spices and strong flavours. They are used to make spicy Indian dal, but they can also be used to thicken soups and casseroles. (See page 277.)

Yellow lentil Also known as chana dal, yellow lentils are slightly larger than red lentils. They disintegrate in the same way when cooked, and can generally be used in exactly the same way. (See page 277.)

SPROUTED BEANS AND SEEDS

Most beans and lentils can be sprouted. With their crisp texture and nutty flavour, sprouted beans are

often richer in nutrients than the whole bean. Look for fresh-looking sprouts and avoid any with brown patches or that appear slimy. Store in the fridge and use within three days. Seeds and some grains can also be sprouted. You can grow your own at home, but it is important to buy ones that are specifically produced for sprouting – Mung beans, aduki beans, alfalfa seeds and fenugreek are all suitable.

PASTA

Quick and easy to cook, pasta can transform vegetables into substantial meals, and can be served as an accompaniment or in soups, bakes and salads.

There are some useful rules about matching certain types of pasta with specific types of sauce.

Egg pasta Northern-Italian egg pasta suits butter and cream sauces that cling to the pasta.

Long, thin shapes Pasta such as spaghetti and vermicelli suit smooth sauces such as garlic and olive oil, as well as tomato sauces and those using olive oil.

Chunky, long shapes Pasta such as pappardelle and tagliatelle suit heavier sauces.

Pasta shapes These can be served with smooth or chunky sauces, as the shapes trap the sauce well.

PASTA FOR LAYERING AND STUFFING

Lasagne These rectangular sheets of pasta can be made from plain or egg dough and they may be coloured with spinach. The sheets may be flat or rippled, with straight or ruffled edges, and are designed to be layered with sauce and baked in the oven. Cook a few sheets of lasagne at a time according to the pack instructions. Layer in a dish alternately with vegetable sauce and béchamel sauce, then bake.

Easy-cook lasagne comes in the same plain, egg or verdi options as traditional lasagne, and may be flat or rippled. The sheets are rolled out thinly when made so that they do not need to be pre-cooked, but must be used with plenty of moist sauce to rehydrate them during cooking. The pasta absorbs the liquid and comes out fully cooked when the lasagne itself is cooked. The baking time is usually slightly longer than when using regular lasagne.

Lasagnette are strips of pasta with a ruffled edge and are used in the same way as lasagne.

PASTA FOR SOUP

Farfalline This tiny bow-shaped pasta is good added to minestrone-style soups. **Farfallette** are a similar shape and used in the same way.

Funghetti are tiny rounds of pasta pinched to form a mushroom shape rather than a bow. Add to soup or broth and cook for a few minutes, or according to the pack instructions.

Conchigliette These have the same shape as conchiglie, but they are much smaller. Both size and shape make them an ideal pasta for minestrone-type soups and chunky broths.

Lumachine are another shell-shaped pasta. Add to soup or broth.

Stelline These tiny stars most often find their way into the mouths of young children, and are perfect for babies – no danger of choking. But they can also be added to clear or chunky broths. Sometimes called **stellete**, which may be somewhat larger (though still never very large). Add to soup or broth.

STUFFED PASTA

Ravioli These stuffed pasta squares with a crimped edge may be made from plain, egg or flavoured dough. Stuffings range from classics such as spinach and ricotta, to new ideas such as artichoke or pumpkin. Ravioli can vary in size from small to very large, where just two or three ravioli would make up a portion. Cook according to the pack instructions.

Tortelloni Tortelloni may be made of egg or flavoured pasta, which is cut into round discs that are stuffed, then folded in half and twisted. They are available with a wide variety of fillings. **Tortelli** are a larger version. **Tortellini** are slightly smaller and are often sold dried. They are a classic addition to broths. Cook according to the pack instructions.

NON-WHEAT PASTA

People with a gluten or wheat intolerance can still enjoy pasta dishes as long as they look for products labelled wheat and gluten free. An increasing range of non-wheat pasta is available, including:

Corn This golden yellow pasta is available in a variety of shapes and sizes similar to traditional pasta. Usually sold dried, it is also available coloured with spinach or beetroot. Take care not to overcook, as it is likely to turn mushy.

Quick pasta sauces

● **CREAMY PESTO** Put 5 tbsp freshly grated Parmesan-style cheese, 25g (1oz) toasted pine nuts, 200g carton low-fat fromage frais and 2 garlic cloves into a food processor. Whiz to a thick paste. Season generously with salt and ground black pepper. Add 40g (1½oz) each torn fresh basil leaves and roughly chopped fresh parsley and whiz for 2–3 seconds.

● **MUSHROOM AND CREAM** Heat 1 tbsp olive oil in a large pan and fry 1 finely chopped onion for 7–10 minutes until soft. Add 300g (11oz) sliced mushrooms and cook for 3–4 minutes. Pour in 125ml (4fl oz) dry white wine and bubble for 1 minute, then stir in 500ml (18fl oz) low-fat crème fraîche. Heat until bubbling, then stir in 2 tbsp freshly chopped tarragon. Season with salt and ground black pepper.

● **WALNUT AND CREAMY BLUE CHEESE** Heat 1 tsp olive oil in a small pan, add 1 crushed garlic clove and 25g (1oz) toasted walnut pieces and cook for 1 minute – the garlic should just be golden. Add 100g (3½oz) cubed Gorgonzola (see Cook's Tip, page 35) and 150ml (¼ pint) single cream. Season with ground black pepper.

● **BROCCOLI AND THYME** Put 900g (2lb) trimmed tenderstem broccoli into a pan with 150ml (¼ pint) hot vegetable stock. Bring to the boil, then cover and simmer for 3–4 minutes until tender – the stock should have evaporated. Add 2 crushed garlic cloves and 2 tbsp olive oil and cook for 1–2 minutes to soften the garlic. Add 250g carton mascarpone, 2 tbsp freshly chopped thyme and 100g (3½ oz) freshly grated pecorino cheese (see Cook's Tip, page 35) and mix together. Season with salt and ground black pepper.

Rice spaghetti made from 100% rice is pale and susceptible to overcooking, but can be used in the same way as regular spaghetti. Other rice–pasta products may include a certain percentage of corn, quinoa or millet.

Gluten-free pasta In an attempt to get closer to the taste and texture of traditional pasta, some products have been developed using a mix of corn, rice, buckwheat and bean or pea starch. Available in various shapes.

POLENTA

This classic Italian staple made of ground cornmeal may be cooked to make a grainy purée to be served immediately, or cooled and then fried or grilled, or it can be baked.

Use coarse cornmeal if you want a slightly gritty texture, or fine cornmeal for a smooth texture.

If you are serving traditional polenta straight from the pan, have all the other dishes ready – the polenta needs to be eaten straightaway, otherwise it becomes thick and difficult to serve.

Traditional polenta Fill a pan with 1.2 litres (2 pints) water and add ¼ tsp salt. Pour in 225g (8oz) polenta and put the pan over a medium heat. As the water starts to heat up, stir the polenta. Bring to the boil, reduce the heat to a simmer and continue cooking, stirring every few minutes, for 15–20 minutes until it comes away from the sides of the pan.

Grilling polenta Make traditional polenta (see above), then pour into an oiled baking dish. Smooth the surface with a spatula and leave to cool. Cut the polenta into squares and brush the pieces with olive oil. Preheat the grill or frying pan and cook for 5–10 minutes until hot and browned on both sides.

Baking polenta Preheat the oven to 200°C (180°C fan oven) mark 6. Fill a pan with 1.2 litres (2 pints) water and add ¼ tsp salt. Pour in 225g (8oz) polenta and put it over the heat. Bring to the boil, stirring, then reduce the heat and simmer for 5 minutes. Pour the polenta into an oiled baking dish, cover with foil and bake for 45–50 minutes. Brown under the grill.

SOYA BEAN PRODUCTS

TOFU

Also known as beancurd, soft white tofu is made from the 'milk' obtained from boiled, mashed soya beans. It is a good source of vegetarian protein and is low in calories; it contains no saturated fat or cholesterol. There are two main types: **firm**, which can be sliced or cut into cubes and added to soups and stir-fries, deep-fried or used for kebabs; and **silken**, which is much softer and smoother and is good for mashing or puréeing in sauces, dips and dairyfree ice creams.

Tofu has a mild, bland flavour, and it readily absorbs other flavourings: it benefits from strong-tasting marinades, such as soy sauce, ginger, sherry, onion, garlic and chilli. Tofu is sold as a chilled product and should be stored in the fridge. Once the packet is opened, tofu should be kept immersed in water in the fridge and eaten within four days. To use, drain away the packing liquid. Use silken tofu as required. Rinse firm tofu, pat dry, then slice or cube as required.

Pressed tofu Sometimes sold as dry or extra-firm tofu, this is made from fresh tofu that has been pressed to extract much of the liquid and to give a firmer texture. Slice or cut into cubes and use as for firm tofu, or it can be panfried as a 'tofu steak'.

Fermented tofu Fermented tofu, a Chinese speciality, takes many months to mature and develop its strong, pungent flavour. The end result has a powerful smell and piquant bite. Use in small quantities as a flavouring ingredient in stir-fries and braised dishes. Two main varieties are available: red fermented tofu and spicy white fermented tofu. Both are an acquired taste. Cut into cubes and use as required.

Smoked tofu This has a distinctive smoky flavour; use in salads, stir-fries or vegetable kebabs, paired with robust flavours such as spinach, pumpkin and butternut squash. Marinated tofu requires no specific preparation. Use it straight from the pack.

Marinated tofu Ready-marinated tofu is often sold in cubes that have been marinated in soy sauce and Chinese-style spices, which give it a brown outer layer and creamy-white interior. The cubes have quite a firm, chewy texture and are good added to stir-fries, braised dishes, soups and casseroles. Less traditional forms of marinated tofu are also becoming available, including Mediterranean flavourings.

Deep-fried tofu Crisp and golden deep-fried tofu is available in various forms: thick blocks, thin sheets, or individual cubes. All are made from fresh firm tofu. The thick blocks are usually grilled and served as 'tofu steaks'; the thin sheets can be split open and filled with vegetables, or sliced or cut into cubes for adding to soups and stir-fries. Cubes of deep-fried tofu can be added to soups, salads, braised dishes and stir-fries. All have a much firmer, chewier texture than fresh tofu. To use, put in a sieve and rinse with boiling water to remove any excess oil, then pat dry.

OTHER SOYA PRODUCTS

Freeze-dried tofu A Japanese speciality, this has a stronger flavour than tofu and a firmer, spongier texture that absorbs other flavours readily. Serve cooked in broth.

Tempeh An Indonesian ingredient made from fermented soya beans, it is sold in creamy-yellow blocks and has a knobbly texture and distinctive, slightly nutty flavour. It can be sliced or cubed and used in the same way as tofu.

Textured vegetable protein (TVP) TVP is made from a mixture of soya flour, flavourings and liquid, which is cooked, then extruded under pressure and cut into chunks or small pieces to resemble mince. It has little natural flavour of its own but is often sold flavoured as either 'beef' or 'chicken'. It has a slightly chewy, meat-like texture. Dried TVP needs to be rehydrated in boiling water for 5 minutes before being added to stews, casseroles and sauces. Frozen TVP mince can be added directly to sauces.

Soya milk is probably the most common dairy product alternative. Sweeter and darker than cow's milk, it has a distinctive flavour that some people find hard to get used to. It's worth trying several brands, however, until you find one you like. Soya milk has almost as much protein as dairy milk, but less fat and no cholesterol. It is sold as longlife or fresh, sweetened or unsweetened, sometimes with added chocolate or fruit flavourings.

Soya yogurts, **desserts** and **ice cream** are widely available.

Soya cream is a good substitute for single cream, and will even whip a little if well chilled.

Soya cream cheese tastes similar to cow's milk cream cheeses and can be used in their place; and the **hard soya cheese** is a good replacement in cooked dishes.

OTHER SOURCES OF PROTEIN

QUORN

Quorn is a vegetarian product derived from a distant relative of the mushroom. Although it is not suitable for vegans because it contains egg albumen, Quorn is a good source of complete protein for vegetarians. Like tofu, Quorn has a bland flavour and benefits from being marinated before cooking. Available from the chiller cabinet, Quorn should be kept in the fridge.

NUTS AND SEEDS

NUTS

Most nuts are highly nutritious, rich in unsaturated fats and consequently have a high calorie content. Many, such as peanuts, walnuts and almonds, are pressed for their oil. Nuts are also rich in protein and are often used in vegetarian dishes instead of meat.

HOW TO BUY AND STORE

Although some nuts are available fresh, or green, most are dried to extend their shelf life. Nuts in the shell should feel relatively heavy for their size; avoid light nuts, which usually indicate that the kernel will be withered and dry. Also avoid any that are damp or appear mouldy. Due to their high oil content, nuts do not keep particularly well and will turn rancid if not used quickly enough. Buy them in small quantities, store in an airtight container in a cool, dark place, and use within three months.

HOW TO PREPARE AND COOK

For hard nuts, you will need to use nutcrackers to crack the hard protective shell, then extract the nut. Use whole shelled nuts for decorating cakes and biscuits. For use in baking and sweet and savoury dishes, nuts are usually chopped, crushed or ground.

OTHER VARIETIES INCLUDE

Tiger nut Also known as chufa. Tiger nuts are not really a nut but a small, wrinkled tuber. They have a crisp texture and sweet, slightly almondy flavour. Tiger nuts can also be pounded and ground to make a sweet milky drink known as *horchata de chufa*, or used to flavour ices.

Lotus nut Also known as lotus seeds, these small, rounded, light brown seeds have a slightly almondy flavour; they are available dried or canned, from Asian food shops. They may be used whole or pounded in Thai soups and desserts, and in China they are often cooked in a sweet soup to serve at the end of a meal. Lotus seed paste is a popular filling for Chinese pastries and dim sum.

Gingko nut Popular in Chinese and Japanese cooking, the small, cream-coloured gingko nut is usually sold canned or dried. It can be used in sweet and savoury dishes, or eaten as a snack.

COCONUT

The coconut is the fruit of palm trees that grow throughout tropical regions. Fresh coconuts are large and green, with a leathery skin. In countries where they are grown, they are often sold on the street as a drink; the top will be sliced off and the juice inside drunk, then the soft flesh inside scooped out and eaten. In the West, you will more often find dry, mature coconuts with a hairy, dark brown skin. When the shell is split open, the juice can be drunk or added to soups and curries. The scooped-out flesh can be eaten as a snack or grated, then added to cakes and desserts as well as savoury dishes. It makes a good addition to soups and stews, particularly those from India, Sri Lanka, South-east Asia and the Caribbean. To prepare mature coconuts, pierce two holes through the 'eyes' in the top using a hammer and screwdriver and drain out the milk. Using the hammer, crack open at the widest part, then prise out the white flesh using a knife.

Coconut is also available in processed forms.

Coconut milk Creamy coconut milk is a thick, rich extract made by shredding coconut and soaking it in water, then draining it through muslin. Regular coconut milk is made using twice the volume of water to shredded coconut. It is high in saturated fat, but you can find cans of low-fat coconut milk.

Coconut cream Thicker than coconut milk, coconut cream can be used in the same way: stirred into curries and soups, or thinned with water to use as if it were coconut milk.

Creamed coconut This thick, creamy paste can be mixed with boiling water, then stirred into curries or into dishes such as soups and rice pudding.

Desiccated coconut Made from the dried flesh of the coconut, this may be sweetened or unsweetened.

Coconut shavings These have a sweet flavour and a texture between crisp and chewy.

SEEDS

Seeds are an excellent, highly nutritious vegetarian ingredient, adding texture flavour and interest to a variety of foods. Poppy, sunflower, sesame and pumpkin are especially popular. To enhance their flavour, toast in a dry frying pan for a few minutes, shaking the pan constantly.

Poppy seeds These tiny little spheres, blue-black or white, are the innocuous seeds of the opium poppy. The darker variety is more commonly available and has a mild, slightly peppery flavour. Use whole, or grind in a food processor.

Sunflower seeds Looking at these small, pointed, greyish seeds, you would never know that they come from the enormous, bright yellow sunflower. Nutty in flavour and tender but slightly crunchy, sunflower seeds can be added to breads and muffins, either mixed into the dough or sprinkled on top before baking. They are also good added to salads and rice pilaus, eaten as a snack, or tossed into muesli. Usually sold shelled; if you buy seeds in the black-and-white stripy shells, you will need to split them open using your thumbnails to extract the seeds. Seeds in the shell are more often eaten as a snack.

Sesame seeds Tiny sesame seeds may be white or black, although the white variety is more common. They have a tender but firm texture and distinctive, mildly bitter flavour. Popularly sprinkled on breads, rolls, bagels, pastries and muffins, sesame seeds can also be added to the dough or mixture before baking, or combined with other seeds such as sunflower and pumpkin. They are good toasted and sprinkled over salads. Sesame seeds are pounded and ground for Middle Eastern tahini (see below) and the sweetmeat halwa. To toast, toss in a dry frying pan until they start to turn golden and give off a toasted aroma, then leave to cool. Take care not to let them brown too deeply, as this will intensify their bitterness.

Tahini Also known as tahina, this thick, creamy, beige-brown paste is made from ground sesame seeds and is used as an ingredient in Middle Eastern cooking. A darker variety made from unhulled seeds is also available, but has a slightly more bitter flavour. With the same nutty but slightly bitter flavour as sesame seeds, tahini is an essential ingredient in the chickpea purée, hummus, and smoky aubergine purée, baba gannoush, and is also used to make sauces for vegetables. Tahini can vary widely in consistency, from a pourable liquid to a very thick paste which needs considerable strength to stir. It is available in jars or plastic tubs and should be stirred or shaken before use, as it may separate when left stationary for long periods. Store in a cool, dark place.

Pumpkin seeds The dried seeds of the pumpkin are nearly flat, with a dark olive-green skin encasing the pale seed. With a crisp texture and mildly nutty flavour, pumpkin seeds are versatile little things. They're good tossed into salads or rice pilaus, or used in breads and muffins (either sprinkled on top or folded into the dough or batter before baking) – or simply eaten as a snack. Often sold shelled; if you buy pumpkin seeds unshelled or pick them straight from the centre of a pumpkin you will need to split open the hard shell to extract the seed. To toast, toss in a dry frying pan for a few minutes until the seeds start to turn brown, then allow to cool.

VEGETARIAN GELLING AGENTS

Gelatine is not suitable for vegetarians but there are various alternative gelling agents.

Agar agar Also known as kanten, this is derived from seaweed and is available as a white powder or threads. It should be dissolved in boiling water and can be used in the same way as gelatine. It doesn't work in all recipes and you may need to use more agar agar than you would gelatine to get a firm set.

Carrageen Also known as Irish moss, carrageen is a reddish-purple seaweed that is bleached by the sun to a pale yellow-pink. It can be used as a gelling agent or for thickening sauces, soups and stews. It is a traditional ingredient in Irish cooking and is often cooked in milk, then strained, sweetened, and set as a blancmange-like dessert.

HERBS

Dried herbs are excellent for adding flavour to cooked dishes, but their fresh counterparts are more lively in flavour and fragrance. Fresh herbs also add visual appeal, especially when left whole or sprinkled on a dish before serving. Buy bunches of fresh herbs from the supermarket or greengrocer and store in the fridge, or buy in pots to grow on a sunny windowsill or in window boxes, or plant a herb garden. All fresh herbs freeze well, and many can be dried. As a general rule, tender, softleafed, delicately flavoured herbs such as basil, coriander and parsley lose their flavour when dried. They should always be used fresh or frozen from fresh. More robust and strongly flavoured herbs, such as thyme, oregano, curry leaves and dill, dry well and make a good alternative if the fresh herb is unavailable. For use in salads and garnishes, where the herb is uncooked, only the fresh herb will do. Frozen herbs will not retain their original appearance and texture, so must be added to dishes during cooking.

USING HERBS

Fresh herbs get their flavour and aroma from the aromatic oils that are released when they are torn, cut or heated. As a general rule, tender herbs such as basil, coriander and mint are good used raw, added to salads, used as a garnish or stirred into dishes at the last minute, but do not bear long cooking. The more robust herbs such as thyme, rosemary and bay are better used in simmered dishes that allow the flavour of the herb to permeate and mingle with the other ingredients.

CLASSIC HERB COMBINATIONS

Bouquet garni A small bunch of herbs tied together with string or inside a piece of muslin, and an essential flavouring for stocks, soups and stews. The herbs can vary but usually include parsley, thyme and bay leaf; spices such as peppercorns and cloves may also be included. It is removed after cooking.

Fines herbes This classic French combination of finely chopped herbs usually includes chives, chervil, parsley and tarragon, and is good sprinkled over vegetables and omelettes.

DRIED SPICES

Many dried spices should be fried before use to remove any harshness of flavour and to enhance their taste. Whole seeds such as coriander and cumin are usually dryfried (fried without any oil) in a heavy frying pan until they give off a rich aroma, then ground. Ground spices may be fried in oil before adding other ingredients such as vegetables.

STORING SPICES

Spices tend to lose their flavour and aroma with age, so unless you use up spices very quickly, buy them in small quantities and store in an airtight container in a cool, dark place. Whole spices retain their flavour better than ground, so ideally buy whole spices such as coriander and cumin seeds and grind them as required.

SPICE BLENDS

Classics include:

Quatre épices A spice mix used in French cooking; the name literally means 'four spices'. It typically contains ground pepper, grated nutmeg, ground cloves and ground cinnamon, and is used in soups and stews.

Chinese five-spice powder A combination of Sichuan peppercorns, cassia, fennel seed, star anise and cloves. This aromatic blend is widely used in Chinese stir-fries and braised dishes.

Japanese seven-spice powder This Japanese spice blend is used as a condiment for sprinkling on dishes such as soups and noodles. Recipes vary, but a classic blend contains two hot spices and five aromatic ones, so a typical seven-spice powder might contain: ground chilli, Sichuan peppercorns, sesame seeds, flax seeds, rape seeds, poppy seeds, dried tangerine or orange peel. The mix frequently includes ground nori seaweed as well.

Garam masala A classic combination of spices used in Indian cooking, this aromatic spice blend is usually added to dishes towards the end of cooking. Combinations and proportions of spices vary, but a typical garam masala could include coriander, cumin, cardamom and black pepper. Other popular ingredients include cinnamon, cloves and ginger.

Curry powder and paste Typically, curry powders and pastes are used to flavour Indianstyle dishes, but it should be noted that in authentic Indian cooking, spices are always freshly ground and blended for each dish. The curry powders and pastes available in supermarkets tend to be generic blends of spices for the Western cook and may not always be vegetarian. Powders are usually described as mild, medium and hot, depending on how much chilli they contain, and would typically include key flavourings such as cumin, coriander and turmeric. There is more variety in jars of paste, but these tend to be created in terms of popular restaurant dishes such as tikka, dopiaza and jalfrezi.

Thai curry pastes There are numerous classic paste blends used in Thai cooking, made from wet and dry spices, herbs and aromatics, but the most widely available readymade ones are red and green curry pastes. Others include yellow curry paste, orange curry paste and mussaman curry paste. **Red curry paste** typically includes red chillies, cumin seeds, coriander seeds, shallots, garlic, galangal, lemongrass, fresh coriander root, peppercorns and shrimp paste, although there are many variations, so check the label to ensure it is vegetarian. **Green curry paste** is similar to red curry paste and would typically include green chillies and herbs.

Harissa This spicy red chilli paste is used throughout North Africa but is particularly associated with the cuisines of Tunisia and Morocco. A blend of soaked dried chillies, garlic, cumin, coriander, salt and olive oil, harissa is a lively and versatile mix that can be used in most types of savoury dish. Rose harissa is a variation made with the addition of rose petals.

Ras el hanout A complex blend of fragrant dried flower petals and dried spices, ras el hanout comes from Morocco, Tunisia and Algeria. Mixtures may vary, but a typical blend might include cardamom, nutmeg, cloves, ginger and black pepper. Lavender and rose petals are also used in some recipes. Tunisian blends tend to be milder, whereas the Moroccan ones are stronger and more pungent. Ras el hanout adds a warming, spicy, fragrant taste and aroma to tagines and soups.

Dukkah Recipes vary for this spice mix from Egypt, but a classic dukkah consists of crushed coriander seeds, hazelnuts and sesame seeds, mixed with ground cumin, ground pepper and salt. It is usually served as an accompaniment to bread dipped in olive oil.

Zahtar A classic blend from the Middle East, this mixture of dried thyme, ground sumac, sesame seeds and salt is sprinkled over dips, vegetables and flatbreads.

Tabil This Tunisian spice mix is a combination of coriander seeds, caraway seeds, garlic and dried chilli or chilli powder, ground together to make a spicy, aromatic mix to use in tagines and vegetable dishes.

Creole seasoning Spice mixes vary, but a classic seasoning might include salt, paprika, onion powder, peppercorns, garlic, cayenne pepper, thyme and oregano. **Filé powder** is a spicy mix popular in Creole cooking. It is based on ground dried sassafras leaves and is added to gumbo at the end of cooking, contributing to its slightly 'gloopy' texture as well as adding flavour.

Piri-piri spice Of African–Portuguese origin, piripiri is the name given to savoury dishes served with a hot pepper sauce made with the tiny, fiery African bird's eye chillies that go by the same name. Piri-piri spice aims to replicate the traditional spicing and flavouring.

Index

CONVERSION TABLES

TEMPERATURE

°C	FAN OVEN	GAS MARK	°C	FAN OVEN	GAS MARK
110	90	¼	190	170	5
130	110	½	200	180	6
140	120	1	220	200	7
150	130	2	230	210	8
170	150	3	240	220	9
180	160	4			

LIQUIDS

METRIC	IMPERIAL	METRIC	IMPERIAL
5ml	1 tsp	200ml	7fl oz
15ml	1 tbsp	250ml	9fl oz
25ml	1fl oz	300ml	½ pint
50ml	2fl oz	500ml	18fl oz
100ml	3½fl oz	600ml	1 pint
125ml	4fl oz	900ml	1½ pints
150ml	5fl oz/¼ pint	1 litre	1¾ pints
175ml	6fl oz		

MEASURES

METRIC	IMPERIAL	METRIC	IMPERIAL
5mm	¼ in	10cm	4in
1cm	½ in	15cm	6in
2cm	¾ in	18cm	7in
2.5cm	1in	20.5cm	8in
3cm	1¼ in	23cm	9in
4cm	1½ in	25.5cm	10in
5cm	2in	28cm	11in
7.5cm	3in	30.5cm	12in